COOPERATION WITHOUT TRUST?

COOPERATION WITHOUT TRUST?

Karen S. Cook, Russell Hardin,
and Margaret Levi

VOLUME IX IN THE RUSSELL SAGE FOUNDATION SERIES ON TRUST

Russell Sage Foundation · New York

The Russell Sage Foundation

The Russell Sage Foundation, one of the oldest of America's general purpose foundations, was established in 1907 by Mrs. Margaret Olivia Sage for "the improvement of social and living conditions in the United States." The Foundation seeks to fulfill this mandate by fostering the development and dissemination of knowledge about the country's political, social, and economic problems. While the Foundation endeavors to assure the accuracy and objectivity of each book it publishes, the conclusions and interpretations in Russell Sage Foundation publications are those of the authors and not of the Foundation, its Trustees, or its staff. Publication by Russell Sage, therefore, does not imply Foundation endorsement.

Library of Congress Cataloging-in-Publication Data

Cook, Karen S.
    Cooperation without trust? / Karen S. Cook, Russell Hardin, Margaret Levi.
        p. cm.—(The Russell Sage Foundation series on trust ; v. 9)
    Includes bibliographical references and index.
    ISBN 0-87154-164-5
    1. Social exchange. 2. Trust—Social aspects. 3. Cooperativeness. I. Hardin, Russell, 1940- II. Levi, Margaret. III. Title. IV. Series.

    HM1111.C666 2005
    302'.14—dc22

                                                                    2004062946

Text design by Suzanne Nichols.

RUSSELL SAGE FOUNDATION
112 East 64th Street, New York, New York 10021
10 9 8 7 6 5 4 3 2 1

Dedicated to those we trust most, our mothers:
Judy, Lucille, and Beatrice

The Russell Sage Foundation
Series on Trust

T HE RUSSELL Sage Foundation Series on Trust examines the conceptual structure and the empirical basis of claims concerning the role of trust and trustworthiness in establishing and maintaining cooperative behavior in a wide variety of social, economic, and political contexts. The focus is on concepts, methods, and findings that will enrich social science and inform public policy.

The books in the series raise questions about how trust can be distinguished from other means of promoting cooperation and explore those analytic and empirical issues that advance our comprehension of the roles and limits of trust in social, political, and economic life. Because trust is at the core of understandings of social order from varied disciplinary perspectives, the series offers the best work of scholars from diverse backgrounds and, through the edited volumes, encourages engagement across disciplines and orientations. The goal of the series is to improve the current state of trust research by providing a clear theoretical account of the causal role of trust within given institutional, organizational, and interpersonal situations, developing sound measures of trust to test theoretical claims within relevant settings, and establishing some common ground among concerned scholars and policymakers.

Karen S. Cook
Russell Hardin
Margaret Levi

SERIES EDITORS

Previous Volumes in the Series

Contents

About the Authors

Karen S. Cook is Ray Lyman Wilbur Professor of Sociology at Stanford University.

Russell Hardin is professor of politics at New York University.

Margaret Levi is Jere L. Bacharach Professor of International Studies in the Department of Political Science at the University of Washington.

Acknowledgments

W E WOULD like to acknowledge the Russell Sage Foundation for its generous support of the program on trust and the trust book series. This is the ninth volume in the series. We thank Eric Wanner, president of the Russell Sage Foundation, in particular, for his continuous encouragement and occasional push to get this volume in print. We also thank the many staff members of the foundation who helped organize our workshops and conferences as well as our visits to the foundation for meetings. We especially thank Nancy Weinberg, program officer, Bindu Chadaga, program support staff, and Suzanne Nichols, director of publications. Other organizations that provided substantial support for our work on trust are the Center for Advanced Study in the Behavioral Sciences, Stanford University, New York University, the University of Washington, the Rockefeller Foundation, the Juan March Institute, the Max Planck Institute for the Study of Societies (Cologne), the Collegium Budapest, and Hokkaido University. A number of very capable and patient research assistants at these universities helped in many ways: Robin Cooper, Coye Cheshire, Alexandra Gerbasi, Irena Stepanikova, John Ahlquist, Theresa Buckley, Matt Moe, Anthony Pezzola, Sharon Redeker, Julianna Rigg, Paul Bullen, Larisa Satara, and Huan Wang. Many individuals, too many to name here, gave us comments on particular chapters or papers presented at various university colloquia over the years. Last but not least, we thank our many colleagues in the social sciences, law, and philosophy who participated in the Trust Advisory Committee meetings and our workshops and conferences on trust-related topics and gave us extensive critical feedback on early versions of this manuscript. In the latter role, we especially thank William Bianco, John Brehm, Jean Ensminger, Robert Gibbons, Jack Knight, Jim Johnson, Jean-Laurent Rosenthal, Toshio Yamagishi, and two anonymous reviewers.

Chapter 1

The Significance of Trust

THE MASSIVE interest in trust in recent years seems to be stimulated by the inarguable view that social order is fundamentally dependent on cooperative relationships. This is a variant of what has historically been the central question in the social sciences: how is social order produced and maintained? General theories of social order range from assuming we need an all-powerful sovereign to coerce us, to requiring that we have shared norms or other mechanisms to generate successful social exchange, to merely supposing we achieve simple coordination to stay out of each other's way.

Some social theorists claim that trust is required to produce cooperation on a large scale in order to make societies function productively. This view is well represented in the work of Francis Fukuyama (1995), Robert Putnam (1995a), and others.[1] We argue, on the contrary, that trust works primarily at the interpersonal level to produce microlevel social order and to lower the costs of monitoring and sanctioning that might be required if individuals were not trustworthy. Trust therefore can play a role in the regime of informal social exchange, where it decreases the need for regulation by state and other institutions and reduces the transaction and monitoring costs of ordinary spontaneous relationships. Generally, however, given the long-term change from small communities to mass urban complexes, mere coordination and state regulation have become far more important, we argue, while *the actual role of trusting relations has declined relatively* (Cook and Hardin 2001).

On this view, trust is no longer the central pillar of social order, and it may not even be very important in most of our cooperative exchanges, which we manage quite effectively even in the absence of interpersonal trust. *Trust is important in many interpersonal contexts, but it cannot carry the weight of making complex societies function productively and effectively.* For that, we require institutions that make it possible for us to exchange and engage in commerce and joint efforts of all kinds, even in contexts in which distrust at the interpersonal level prevails and certainly in contexts in which we simply may never know enough actually to trust the persons with whom we must interact even on a daily basis.

We take a relational view of trust: we treat trust as an aspect of a relationship between two or more actors.[2] *Trust exists when one party to the relation believes the other party has incentive to act in his or her interest or to take his or her interests to heart.* We refer to this view of trust as the "encapsulated interest" model of trust relations, and we emphasize the importance of an interest in maintaining the relationship into the future as the primary foundation of the trustworthiness of each party in the relationship (see also Hardin 2002b). A trust relation emerges out of mutual interdependence and the knowledge developed over time of reciprocal trustworthiness. We spell out what we mean by relational trust in this chapter, and we contrast our view of trust with more psychological orientations to trust.

Our approach challenges much of the current theorizing about how to improve organizations, governments, businesses, and societies. Many observers argue that we need more trust in organizations and institutions. We argue that some organizations and institutions serve us well just because they substitute for trust relations. Furthermore, we suggest that distrust may be good in many contexts, since it grounds forms of social structure that help to limit exploitation and protect those who cannot protect themselves (Levi 2000). When distrust stimulates the development of improved institutions, it may facilitate cooperation, not hinder it. In contrast, networks of trust relations that are closed can promote ethnic clashes or racism and can even unproductively restrict economic exchange and significant forms of social exchange. Trust in such contexts may restrict opportunity, and such restrictions may in turn retard economic growth and development.

We emphasize the role of institutions and other arrangements for ensuring the reliability that makes it possible to sustain complex markets, accountable and responsive government, and a wide range of social and organizational devices for managing conflict and improving productivity at the workplace and in society. We therefore envision the role of trust as most active in the realm of personal relationships and in some settings as a *complement* to (not a substitute for) organizational arrangements that make cooperation possible. Trusting one's coworkers (when they have proven themselves trustworthy) makes it possible to widen the range of cooperative enterprises and lower the costs of managing such activities. But the contexts that make it possible to assess trustworthiness tend to involve ongoing relationships in which the individuals have personal knowledge of each other or knowledge acquired through inclusion in a well-connected network.

Where the risks are high, the relevant knowledge about trustworthiness is unobtainable, power is highly unequal, or distrust prevails, we

are likely to turn to institutional arrangements and other devices to ensure the reliability of partners in our exchanges and interactions. In these
circumstances, it is not trust (or more precisely, belief in the trustworthiness of others) that facilitates cooperation. As discussed later in the
chapter, this is because we cannot know that the other person's interests
encapsulate our own (see also Hardin 2002b). Indeed, we may even
know for sure that the other party has interests that conflict with our
own. If we cooperate at all in such cases, we do so because we believe
our partners have incentives to behave consistently with our interests.
These incentives, however, are built into the social structure; they are
not inherent in our personal trust relations. Incentive compatibility
may make our partners reliable but not necessarily trustworthy.

Even within families, friendships, and other very dense networked relationships, trust beliefs and relationships are variable and depend on
knowledge conditions, the kinds of tasks the other is being trusted to perform, and the context. When the costs of mistaken judgments become
high, or when the temptations to become untrustworthy are great, we
tend to turn to other ways of ensuring the competence and motivation of
those on whom we are taking a risk. This is often true even within families. It is almost always the case in business, government, and professional
relationships.

We discuss many of the mechanisms that society has devised for ensuring the reliability and competence of those on whom we need to rely.
Relying on trust relations is not the most common such mechanism. And
even when trust relations do facilitate one kind of cooperation, they may
inhibit others. For example, trust relations among those in a group can
create boundaries that inhibit relations with those outside the group.
Similarly, groups of trusted colleagues within an organization can build
power that is used to inhibit technological innovation, slow production,
or otherwise hold the firm hostage. Trust relations among cronies are a
major source of corrupt and inefficient government.

Yet under some circumstances trust and trustworthiness can *improve*
the workings of organizations and markets, as many writers have noted.
In these instances, trust and trustworthiness are *complements* to structured
incentives and to monitoring and enforcement mechanisms (see Arrow
1974, 24). The backdrop of third-party enforcement can give individuals
the confidence to treat each other as if they are trustworthy at least in those
domains where violations of trust will be punished or in which little is at
stake. Such a context may enable individuals to learn more about each
other, to begin to take risks with each other, and in time to become trustworthy to each other. Examples of third-party enforcers abound: legal
institutions that enforce contracts, managers who supervise employee relationships with clients, professional associations that investigate unethical behavior of their members, hospital boards that inhibit malpractice.

Third-party enforcers not only boost the probability of reliable behaviors but also create circumstances in which trust within certain relationships over certain issues becomes viable.

Trust is most likely to emerge in contexts in which the parties find themselves in ongoing relationships. This probability is enhanced to the extent that each party depends on the goodwill of the other to make things run more smoothly. Thus, the managers of firms and their subcontractors can become trustworthy with respect to their exchanges. Bankers and their lendees, social workers and their clients, physicians and their patients, supervisors and their subordinates in the workplace—all may perform better when they are able to take risks. But grants of discretion are unlikely unless some degree of trustworthiness becomes evident.

In many settings, unequal power may make it nearly impossible for the more powerful to convince the less powerful of the credibility of their trustworthiness. Yet when the relationship becomes personal and long-lived, trustworthiness may develop. Often trust seems to require that the more powerful treat the less powerful with respect and fairness, or that the more powerful treat the subordinate in the relationship as trustworthy by reducing monitoring and other intrusive interventions. Patron-client, physician-patient, and employer-employee relations are among the examples we cite as having this quality under certain circumstances. However, these trust relationships are fragile. Trust is generally about a very narrow set of tasks in a specific context. Trust is more easily broken and probably less easy to repair in these relatively one-dimensional relationships than in multifaceted relationships in which there may be more latitude and thus room for repair.

When trust does develop in power-dependent relationships, there may still need to be some form of third-party enforcement to ensure against the worst abuses or exploitation of the relationship, even when the basis of trust is the ongoing dyadic interaction. The most important means for creating the potential for a trust relationship based on encapsulated interest may well be the threat of ending the relationship. Such a threat is viable only when there is some level of mutual dependence. This is true even when the third party is far in the background. However, even in those cases in which trustworthiness seems to emerge, it may be an effect not of a belief that each party encapsulates the other's interest but rather of the more straightforward fear of loss of a loan, a welfare payment, or a livelihood. Given this dependence, demonstrating trustworthiness is important in maintaining the relationship with the more powerful party.

Most of the contemporary treatises on trust and its benefits are not attentive to the questions we raise. The authors of some of these works may define trust and trustworthiness differently. Ours is a relatively specific definition that imposes clear requirements on those we claim are trusting. Trust requires considerable knowledge. It is impossible by our definition to trust strangers and even many of our acquaintances, and it is virtually impossible by our definition to trust institutions, governments, or other large collectivities. Anyone who wants to make claims about trust or trustworthiness must have a definition that allows them to account for variation in its intensity, consequences, and probability.

There appear to be only three conceptions of trust that are at least moderately articulated and developed in the existing literature. These conceptions are differentiated by their grounds for supposing another is trustworthy. We can suppose you are trustworthy because we think you are morally committed to being so, because you have a relevant character disposition, or because you encapsulate our interests. In this chapter, we spell out the three conceptions of trust that are grounded in some kind of judgment of the trustworthiness of the potentially trusted agent or person. The first two are presumably clear enough, but it is worthwhile to spell them out so as to see what force they have in explaining behavior or social structures. We focus first on the encapsulated interest conception and then briefly discuss the other common theories.

Trust as Encapsulated Interest

Most of the discussion in this book is based on the encapsulated interest model of trust (Hardin 1991b, 2002b). According to this conception of trust, *we trust you because we think you take our interests to heart and encapsulate our interests in your own.* You do so typically because you want to continue our relationship, and you therefore want to act in our interests. By "encapsulate" we mean that to some extent our interests become yours in the trust relation between us. From this perspective, the trusted party has an important incentive to be trustworthy, and this incentive is grounded in the value of maintaining a relationship with the truster into the future. Of course, it is always possible that your concern for your own separate interests will sometimes trump your concern with ours, and thus we may face some risk in trusting you. In this case, you may sometimes act against our interests.

Such a violation of trust is especially likely to happen when there is a systematic conflict of interest between us, as when I could profit at your expense while seeming to act as your agent. There are many examples of such betrayals coming to light, often ending relationships once based on trust. Conflict of interest is a broader phenomenon, however, that can happen in simple business and other relationships in which there need not have been any trust. A disturbing recent example is the practice of many major investment and banking firms—including Merrill Lynch, Citigroup, Morgan Stanley, and UBS—of running "both investment banks and brokerages. Investment bankers help companies sell stocks and bonds. Brokers help investors buy stocks and bonds. Companies want to sell high; investors want to buy low. Companies want Wall Street to make them look good; investors want Wall Street to tell them which companies actually are good. When the same firm is advising both sides, someone is going to get a raw deal, *"even if everyone is acting honestly"* (Surowiecki 2003, 40, emphasis added). For examples of such conflicts of interest from professional practice and science, see chapter 6. On the encapsulated interest conception, when we trust you, our expectations are grounded in an assessment (perhaps inaccurate) of your interests specifically with respect to us. If we have a conflict of interest with you over the matter on which we might wish to be able to trust you, we have good reason to doubt your trustworthiness.

While superficial objections could be made to bringing interests into trusting relationships, such as one's relationship with a close relative or friend, they are clearly there much of the time. For many other trusting relationships, the whole point is likely to be interests. For example, people may have ongoing commercial relationships with local merchants or business people that become trust relationships. Such a view of trust fits quite well with a wide array of trust relationships. In fact, we most often trust those with whom we have ongoing relationships. And the richer the ongoing relationships and the more valuable they are to us, the more trusting and trustworthy we are likely to be.

This model of trust has been used in explanations of many behaviors and social phenomena, as it is in this book. For example, it is used here to explain the effects of asymmetric power on trust relationships (chapter 3); the ways in which distrust and trust can be asymmetric and how distrust grounds liberal theories of government (chapter 4); informal social devices for eliciting cooperation (chapter 5); quasi-institutional devices for overcoming conflicts of interest in our relationships with professionals acting as our agents (chapter 6); intraorganizational trust and distrust (chapter 7); devices of government and law to overcome lack of trust (chapter 8); and many issues in the transition from one form of social order to another on both the small and large scales (chapter 9).

The main factor that distinguishes trusting from other types of social relations, such as relations of simple coordination, is *the concern of the trusted with the truster's interests.* To say that we "trust" someone to coordinate with us when doing so directly serves their own interests is not a compelling use of the term "trust." The only issue at stake in the case of mere coordination is the other party's competence and understanding of the situation, such as another motorist driving in ways that do not lead to harm. In driving and many other contexts in which we are primarily concerned with successful coordination, we need not care very much about the others involved in that coordination effort, and in fact we are likely not to know them at all. Trust entails a stronger claim. For us to trust you requires both that *we suppose you are competent to perform what we trust you to do and that we suppose your reason for doing so is not merely your immediate interest but also your concern with our interests and well-being.* Although much of the discussion of trust is general and not very specific, actual trusting seems to be quite specific. I trust you to do certain things (and not other things). In our model, trust is a three-part relation. A trusts B with respect to issue x or issues x, y. . . . A is very unlikely just to trust B tout court. We expand this model in chapter 2.

One can argue that A trusts B with respect to x under a specific set of conditions that have as much to do with the nature of the relationship between A and B (that is, trust is a property of the social relation) as with the nature of A's interests and B's interests and with their levels of relevant knowledge or any other individual attribute (gender, education level, occupation). The analysis of trust based on factors such as interest and knowledge can then be embedded in the context of social relations and what we know about aspects of the relationship and the broader network of relations surrounding the A-B relation (for example, with actors C, D, E . . .).

Developing a relational model of trust should aid in the study of the diffusion of trust and distrust in social settings, such as within organizations or communities. Presumably these take quite different paths. For example, the diffusion of distrust in a social system or network of social relations might be quite rapid, whereas trust would be diffused only under a highly special set of circumstances. Such analyses should also put into relief the asymmetries between trust and distrust and help to sort out the significance of changing units of analysis (individual-level, relational-level, system-level). At least two broad substantive issues are raised by these considerations: the nature of the relation between any two particular actors and the determinants of trust between them (a dyadic focus), and the nature of the network surrounding these actors that might facilitate trust or the reconstruction of trust where it has been destroyed (the embedded conception).

This book assumes an essentially dyadic account of trust and trustworthiness based on the analysis of trust as encapsulated interest. We extend the model by assuming that relations of trust are embedded in a larger social context (see, for example, Granovetter 1985). On this account, the truster's expectations of the trusted's behavior depend primarily on assessments of the trusted's motivations. These assessments can be based on knowledge of the actor or knowledge of the structures in which the relationship is embedded. We expand on both of these bases of trust in chapter 2 on trustworthiness.

The purpose of the account offered here is to explain some trust-related behaviors and the implications of trust and distrust in many social and institutional contexts in order to make sense of a wide array of devices for organizing cooperative behavior in the absence of trust or in the presence of very weak trust. In general, we suppose that the success of cooperation under such conditions is a far more important social issue than are trust relations in many other contexts.

Note that the conception of trust as encapsulated interest implies that *many interactions in which there is successful coordination or cooperation do not actually involve trust.* In this book, this observation is fundamentally important because it is success in just such interactions that we wish to explain, whereas many discussions of trust take cooperation to be virtually defining proof of trust. Consider a very important daily interaction that we resolve with apparent ease and with neither knowledge of the other parties involved nor real concern for their welfare. We usually walk on sidewalks and drive on streets without difficulty. We coordinate with all the other pedestrians or drivers without running into them. You might be an unusually nice person who is deeply concerned with the welfare of others, but you need not have any such concern to be adequately motivated to avoid bumping into others. Your own interest in survival typically suffices. Indeed, you might wish you could simply will the others off the sidewalk or the road to let you pass more easily or safely. Trust is not at issue.

Similarly, in the cooperative venture of trying to elect a candidate whom you favor, you might vote because of the effects you want to have, not because you are concerned with the desire or interests of others who are also voting your way. This is yet another context that typically involves coordination in which trust as encapsulated interest is not at issue. You may have confidence in others to vote your way, but you need not trust them. In fact, there need be no trust whatsoever for you to succeed in these interactions.

There are many such daily interactions. *Trust involves a genuine involvement between you and the trusted other and a specific, not abstract, assessment of that other's motivations toward you.* If you have never met or in any way dealt with the other person—perhaps you cannot even see the driver of an unknown car—it is meaningless to say you trust that person. The word *trust* has no real meaning if it does not differentiate our relationships with others because trust is inherently about our relationships. Indeed, it differentiates our relationships because we trust some people but not others. For trust to yield explanations of behavior, it must tell us something distinctive about our relations with others.

Other Conceptions of Trust

In two alternative conceptions, trust depends on the moral commitments or the character of the potentially trusted person or agent. Despite the fact that moral commitments seem to be very important in motivating trustworthiness in the lives of many of us and therefore in evoking trust for us, and despite the fact that many writers on trust assert the centrality of such commitments, there is apparently no systematic work on the role and effects of morally motivated trustworthiness. From the sheer number of scholars who assert the importance of morally grounded trustworthiness, one could say that this is the chief alternative to the account of trust and trustworthiness as grounded in encapsulated interest. Unfortunately, however, the moral theory of trustworthiness and therefore trust is almost entirely undeveloped.

In the trust literature, the moral account leads to almost no explanations of social behaviors in general or of the social structures that result from it. Furthermore, such literature may offer no compelling accounts of why some are morally motivated to be trustworthy while others are not. The moral account of trustworthiness is more often asserted than either of the other two main candidate theories of trust—the dispositions and encapsulated interest theories—but it is generally asserted without argument, as though it were an obvious conceptual point or an undeniable fact of human nature. And it is seldom put to the empirical task of explaining different categories of important behaviors (Becker 1996; Held 1968; Hertzberg 1988; Horsburgh 1960; Jones 1996; Mansbridge 1999). Some data, however, seem to show that ordinary people characterize *trust* as moral, just as many scholars do (see, for example, Uslaner 2002).

Many, perhaps most, of the proponents of the moral theory mistakenly refer to trust as moral, although their actual claims and discussions are most often very clearly about the *moral commitment to be trustworthy.*[3] Of course, if others believe you have such a commitment, they can attempt to cooperate with you with relative confidence that you will live up to their expectations. But such knowledge of moral commitments realistically derives from information most likely obtained from ongoing relationships. It is something I come to know about you over time, and it is particular to our relationship as articulated in the encapsulated interest account. Occasionally you might assume that all those in a particular social category are morally committed to be trustworthy, but such categorical judgments are often wrong (see chapter 2).

Perhaps the leading recent proponents of a dispositional account of trustworthiness are Toshio Yamagishi and his colleagues (for example, Yamagishi and Yamagishi 1994), who include moral and other dispositions in their accounts. Bernard Barber (1983) and Tom Tyler (2001) similarly tend to have dispositional accounts of trustworthiness. One can imagine, however, focusing only on the disposition to have a particular character, as a stoic might do, and here we restrict the dispositional model to such dispositions.

It is commonplace that we each trust different people. This fact makes eminently good sense on the relational view of trust as encapsulated interest, but it does not fit well with the two accounts of trustworthiness as based on very general features of people (for example, the dispositional and moral accounts). When you trust someone whom others distrust, either you or they must be mistaken in assessments of that person's moral or character dispositions. The person's trustworthiness, on the moral and dispositional accounts, is independent of who is dealing with her; it is purely a feature of her morality or her character. In other words, *a person's trustworthiness is wholly nonrelational.* Yamagishi (2001) connects his dispositional account with what he calls "social intelligence." Some people are better judges of who is likely to be trustworthy or untrustworthy. Without an account of something like social intelligence, the dispositional model of trust would make little empirical sense of actual trust relations. We review this discussion more fully in chapter 2.

On the encapsulated interest view, some of us can trust while others distrust a particular person A, because some of us have ongoing relations with A that others do not have; those ongoing relations might be valuable enough to A to induce A to be trustworthy toward us. The universality of the moral and character views with respect to who is or is not trusted is not substantiated by our actual experience, and it suggests that these views of trust are not views that actually drive real people in their assessments of their own relationships with those whom they trust and those whom they distrust.

Parallel to the dispositional model of trustworthiness is a long-standing view that some people have a *disposition to trust.* One could usually reframe this claim as a matter of optimism, learned perhaps through experience, that others (and perhaps only certain classes of others) will be trustworthy toward us if we try to deal with them. Julian Rotter's (1967, 1980) interpersonal trust scale is intended to measure the disposition to be trusting, independently of any inquiry into the trustworthiness of those trusted. It is not a scale of the trustworthiness of the person or agent who is trusted. We discuss this empirical work in chapter 2, but in general we are not concerned with the possible *disposition to trust* in this book. In the context of trust relations, we treat any such disposition as a summary of one's experience. If most of the people you have dealt with have been trustworthy, you may typically expect to find it easy to develop relationships of trust with new people with whom you come to deal. That is, you are more willing to take a risk on someone unless the stakes are too high. Note, incidentally, that the moral theory of trust (that it is moral to trust) is far less developed and researched than the psychological disposition-to-trust theory, as represented in the extensive work of Rotter and many others.

Generalized Trust

Related to the view that some people have a disposition to trust is the somewhat complex and much grander claim that we have generalized trust in other people, independently of who the other people are. This is sometimes called social trust. It has arisen as a concept perhaps only because poorly worded, imprecise questions in the two main surveys of political attitudes in the United States have forced fairly grand answers. The National Election Studies (NES) surveys measure attitudes toward government, and the General Social Survey (GSS) of the National Opinion Research Center (NORC) taps attitudes toward the general other person in society. The latter seems to allow people to say that they trust just anyone at all. Quite possibly, no one would ever have thought it plausible that anyone trusts literally everyone in the world, but thousands of people answering these survey questions are virtually forced to say that they are either *generally* untrusting or *generally* trusting. The thesis that science is socially constructed may well be apt in this case. Here are the GSS questions that are used to measure generalized trust:

1. Do you think most people would try to take advantage of you, or would they try to be fair?

2. Would you say that most of the time people try to be helpful, or that they are mostly looking out for themselves?

3. Generally speaking, would you say that most people can be trusted, or that you can't be too careful dealing with people?

It seems sensible to suppose that someone might distrust almost everyone and even literally everyone in certain groups. That same person is unlikely to trust almost everyone or even everyone in any particular, broadly defined group. Hence, we could have group-generalized distrust, although it is unlikely that we would have group-generalized trust (see chapter 4). Some people might be more or less likely to take a risk on interacting with certain groups of people based on fairly naive conceptions derived from their past experiences, but that is not to say that they would *trust* these other groups of people in any meaningful sense (see chapter 2 on social cognition). Also, many people might have very general distrust in government and all its agents in certain contexts. For example, Jews in Nazi Germany must have come to distrust the Nazi government and virtually all German soldiers and police officials.

The idea of trust in government has some of the quality of the idea of generalized trust in everyone in some broadly defined group. The government of a large nation such as the United States or the United Kingdom has hundreds of thousands of employees, all of whom are in some vague sense the agents of citizens but very few of whom take our particular individual interests seriously or even know anything about most of us. We could readily distrust all of these people as a class, and therefore distrust government, for the simple reason that we cannot see how our interests are encapsulated in theirs.

Ironically, the battery of four questions that constitute the trust scale in the National Election Studies surveys were originally proposed as a cynicism scale. That scale was invented in an effort to understand lack of participation in democratic politics, especially in the United States, where turnouts in national elections were typically below 60 percent when the scale was introduced around 1960. Couched as a general attitude toward government, the questions in this cynicism scale are:

1.   How much of the time do you think you can trust the government in Washington to do what is right—just about always, most of the time, or only some of the time?

2.   Would you say the government is pretty much run by a few big interests looking out for themselves or that it is run for the benefit of all the people?

3.   Do you think that people in the government waste a lot of money we pay in taxes, waste some of it, or don't waste very much of it?

4.   Do you think that quite a few of the people running the government are crooked, not very many are, or do you think hardly any of them are crooked?

Cynicism is essentially the belief that others are motivated only by self-interest. That suggests that high cynicism should be a very neat, although not perfect, analogue of distrust. Hence, generalized cynicism can make sense just as generalized distrust can make sense.

Inverting the cynicism scale to make it a measure of generalized trust makes much less sense. The questions in the scale seem to be a fair guide to cynicism, hence to distrust, but no guide at all to trust on any of the three standard conceptions of trust.[4] The trust questions in the General Social Survey should also be good for tapping cynicism. We view many of the empirical claims about the seeming goodness of generalized trust as actually about the benefits that would follow from generalized trustworthiness; hence, our focus in this book is primarily on devices used to ensure trustworthiness and cooperation in the absence of the possibility of assessing trustworthiness accurately or at all.

Declining Trust?

The central question about trust in larger social contexts is what makes people trust each other when they have relatively little direct relationship with one another. It is unproblematic that trust emerges in smaller communities and is maintained among small groups or dyads when individuals interact regularly over time. To be beneficial, trust must be maintained and even constructed, but there is relatively little under-

standing of how this is done or can be fostered. There are extensive literatures on property rights, appropriate organizational forms for solving principal-agent problems, and correctives for high information and
transaction costs. Contracts cannot be perfectly specified, information is
imperfect at the margin, private incentives do not always work, and enforcement costs can outweigh the benefits of many transactions. Yet explicit and implicit contracts continue to be made, people believe they can
predict the relevant behavior of others, and collective action problems
are sometimes solved despite evidently contrary incentives.

Often the combination of trust and reputations for trustworthiness resolves these problems. Putnam (2000) argues that trust, produced by a
dense network of secondary associations, improves the quality of representative government, leads to economic development, and makes neighborhoods safer and more livable. Russell Hardin (2002b) suggests that the
long-term persistence of structural inequalities between certain groups or
individuals is a consequence in part of initial differences in the learning
of trust, which is to say in learning how to distinguish who is likely to be
trustworthy; such learning must be difficult for those who seldom see
examples of trustworthiness (see chapter 5). By implication, policies designed to reduce economic and political disparities must build a social
infrastructure that ensures a rupture with the past and that promotes substantial relearning of the likelihood of trustworthiness.

Survey research findings on trust have been interpreted to suggest that
both overall levels of interpersonal trust and general levels of trust in
government and other major social institutions are in steady decline in
the United States and some other industrial states, especially Canada,
Sweden, and the United Kingdom. The popularization of the general conclusion of these studies has become a major part of public debates about
the performance of government and the viability of democracy in an age
of apparent distrust. Indeed, most of the recent literature on the supposed
decline of trust in the United States and on its putative effects is based on
such survey research. Putnam (2000) examines numerous possible explanations of the seeming decline in trust. Some of these explanations suggest that it is a problem of individual-level psychological changes, and
others suggest that it might be an artifact of structural changes.

Consider various individual-level explanations that have been offered.
Putnam (2000) has suggested that the rise in television viewing undercuts
social participation; lower levels of social participation lead in turn, he argues, to lower levels of trust in varied contexts. John Brehm and Wendy
Rahn (1997) argue that materialism is rising and that it undercuts trust.
One possible motor for this effect is that a society's single-minded focus
on economic success leads its members to pay less attention to others and
therefore to trust each other less. Laura Stoker (personal communication,
May 6, 2000) argues that deliberate programs to induce people to make

demands on government (under the Great Society and other initiatives at various levels of government) succeeded in stimulating direct participation, but that the subsequent failure of government to resolve the relevant problems led to a loss of trust in government. William Julius Wilson (1987, 144) argues that the hard-core poor, especially in racial ghettos, develop little social capital. The departure of the more nearly affluent ghetto dwellers makes it "more difficult to sustain the basic institutions in the inner city," and those who remain behind face the decline of their "social organization." We argue in chapter 5 (see also Hardin 2002b) that this problem is exacerbated by the difficulty of learning to trust in a context in which networks of beneficial interaction are poorly developed, beginning already at the level of weak familial networks but extending outward to larger social networks that are weak and even unreliable. A child who suffers abuse whenever he or she interacts with adults is unlikely to risk interactions and therefore is unlikely to learn that some adults can be trustworthy.

There have been two large structural changes that might have changed the meaning of the responses to the standard trust questions used in most survey research on these issues. Increasing urbanization entails interactions with larger numbers of people, so that "most people" is a much larger category for current generations than for respondents forty or fifty years ago. Similarly, increasing immigration and increased mixing across ethnic groups make it likely that in many advanced industrial societies "most people" is a more diverse category than it was earlier. This effect might be part of the reason blacks in the United States are reported to be less trusting than whites: as a mere structural fact, a black must have about seven times more interactions with whites than a white has with blacks (Blau 1994, 30–31). The standard survey research questions about trust do not easily address these causal claims. In this book, we focus directly on causal claims, specifying the nature of the role of trust in society, its limits, and its alternatives.

An Overview of the Book

We have discussed the most developed approaches to trust in the social science literature, and we have introduced the conception of trust as encapsulated interest. In this book, we extend and apply this model to a wide range of phenomena traditionally viewed as central to the understanding of the production of social order in many contexts, from small groups to nation-states. We evaluate the existing evidence and clarify the role that trust plays in the construction and maintenance of social order. Contrary to much of the literature on trust produced over the past quarter-century, we argue that trust plays a relatively small role on the grand scale in producing and maintaining social order. We usually rely on and cooperate with each other, not because we have come to trust each other, but because of the incentives in place that make cooperation safe and productive for us. We can take risks on one another even as complete strangers in many situations because of the presence of institutions, organizations, and networks that constrain exploitation and provide individual and collective incentives that reduce externalities.

In chapter 2, we consider the bases for beliefs in the trustworthiness of others. Such beliefs derive from cognitive processes that help us assess the role of social structure in the actual production of trustworthiness. Stereotypes, reputations, norms, communities, networks, and incentives all come into play. We do not rely primarily on morality or personal dispositions to produce trustworthiness in most contexts. In the encapsulated interest view of trust, judgments of trustworthiness are most often grounded in specific evaluations of the actors involved, the nature of the issues at stake, and the social context. Few can be said to be trustworthy in any meaningful sense of the term under all conditions. Yet the bulk of the existing empirical evidence, especially that derived from general social surveys, as noted earlier, fails to take context into account, even though the data come from many different cultures. We discuss the limits of evidence as well as the limits of the theoretical claims based on such evidence.

Chapter 3 addresses an undeveloped topic in the extensive literature on trust. Given that trust is often treated as an individual character trait or moral disposition in this literature, few have explored the topic of power and its relationship to the possibility for trust. Once trust, like power (Emerson 1964), is defined as *a property of a social relation,* other aspects of the relationship beg for analysis. The vast array of social relations characterized by power inequality comes under the microscope in this chapter. Two features of the power relation that affect trust are the degree of mutual dependence on the relationship and the nature of the alternatives to the relationship for each party. Greater access to alternatives yields greater power, lower dependence, and less possibility for trust. High mutual dependence creates the grounds for high trust as encapsulated interest as well as trustworthiness.

Various devices are used by the powerless to reduce their dependence and thus their vulnerability. Where trust relations are desired, powerful actors can attempt to make credible their commitments not to exploit others, or they can use various strategies that increase the possibility that they can be trusted by making their decisions and actions transparent, avoiding secrecy and the appearance of unfairness, and embracing principles of distributive and procedural justice. Similar issues arise at the macro level with respect to dishonesty, corruption, and the exploitation of power inequalities, topics we explore in our discussion of economic and political transitions in society in chapter 9.

Chapter 4 focuses on power inequalities, which, among other forces, sow the seeds of distrust. Distrust can create barriers to cooperation and exchange when there is little institutional backing to block the worst possible outcomes. But under some circumstances, distrust is warranted and sometimes desired as an approach to limiting possible abuses of power, as in the design of democratic government. In this chapter, we analyze various devices for managing relationships pervaded by distrust, as well as the devices we employ in settings in which distrust is warranted and in settings in which there is simply a lack of trust. These different conditions result in different outcomes. Interesting conclusions can also be drawn from the fact that there are asymmetries of trust and distrust, which, when acknowledged, clarify many of the grander claims about the role of trust in society and the "problem" of distrust. In particular, there are significant asymmetries in both the knowledge and the motivational elements of trust and distrust.

Important social consequences also emerge from the interrelationship between trusting relations and relations dominated by distrust. Sometimes trust networks, for example, are based on ascriptive characteristics that solve problems of within-group exchange and cooperation and lead to increased within-group social cohesion. But these same trust networks may impede the development of crosscutting social ties and lead not only to a lack of trust of "outsiders" but to active distrust. In addition to exploring such social consequences of trust relations in the context of distrust, we examine the role of liberal distrust of government in the production of good government. And we comment on the difficulties that are created, especially during political and economic transitions, by corrupt and unreliable governments (see also chapter 9). In some circumstances, the state itself can be a major source of distrust in society.

In the face of distrust or even the lack of trust, we commonly attempt to create structures—at the interpersonal, small-group, organizational, or societal level—to protect us against the potential for harm. In some arenas, it is not likely that even a strong state or a powerful oligarch could secure for us the conditions that make certain cooperative relations possible. For this, we rely on *informal social and organizational mechanisms* to give potentially useful partners the incentive to be cooperative. Such devices, the subject of chapter 5, have long been the focus of anthropology, sociology, and even economic history. This class of cooperative interactions may be the most numerous in our lives, lying somewhere between those that can be managed with trust relations secured by encapsulated interest and those that are significant enough to be managed by the state and by legal institutions, such as the courts. We explore devices such as reputational mechanisms, networks of social capital that enable cooperation without trust, and norms backed by communal sanctions. For color, we include a discussion of the duel as a social device for controlling interpersonal behavior among aristocrats and the use of fictive kin relations in such places as Japan and Kenya to secure cooperation and in some instances genuine trustworthiness when familial ties do not exist. We also discuss numerous forms of lending without legal backing, as in the interesting case of the Grameen Bank.

In the absence of such informal social devices that enable cooperation, we sometimes rely on nongovernmental institutions, some of which have the force of the state behind them if backed by legal institutions such as the courts. These are the subject of chapter 6. Professional organizations are one class of such devices that create the framework within which trust relations between professionals and their clients, or between agents and their principals more generally, can emerge as ongoing relations of encapsulated interest. Two cases are discussed briefly: the American Medical Association (AMA) for doctors in relation to patients, and the American Bar Association (ABA) for lawyers in relation to their clients. We offer more extended discussion of the kind of regulation of science and business that can lead to conflicts of interest in which perverse incentives arise that, if unchecked, threaten to destroy the very basis for productive enterprise in these realms.

When people have little confidence not only in politicians, doctors, and lawyers but also in business executives who distort stock prices (as at Enron and WorldCom) and scientists who fake results (such as the physicists Viktor Ninov and Jan Hendrik Schön, as discussed in chapter 6), our attention as social scientists is drawn to the failure of organizational incentive structures to restrain opportunism or to sanction the untrustworthy and even the incompetent. These issues and their relationship to trust are explored in depth in chapter 6. Three major institutional structures that have emerged to constrain the behavior of specific actors to act in our interest come under scrutiny: professional regulation, the competitive self-regulation of scientists, and the market regulation of business.

Managing conflicts of interest and creating wide-ranging devices for aligning individual and collective interests are the main goals of organizational design, we argue in chapter 7. But supervision, rules, monitoring, and clever pay schemes cannot fully constrain opportunism in the face of relatively powerful incentives for profit-seeking or gain. Furthermore, contracts are almost always incomplete, and the parties involved often have asymmetric information, if not differential power. Even though creating and sustaining trust relations in most organizational contexts can be very difficult, their value is clear.

Organizations have to deal with several types of general problems with respect to performance: problems of adverse selection and moral hazard. Adverse selection can be mitigated to some extent by training and, at the extremes, firing. Moral hazards arise when monitoring is impossible or impractical. Typically in such cases more resources are invested in the selection process and in reliable networks that produce high-quality employees. Reliance on incentives to reward competence, commitment, and loyalty is the cornerstone of the human relations industry. But incentives do not always work, and conflicting interests may result in unanticipated consequences. Monitoring and sanctioning can fill the gap, sometimes with negative consequences if practiced too intrusively or too severely. Under circumstances we survey in this chapter, treating employees *as if* they can be trusted may generate not only trustworthiness but also greater satisfaction, better performance, and reduced transaction costs. But there are limits to the extent to which this strategy can be successful in many organizational and institutional contexts. Even professionals—such as priests, teachers, physicians, or investment counselors—violate the trust placed in them.

The devices discussed in chapters 5 through 7 often cannot adequately ensure cooperation and block opportunism in the absence of a stable state, as we argue in chapter 8. Reliable and stable state institutions can produce the conditions necessary to facilitate exchange and cooperation in the market and in civil society even when there is low interpersonal trust (chapter 8). Democratic forms of government, an independent judiciary, and the public accountability of elected and appointed officials can increase the confidence of citizens, even if these features of state institutions do not always lead to accurate assessments of the trustworthiness of their political representatives.

States that engender willing compliance from citizens tend to be those that are viewed as fair, competent, and relatively good at serving the public interest (Levi 1997, 1998). Democratic regimes are more likely than other forms of government to reach this goal in the modern era. But doing so may require institutionalizing distrust in the design of government to create the checks and balances required to limit abuse of power. If so, then the very general claim that "trust" in government is good is wrong. We explore the complexities of this set of debates both in chapter 8 and in chapter 4.

But states change, sometimes overnight (as in Eastern Europe and the Soviet Union in 1989), and the political and economic landscape can be dramatically altered in the process. Also, people who move from one state to another (or from one country to another) must come to terms with new political, economic, and social conditions. These are among the types of transitions we discuss in chapter 9. Transitions create uncertainty and often risk. Under these conditions, people tend to cooperate and exchange with those they know or are connected to in some significant way. Immigrants are drawn into ethnic enclaves at the end of a migration chain that provides them with the resources, however minimal, to become productive and to settle into a new environment. Networks of trusted family, friends, and acquaintances can aid adjustment but can also block access outside the group and reduce the capacity for assimilation into the larger culture, and thus such networks can actually decrease economic and social opportunity. In this way, extant social capital may reduce the possibility for further accumulation of human capital (see Cook 2005; Cook, Rice, and Gerbasi 2004). These and other complex links between trust, social networks, social capital, and successful cooperation, exchange, and economic growth are discussed in chapter 9.

We explore the many disruptions that large-scale economic and political transitions have entailed in a number of historical and cultural contexts, from early modern Europe to contemporary Vietnam, Africa, Eastern Europe, and Russia. Reliable and stable institutions that reduce corruption and make possible economic growth are critical. Institutional legitimacy is based on reliability, consistency, and fairness. These factors may lead to perceptions that institutional and state agents are likely to be reliable. We need a more complete model of the process of transition from one state to another if we are to understand more fully the production of social order based on devices for securing cooperation without trust. To suppose that social order and economic growth depend critically on trust relations within society is sociologically and politically naive.

The fundamental problem of social order in society is the main focus of our book. How is social order produced? How is cooperation sustained? What is the role of trust in the production of cooperation and social order? How is distrust managed? What are the consequences for social systems of the lack of trust? How do social systems shift from one state to another? What factors hinder or facilitate the production of trust in society? Who trusts whom, under what conditions, with what consequences? And most fundamentally, how do we secure cooperation and social order in society when there is little trust or trust is impossible?

Our primary aim in this book is to provide conceptual clarity about a subject that is fraught with vagueness in the social science literature as well as in popular writings. If we succeed in this task, we will have made a major contribution to the understanding of the limited role that trust typically plays in the production of social order in the modern era.

Chapter 2

Trustworthiness

TRUST IS unproblematic in a world in which everyone is trustworthy, but it is often not easy to know the extent to which others will be trustworthy with respect to matters of concern to us. They may turn out to be trustworthy in all respects, but we may not know that and may not be in a position to ever know it. In this book, we focus on how actors come to cooperate with and rely on each other even when they cannot expect each other to be trustworthy. The degree of uncertainty often determines the nature of the mechanisms put in place to guard against misjudged trust. Another key factor is the nature of what is at stake. If the stakes are high, we are much more likely to require that there be organizational or institutional mechanisms in place before we are willing to rely on others.

In this chapter, we investigate trustworthiness: how we attempt to assess the trustworthiness of others; how our own characteristics make us more or less likely to take risks on others, especially those we do not know; and how various devices protect us against exploitation or betrayal. Our primary focus is on interpersonal relations, although in subsequent chapters we explore social devices at the organizational and institutional levels that facilitate reliability and cooperation in the absence of trust.

To recapitulate the definition from chapter 1, trust in our framework is a three-part relation: an actor A trusts another actor B with respect to matter x or matters x . . . z in situation S. A is said to trust B (or an agent of a larger collectivity) in situation S when A believes that B is trustworthy with respect to the matters at hand (x . . . z). In particular, A believes that B's interests encapsulate her own interests. This implies that A knows or can assess the trustworthiness of B with respect to x in situations like S. Judgments about the trustworthiness of B involve judgments made by A (the truster) based on the assessments of B (the trusted) of the nature of x (the focus or object of the trust relation) *and* of features of the situation S in which the relation is embedded.

The focus of much of the psychological work on trust is the individual, not the social relation or social structure in which the individual is embedded. This is especially true of models of trust based on the morality or psychological dispositions of the potential trusted party. We discuss some of this psychological work and its limitations before moving to the focus of the book: the more relational analysis of trust and trustworthiness. The role of psychology is to give us a window into the cognitive elements involved in assessments of trustworthiness and the characteristics of the truster that may make trust more likely to develop under some circumstances.

We take trustworthiness to have a meaning that is relevant to the theory or conception of trust with which it is used. As we argue, people can be reliable for many reasons, including the mere compatibility of their incentives with our own. Those incentives can be imposed on them by us or by organizations of various kinds. Or they can just happen to be the same as ours. We say that someone is trustworthy, however, only if they are morally committed to being so, have a disposition to maintain a trustworthy character, or encapsulate our interests. The last of these characteristics makes trustworthiness a relational concept, just as trust as encapsulated interest is relational. A person can be trustworthy to us but not to others. The other two ways of being trustworthy are not relational in this way. Someone who is trustworthy in some respect is also reliable in that respect, but the converse is not true. One can be reliable without being trustworthy in any of the three senses here.

First, we discuss the characteristics of the truster (A) that are related to risk-taking and may facilitate or hinder the development of trusting relations. Next, we focus on A's assessments of the person potentially to be trusted (B), and we discuss determinants of the accuracy of such judgments. Before examining how features of the situation S or the social context affect the possibility of trust, we discuss how *the nature of the relationship between A and B* affects A's assessments of B's trustworthiness. We acknowledge the reciprocal dependence and interdependent interests that emerge when individuals are in relationships that involve repeated interactions as key features of trust relations. The extent to which their interests become interdependent such that the interests of one party encapsulate those of the other is central to our analysis. Then we move to a focus on the situation S in which the actors are embedded, and we examine how some social contexts facilitate trust while other contexts clearly make the formation of trust relations difficult, if not impossible.

Like many other analysts, we see competence and motivation as the two main aspects of trustworthiness. In many situations, both aspects are important, as when a mother decides to trust a babysitter with her newborn infant for the evening. In other situations, competence may well be the primary concern, as in physician-patient or lawyer-client relationships.

But even in this latter category, if there is much at stake, we are also concerned about the motivations of the trusted to take our interests to heart. Among the class of competent physicians who are reliable by reputation (or certification), we want for our open-heart surgery the one who cares the most about our well-being, not the one who prefers the golf course to the operating room. And among those classified as competent lawyers, we want one who does not have a conflict of interest in pursuing our case.

In the final section of this chapter, we provide a brief overview of the various organizational and institutional mechanisms that compensate for the absence of trust. These mechanisms form the core of the remaining chapters. Many problems arise in our efforts to assess the trustworthiness or reliability of others. These problems multiply when those others have power over us, especially when they are agents of larger social entities or institutions, such as tax authorities or government more generally.

The Psychology of Trusting

In some of the earliest work on trust, Julian Rotter (1967, 1971, 1980) found that actors (the trusters in our model) differ in their capacities for "trust." Some people are more likely to be trusting than others in any situation; thus, we have "high trusters" and "low trusters" in society. The underlying argument is that people either are born this way or learn to be more or less trusting as a result of their experiences, especially in their early interactions, most likely with family members (see Hardin 1993; 2002b, ch. 5). In much of this literature, the key variable is the individual's propensity for risk-taking or, conversely, the individual's level of cautiousness in pursuing social opportunities. In addition, some people are more willing than others to believe that the world is a benign place, often with good reason. We examine this tendency to be trusting before moving to a discussion of the more significant determinant of trust: the assessment of the trustworthiness of others.

Rotter (1967, 65) defines trust not in relational terms, as we do, but in psychological learning-theory terms as a "generalized expectancy held by an individual that the word, promise, oral or written statement of another individual or group can be relied on." This psychological definition of trust focuses on the issue of the expected reliability of another, and it appears to include both the competence dimension of trustworthiness and the intentions or motivations of the recipient of trust. It is quite different from our encapsulated interest model of trust as relational.

Though some argue that we are born trusting (as in Annette Baier's [1986] claim for "infant trust"), a presumption about which we have little evidence, most argue that we learn to trust. For this reason, developmental psychologists focus a great deal of attention on early childhood experiences and their effects on the capacities of children to trust. If a child's primary caretakers are not trustworthy toward the child, it is unlikely that the child will learn to trust others. Ken Rotenburg (1995) finds positive correlations between mothers' fulfillment of promises to their children and their children's trust in their parents and their teachers, as well as positive correlations between mothers' trust beliefs and their children's trust beliefs in their teachers. Fathers' promised cooperation in a prisoner's dilemma (PD) game, he finds, is positively correlated with their children's promised cooperation in the game. Other clinical psychologists have studied the development of trust and its consequences (King 2002; Weissman and LaRue 1998). In a similar vein, Rotter and other social psychologists focus on the capacity for trust as learned from experience (see also Hardin 2002b, ch. 5).

In surveys conducted over two decades (the 1960s and 1970s), Rotter explored the differences between high and low trusters as well as the nature of the relationship between trust and trustworthiness. There is an overall positive correlation between trust and trustworthiness in his data, as well as a positive correlation between low trust and untrustworthy behavior (indicators of cheating and lying). High trusters are more trustworthy, find it difficult to lie, and are generally more likable. They are also more likely to contribute to the provision of public goods through volunteering, and they report engagement in other socially valuable behaviors (Rotter 1967, 1971, 1980; Yamagishi and Yamagishi 1994; Mackie 2001). The generality of these findings has not been fully determined, but if they hold they imply that knowing whether someone has a general tendency to be trusting also provides some information about her likely trustworthiness. The difficulty with drawing such inferences from survey data, however, is that *the responses are generic and not specific to particular social relationships.*

In addition to reportedly being more trustworthy, Rotter finds two other important characteristics of high trusters. First, high and low trusters differ in their approach to strangers. High trusters are more likely to take a risk on a stranger than are low trusters. According to Rotter (1980), the difference is captured in the following stylistic quotes. The high truster says: I will trust him or her until we have clear evidence that he or she can't be trusted. The low truster, in contrast, says: I will not trust him or her until there is clear evidence that he or she can be trusted. The main divide is reflected in their *levels of cautiousness.*[1]

Second, high trusters are more likely to have the *capacity* to differentiate whom to trust from whom not to trust on the basis of fairly specific cues. Toshio Yamagishi (2001) calls this capacity "social intelligence" (see also Yamagishi, Kikuchi, and Kosugi 1999). This result is important for our relational analysis of trust since it implies that some actors are simply more likely to be able to form trust relations based on their own psychological makeup, derived in part from the social settings in which they live and their past experiences.

Rotter's results indicating that high trusters are less cautious than low trusters *and* that high trusters have a greater capacity to discern which individuals are trustworthy and which are untrustworthy are derived from survey work on trust. Other studies suggest, however, that the generality of the survey measures of trust is problematic for predicting actual behavior. For example, in an analysis of Rotter's Interpersonal Trust Scale (ITS), Thomas Wright and Richard Tedeschi (1975) detect three orthogonal factors suggesting that there may be several independent dimensions of trust. A general trust measure (based on survey items such as "Generally speaking, would you say that most people can be trusted or that you can't be too careful dealing with people?") would not differentiate between these dimensions. The three factors that emerge are: political trust—beliefs that politicians and the media are trustworthy; paternal trust—measures of the perceived trustworthiness of benign authorities (for example, parents, salesmen, or experts); and trust of strangers—measures of the degree to which potentially exploitative, anonymous others are trusted (typically the focus of measures of what has come to be called "generalized" trust). Trust of strangers refers to the notion that people are generally selfish and thus we must be cautious in dealing with them or they may take advantage of us or cheat us (Wright and Tedeschi 1975, 472). The implication of these findings is that the general trust scale is much less able to predict behavior in certain domains than are the more specific factors (see also Levi and Stoker 2000).

Ironically, one of the reasons Rotter (1971) pursued survey work on trust was that he was dissatisfied with the seemingly exclusive focus of other social psychologists at that time on prisoner's dilemma games. Rotter's primary purpose was to investigate the extent to which trust was a *general* personality factor that could be used as a predictor of socially oriented cooperative behavior in a wide range of settings. He argued that the PD and other games might produce relatively specific reactions more characteristic of competitive situations and thus might not generalize to other types of interpersonal interactions. In addition, Rotter was concerned with the validity of the existing survey measures of trust. He worked for almost two decades on measurement issues before turning back to experimental work on trust (for a review, see Cook and Cooper 2003).

Although the development of Rotter's Interpersonal Trust Scale fell under scrutiny, his findings regarding high trusters' lower levels of cautiousness and greater capacity to differentiate whom to trust from whom not to trust were later replicated and investigated more fully in experimental work on cooperation. Early attempts to validate Rotter's work by assessing its capacity to predict behavior found that low trusters are more suspicious of experimenters (Roberts 1967) as well as peers (Wright 1972) in PD games. Toshio Yamagishi and Karen Cook (1993) have found support for this result in a study comparing high and low trusters in the United States and Japan. The low trusters in both cultures are more cautious when dealing with strangers than are the high trusters, although low trusters in Japan are more cautious than those in the United States overall. In part, this reflects the differences in levels of trust in the two cultures. General trust levels are higher in the United States than in Japan (Hayashi 1995; Yamagishi and Yamagishi 1994). Specifically why psychological levels of general trust vary from culture to culture is not well understood (but see Buchan, Croson, and Dawes 2002). These differences may derive from social structural differences across cultures, or they may be a residual of past histories involving political and economic factors that generated cultures of trust or distrust.

Because high trusters are more likely to interact with strangers than are low trusters, at least on first encounter, their expectations concerning the other's reliability are thus more likely to be confirmed. Risk-taking based on their lower levels of cautiousness provides them with the opportunity for more profitable interactions over time. Low trusters, on the other hand, are simply less willing to engage strangers at all; thus, their higher levels of caution lead them to enter fewer beneficial interactions (Hardin 1993; Orbell and Dawes 1993). This characteristic of high trusters *benefits* them, especially in the face of substantial opportunity costs (Hayashi 1995).

Optimism about the likely reliability of others, which Yamagishi calls "general trust," may be a by-product of the development of the kind of social intelligence that provides clues to the potential trustworthiness of others in a society. Encounters with trustworthy people, however, are a prerequisite for developing this kind of social intelligence. Low trusters may not have had many such encounters (Yamagishi 2001). If anything, John Holmes and John Rempel (1985, 190) conclude, "there is some evidence that distrusting individuals adjust less effectively to the features of particular relationships than do trusting individuals." This may be the result of limited past opportunity to learn the contours of trusting relationships (Hardin 2002b, ch. 5).

Hence, the experimental and survey approaches reach similar conclusions. Yamagishi's (2001) experimental work on social intelligence helps to explain some of the observed differences between high trusters and low trusters. In addition, it implies that high trusters may be more trustworthy than low trusters because they have found it to be more rewarding than have low trusters, for whom being trustworthy may have had much poorer payoff. Rotter's (1971, 1980) survey work provides some evidence to support the claim that there is a positive correlation between being trusting and being trustworthy, but he offers no clear explanation for this finding, except to argue that high trusters are less cautious and thus may engage over time in more profitable interactions. This would be the case, however, only if high trusters encountered primarily trustworthy others. This may partly be a matter of projection, or of generalization from one's own tendencies. Differences in the processing of evidence and in social intelligence more broadly also have implications for the accuracy of judgments based on cultural and social stereotypes of the type often employed in assessments of trustworthiness in the absence of more reliable evidence based on experience and past behavior. We explore these topics later in the chapter.

Differences in general optimism about others thus seem to predict some aspects of behavior. Guided by Rotter's survey work on the differences between high trusters and low trusters, experimentalists explore the correlations between trust and cautiousness as well as the correlations between trust and the capacity to assess the trustworthiness of others. Not only are high trusters more willing to take risks than low trusters, but when they do they have resources, such as social intelligence, that allow them to make more accurate assessments of the other party's trustworthiness. This work, with its implication that some actors are more likely than others to enter into potentially trusting relations, sets the stage for our relational account of trustworthiness.

In the next section, we move from discussing the psychological research on the characteristics of trusters and its implications for trust relations to a discussion of the psychological work on the ways in which we assess the trustworthiness of others.

Assessing Trustworthiness: Socially Significant Cognitions

Although people may vary in their general levels of optimism or willingness to take risks on others, the level of trust in a society is primarily a function of the extent to which individuals deem relevant others to be trustworthy in specific relational contexts. For this reason, examining the factors that determine our perceptions of trustworthiness is important for the study of trust. What affects our judgments of trustworthiness, however, is a complicated question. The extent to which the truster believes her interests are encapsulated in the interests of the potentially trusted party is affected not only by the larger social context but by features of the immediate situation. It is also affected by characteristics of the person whom she may or may not trust as well as by characteristics of the relationship between her and the potentially trusted party.

Organizational and institutional mechanisms often help us determine the reliability of others or reduce the risk of failed trust (see chapters 5 through 9). In this section, we focus primarily on the social psychological literature on the cognitive processes involved in assessments of trustworthiness, although our relational account of trust implies that such assessments are most often derived from judgments we make about others with whom we have specific social or organizational relations.

For trust as encapsulated interest, the main issue is how a relationship that leads to trust gets under way in the first place. Once a relationship is under way, the incentive for trustworthiness is often built into the relationship itself if it is valued. The "shadow of the future" may be enough to ensure trustworthy behavior. For trust that is grounded instead in an assessment of the other party's moral commitments or character, the main issue is how one can assess either of these well enough to judge whether that person will be trustworthy. In both cases, the initial problem is cognitive: how can we infer trustworthiness from another person's traits or their revealed actions, past and present?

Aside from our relations with our closest friends, colleagues, and family members, whom we generally know quite well, it is difficult to determine whether the new people with whom we come into contact will be trustworthy in a particular interaction. On small matters, this poses no real problem. We can afford the risk that the stranded traveler at the airport to whom we lend twenty dollars might not fulfill her promise to mail us a check repaying the loan. The loss will not be great if the money is never returned. More commonly, however, we refrain from taking such risks even when the stakes are low. If we do enter a relationship with a complete stranger, we do so by first taking a minimal risk to gather more information through interaction before investing very much in the relationship and eventually taking larger risks (Cook et al., forthcoming). Literature is full of examples of those who initially trust someone and then are later disappointed by them.

How do we know when and with whom to take the risk of cooperating on initial encounter? First, we focus on the inferences a person makes *about another person.* (Later we discuss the inferences a person draws from the social context.) Making inferences about another person is a general problem for both dimensions of assessing another's likely trustworthiness: competence and motivation. In trying to assess my trustworthiness, you might focus on characteristics that reveal or at least suggest my character or my moral commitment, my capacity to recognize how my trustworthiness toward you affects my further interests, and my competence to do what would fulfill your trust. The traits that become salient for individuals assessing the trustworthiness of other persons fall into two categories: cultural stereotypes or socially significant (socially valued) characteristics, and the similarities of those other persons to themselves.

Status characteristics such as age, gender, occupation, educational achievement, and race or ethnicity often form the basis for performance expectations and judgments about competence in specific situations, especially task settings (see Ridgeway and Walker 1995). They may also form the basis of judgments about likely motivations to be trustworthy. Available cultural stereotypes and schemata fill in for the details we are missing in our efforts to evaluate others. Under certain conditions, as for example when we are under time pressure, we use stereotype-based inference strategies as cognitive shortcuts (Andersen, Klatzky, and Murray 1990). Under cognitive overload we even prefer the use of stereotypes, tend to recall information that is consistent with our stereotypes (Macrae, Hewstone, and Griffiths 1993), and fail to process information that disconfirms them (Dijksterhuis and van Knippenberg 1996). We generalize on the basis of such socially valued characteristics well beyond the evidence at hand in making assessments of the likely performance capacities and competence of others. Similarly, we may expect that others with these characteristics are more likely to be trustworthy in the sense that they are competent to manage the matter at hand.

It is much harder to evaluate motivations on the basis of these socially valued characteristics, although under some circumstances we do so. For example, a mother might judge a middle-aged female to be potentially more competent than a male to manage the task of caring for her infant while she runs into a store for a moment. However, she would be on riskier ground in making a judgment about whether someone might be motivated to harm the infant. In sum, in making judgments based on the characteristics of the actors with whom we are involved, we might first rely on stereotypes and deem those individuals with socially valued characteristics as more trustworthy than individuals without such characteristics.

Besides relying on the stereotypes dictated by the stratification system in our particular culture, we may make judgments of the trustworthiness or reliability of others by assuming that those *similar* to us are trustworthy while those not similar to us are not trustworthy. For example, if we must decide whom to trust with a suitcase while we step into a restroom at a train depot in a foreign country, we are likely to first look for those who are similar to us in some significant way. Typically, we assess those similar to us in somewhat superficial ways (for example, those of the same age, gender, and nationality) as more likely to be reliable under these circumstances. As Eleanor Singer (1981, 78) notes, in many situations, "similarity with respect to one or more statuses may be used as a clue to probable similarity in opinion, attitude, ability or values." Although we may not use these clues very often or may not use them at all when the risk is very great, in some settings such information suffices at least for a while.

As an example of the tendency to focus on similarity as a basis for assessing the trustworthiness of others when family and kin ties are not available, Chinese entrepreneurs rely on secondary characteristics, such as birthplace, to assess reliability (Hamilton and Cheng-Shu 1990). For certain business purposes, others from the same place of origin are treated as if they were kin and expected to be honorable associates or partners in trade. In this case the individuals rely on the probability that, being linked through a social network, they know people who know both of them even though they are strangers to each other. Such relations act as a surrogate for reputation.

In settings in which actors have other bases for their judgments of trustworthiness, similarity assessments may play only a minor role. For example, in a study of interpersonal trust among managers and professionals in organizations, Daniel McAllister (1995) finds that supervisors' assessments of peer performance are strongly associated ($r = .40, p < .001$) with assessments of the trustworthiness of the peer, whereas social and ethnic similarity are not associated with "cognition-based" trust (but for an argument on "social trust," see Tyler 2001; see also Costigan, Ilter, and Berman 1998). Similarity on social and ethnic dimensions is a determinant of what McAllister calls "affect-based trust," which is closer to friendship and less predictive of competence assessments. Essentially, McAllister finds that when other, more reliable indicators of trustworthiness are available, such as job performance, people are less likely to use similarity as a proxy for trustworthiness.

P. C. Wason (1960) and others present psychological findings to support the argument that individuals, besides attributing high levels of trustworthiness to those with highly valued social characteristics and to similar others, often have a strong confirmation-seeking (cognitive) bias in their work (Mitroff 1974; Good 1988, 40) and in their judgments of others. That is, individuals may seek evidence that confirms their actions, decisions, and judgments of others rather than weigh the evidence more carefully. This bias is an example of cognitive inertia (see, for example, Good 1988), based on the more general "cognitive miser" model of information processing (see, for example, Howard 1995).

As a result of the operation of a confirmation bias, reputations (discussed more fully in a later section) can be self-enforcing. Much of the time reputations are more likely to be confirmed than disconfirmed, even in the face of evidence to the contrary, because evidence that does *not* support the reputation (as it is initially perceived) is given less weight (Levin, Wasserman, and Kao 1993). For example, Carmen Huici and her colleagues (1996) examined the effect of information that disconfirms an individual's original evaluation of a group. When information is presented that disconfirms the initial negative evaluation of a group, subjects do not change their description of the group. The disconfirming information has little impact.[2]

The role of evidence is significant in judgments of trustworthiness in part for the reasons understood by cognitive psychologists. Cognitive inertia can be blind—good or bad reputations are equally subject to the confirmation bias. There is one asymmetry, however, that is substantial in the case of trust. If someone breaches our trust, our faith in that person is seriously undermined; however, "if an untrustworthy person behaves well on one occasion, it is not nearly so likely that the converse inference will be made" (Wason 1960, 43; Hardin 2002b, ch. 4). A good reputation can easily become tarnished, but a bad reputation is very difficult to overcome.

Competence and motivation are the two main aspects of trustworthiness that actors assess when making judgments. Although evaluations of both aspects should perhaps be part of every judgment of trustworthiness, individuals may focus on competence more than motivation in some cases, as noted earlier, or they may focus on motivation when competence is not particularly at issue. For example, when an individual relies on cultural stereotypes to assess the trustworthiness of another person, she may be focusing on the competence of the other person, not his motivations. Socially valued characteristics (race, age, gender) are often associated with greater competence. Status characteristics theory is organized around the principle that individuals with high-status characteristics have higher "performance expectations" (Berger, Cohen, and Zelditch 1966, 1972). A performance expectation is defined as a "prediction about the quality of the performance" of an individual (Meeker 1994, 103). Status characteristics and the performance expectations associated with them "reflect cultural beliefs that may or may not be objectively true" (Balkwell 1994, 125). Yet these stereotypes are *believed* to be true and thus are acted on as if they were true. The principles in status characteristics theory highlight the point that when actors rely on cultural stereotypes to assess someone's trustworthiness, they are often assessing that person's competence.

In contrast, when an individual relies on the degree to which the other person is *similar* to her, she may be focusing on the *motivation* of that other person. She might also, of course, be making an assessment of competence. But motivation may be the aspect of trustworthiness that is more salient when inferences are based on similarity—perhaps because actors know their own motivations, which they feel are cooperative and benign. They may assume that similar persons have similar motivations of cooperativeness.

The accuracy of judgments of trustworthiness is important, since those judgments may put individuals at risk if they are inaccurate. Psychological research based on social cognition indicates both that we frequently use cultural stereotypes as bases for judgments, especially as shortcuts to more complex forms of information processing, and that these judgments can be wrong because they overemphasize stereotypic characteristics. In a later section, we comment on individuals' capacity to exploit this tendency for their own ends by mimicking traits or manipulating the situation to appear to be trustworthy (see especially Bacharach and Gambetta 2001).

In sum, the psychological literature provides evidence that individuals tend to be more or less optimistic about the reliability of others. In addition, in comparison to low trusters, those who are more optimistic often are more trustworthy, more willing to take risks (less cautious), and better able to assess accurately the trustworthiness of others. Individuals typically focus on the traits of others and rely on cultural stereotypes or on the degree to which others are similar to themselves in determining their trustworthiness in the absence of information derived directly from social relationships. Individuals can also be stuck in a kind of cognitive inertia in which they focus only on traits that confirm their original assessment (sometimes derived from reputations). In the following section, we turn to a more relational account of the nature of trust and examine the nature of the actual relationship between A and B as a determinant of A's assessment of B's trustworthiness.

One of our main arguments is that *trustworthiness and reliability are generally too important in society to leave to the vagaries of interpersonal relations or to the unpredictability of individual behavior.* Thus, we quickly leave behind the more psychological work on trust. A primary task in the design of social systems is devising mechanisms for ensuring, reinforcing, and requiring the reliability of the actors involved. For this analysis, we first need to understand the nature of trust *relations* based on encapsulated interest. The institutional design aspects of this argument introduced at the end of this chapter foreshadow later chapters of this book.

Repeated Interaction and the Larger Social Context

Because actors depend on one another for resources, among other things, they need to evaluate each other's trustworthiness. This is especially problematic in the initial stages of an interaction, when there is little or no knowledge base for assessing trustworthiness (Holmes and Rempel 1985). We may have limited knowledge of the other, except for what we see of their visible characteristics, and we have no interaction history from which to draw information. We discussed earlier how we make temporary assessments of trustworthiness based on inferences derived from traits or characteristics of the actors we confront, but these judgments are often erroneous and thus risky. The emergence of reciprocal dependence early in a relationship (see Molm and Cook 1995) provides a potential foundation for the development of trust (Holmes and Rempel 1985, 195). Trust forms in a relationship as an exchange of messages and actions gradually reduces uncertainty, so that trust is grounded in the interactions of the partners over time (Kelley and Thibaut 1977). Repeated interaction forms the primary basis for trust as articulated in the encapsulated interest theory of trust (see Hardin 2002b).

Our evaluations of trustworthiness thus depend more on the nature of the relationship involved, the network in which that relationship is embedded, and other features of the social context or environment than on our initial individual judgments of the actors involved, which in some instances may be quite misleading. Clearly some risks pay off and others do not in the development of trust relations. One way in which the social context matters is that it can determine the nature of the events or the class of communications for which trust is an issue. For example, if the setting is an office and you are a potential new officemate, there is a limited range of actions over which we would need to assess your trustworthiness. Initially, we might simply need to know whether you can be trusted with gossip about the boss. Trustworthiness in this case would mean that we can trust you not to reveal to the boss what we have conveyed to you in confidence, especially if such a revelation would be damaging to our relationship with her. Later we might need to know whether we can trust you to meet deadlines and to cover for us when we are unable to complete our work on time. Our trust relations thus may be quite specialized, covering only a small subset of the aspects of our work lives. It is a small set of individuals whom we might trust with virtually all aspects of our lives—perhaps a parent, a spouse, or a sibling, but not many others.

To the extent that we are mutually dependent on one another, we are likely to develop a method for assessing each other's trustworthiness over time and to find ways of managing the risks involved for both of us or giving each other incentive to be trustworthy. In the office example, it is the repeated nature of our interaction and the opportunity for continued future contact that give us reason to maintain our commitments and become trustworthy partners in our employment situation. In addition, the larger social context often provides a "safe" environment in which we can come to trust each other. It does so by reducing some of the uncertainties that might surround our interactions, making it less likely that we would have to rely entirely on trust. Moreover, the social context can help determine the type of events and communications for which trust is relevant. However, just as some social contexts can provide a safe haven by ensuring repeated interactions and limiting the range of events in which trust is at issue, some social contexts provide little or no such contextual assurance. In the next section, we look more closely at social contexts and the effects of features of the social context on assessments of trustworthiness.

What types of knowledge do we have access to, and how does this knowledge help in our assessments of trustworthiness? The social context in which we are embedded provides some relevant knowledge. Being embedded in a web of social relations reduces uncertainty and increases the likelihood that we will trust you in at least two ways. First, your ties to people in our network give us some knowledge about your trustworthiness. We can seek out information about you through our connections to others in the network. Your reputation, then, helps us determine whether to risk cooperating with you. Reputation is relevant to this situation in another, perhaps more important way. To the extent that we are connected in a web of relations, even when we do not know each other at all we have some assurance that if we are the objects of a failed trust we can take action to rectify the situation. At a minimum we can use these social ties to pass along information that might harm your reputation for further interactions with those who are willing to take an initial risk in interacting with you as a stranger.[3] If you are not trustworthy, we can take actions that will affect your future interaction opportunities. Therefore, the network of social relations to which we both belong provides not only a source of information about you but also the opportunity for us to contribute to your reputation should we choose to provide information about your lack of trustworthiness. And your interest in maintaining a good reputation reduces some of the uncertainty we face in deciding whether you are trustworthy in the first place.

The role of reputation systems varies depending on whether the social system is closed or open. Closed systems or networks do not permit entry and operate as closed communities (see Cook and Hardin 2001). Open systems involve opportunities for entry and exit and are open-ended in their network of social relations. In closed trading communities, reputation schemes that codify the trustworthiness of the actors in terms of their tendency to default can be effective because negative reputations force the exclusion of those who violate communal norms (Yamagishi et al. 2003; Cook and Hardin 2001). In more open societies or networks, negative reputation schemes are less effective because they are limited in the extent to which they are transferred to all members in the network—information flows only to those actors who are linked directly or indirectly.

In addition, actors can alter their identities in ways that make it easier to reenter trade networks without being recognized as having had a negative reputation. In Yamagishi's experimental study on Internet trading networks (Yamagishi et al. 2003), both the level of honesty of the traders and the price of the commodities could be tracked. While negative reputation systems are more effective than positive systems in building trust in closed systems, positive reputation systems are more effective than negative systems in building trust in open systems. Traders are rated on their honesty and thus accumulate reputation points that are published on the network during each transaction. Negative reputation systems typically drive "bad" actors to change identities to make this reputation mechanism generally ineffective.

Reputational mechanisms are central to the study of the nature of credit reports and their impact on the efficiency of credit markets and ultimately consumer prices for loans as well as for goods and services. In some countries, such as Australia, credit reporting systems include only negative information, such as default rates or late payment information. These credit markets, compared to more comprehensive credit reporting systems that include both positive (on-time payment rate, account histories, and so forth) and negative information, lower access to credit, especially for those who are at greater risk. More inclusive credit systems (such as in the United States) open the market for credit, making it more effective and typically more efficient (Barron and Staten 2003).

Reputation is important in embedded social relations because it gives us information about you. In this respect, it is past-oriented. And if you value your reputation for the opportunities it gives you, then it is also a means by which we can affect your actions toward us, because we can disseminate information about you if you prove to be untrustworthy. In this respect, it is future-oriented. However, our *own* reputation is important as well when considering whether we should be trustworthy. We are less likely to cheat someone we know, or even someone we do not know, if he or she happens to be connected to our friends or business contacts. Our concern in this case is with the quality and veracity of our own reputation. Realizing that a person we deceive might disseminate information that discredits us through various networks encourages us to be trustworthy.[4]

Although reputation is important in trust relations, it is not the only thing we worry about if we choose to take advantage of someone. Social networks can often implement informal (or formal) sanctions to address "bad" behavior. Yet, as Cook and Hardin (2001) argue, norms of exclusion work well in closed groups and are much less effective in open networks. Norms of exclusion eliminate those who have "cheated" from the group or system of trade (Hardin 1995, ch. 5; 2002b). Open networks, as noted earlier, cannot operate as easily on the basis of exclusion since actors may simply adopt new identities or relocate to enter a new community. Sanctioning is based on the capacity to monitor, but monitoring can occur only under certain circumstances, and it usually has costs.

Monitoring is a feature of social networks that can reduce the likelihood of mistrust in some contexts (for example, in closed versus open networks). To the extent that both sanctioning and monitoring can easily occur in the network, reliance on trustworthiness as an individual-level trait is greatly reduced. We can rely on the social structure instead. In fact, in most circumstances those we come to trust are embedded in a network of relations that provides assurance of their trustworthiness.

The more problematic cases are those in which there is no embeddedness and we confront a strange person perhaps in a strange location. Here embeddedness is at best a very weak constraint, and our knowledge base is clearly inadequate. Thus, people often lean on schemata, stereotypes, and other cognitive processes as bases for action under such circumstances, in ways we have described earlier in this chapter. Interestingly, many of the strategies people use to overcome the difficulties of traveling in strange lands without much knowledge of the local culture or any personal ties involve creating social connections that serve as surrogates for a network of relations that matter. Such strategies mimic efforts to develop more enduring social structures as constraints on opportunism. Taxi drivers, desk clerks, waiters, and even merchants fill the void, not always reliably. Repeat interaction forms the basis for these "proto-trust" relations, at least from the point of view of the tourist. Shifting from a one-shot interaction to a repeat interaction opens the door for norms of reciprocity to operate and for the dyadic sanctioning of behavior. Your failure to be trustworthy or to engage in mutually rewarding reciprocal behavior can then be met with my withdrawal from the relation. No such contingent behavioral mechanisms operate in a one-shot interaction, unless the interaction is embedded in a larger context that provides some recourse for failed trust.

Thus far, this chapter has focused on the three-part trust relation involving only individual actors. Individual actor A trusts individual actor B with respect to matter x or matters x . . . z in situation S. We have looked at the nature of actor A (tendency to be more or less trusting), how A assesses the trustworthiness of B by focusing on B (status characteristics, similarity to self, repeated interaction, and so on), and how A assesses the trustworthiness of B by focusing on the situation S (for example, embeddedness, reputation, and possibility for sanctioning and monitoring). However, individual actors also attempt to assess the reliability of organizations or companies from which they want to purchase commodities or with which they want to enter into agreements.

The marketing literature is a great source of information about brand names and reputations since firms invest significant levels of resources in establishing and protecting brand names that consumers can "trust." In much the same way individuals are often concerned with protecting their perceived trustworthiness and integrity, organizations are also concerned with being perceived as reliable, especially when future professional opportunities hinge on these judgments. In this context, trustworthiness often means nothing more than reliability. What firms want is to inspire confidence in their product or service and to obtain consumer loyalty. They do this through brand names—established trademarks and copyrights that are most often viewed as reliable indicators of trustworthiness. Decisions about whom to trust are often based on reputations, in which we can invest and which therefore we can manipulate. Reputations at the individual level thus function like brand names or trademarks at the organizational level (Dasgupta 1988).

Can we trust the standard signs and symbols of trustworthiness in an uncertain world in which mimicry pays? Signals include a wide range of phenomena, including brand names, accents, religious affiliation, even facial expressions (Bacharach and Gambetta 2001). The work on social cognition reviewed earlier in this chapter also addresses issues of the veracity of social signals and the inferences we draw from them (including those based on traits and other individual-level characteristics). Signals may be especially effective when providing them is differentially costly to the false signaler. Even signals that are more easily subject to abuse and fraud, such as trademarks and copyrights, may yet remain effective owing to an extensive legal and regulatory apparatus (Bacharach and Gambetta 2001).[5]

A recent study of taxi drivers in Belfast and New York City (Gambetta and Hamill, forthcoming) examines how taxi drivers use cues or signs to determine the trustworthiness of potential customers. Because they do not have enough time or the luxury of repeated interactions to learn about their customers, taxi drivers quickly assess the trustworthiness of those customers. They have to decide quickly whether to pick up a passenger, and this can be a dangerous affair. While taxi drivers are only 0.2 percent of the population, they account for 7 percent of all work-related homicides in Belfast. One technique the drivers use approximates "statistical discrimination." Being a member of a category that is statistically more or less dangerous is a type of signal that provides a basis for risk assessment; thus, drivers look for the signs of membership in these categories. Gender and age are similarly profiled in both locales: older passengers are preferred over younger ones, and females over males. Ethnicity and religion are clearly relevant, but they differ depending on the driver's own ethnic or religious background, especially in Belfast. This is not to imply that drivers are racist, sexist, or ageist, but rather that drivers select fares from categories of people they believe are less likely to be harmful.

Another technique used by taxi drivers to assess trustworthiness is based on experience—in the form of either direct experience themselves or vicarious information they acquire about groups, places, or times. These experiences provide reputations for groups (if identifiable) as being good or bad customers (reliable or not). Drivers are not satisfied by cheap signals (those that are easy to mimic) with regard to passengers' trustworthiness. They do not take elementary signs at face value, and they look for multiple signs over a wide range of possibilities. They also look for contextual cues. For example, while being young and male often combines bad signals, a young man leaving a certain type of church is more likely to get a taxi ride than a young man just walking along a street. Case studies of such patterned risk-taking as this one provide rich detail about the social and contextual cues used by those whose profession requires that they be competent at accurately judging reliability. In the case of taxi drivers, their lives depend on their capacity to process trust-related information quickly and carefully.

Credible Commitments

Consider briefly the types of mechanisms we believe are commonly put into place to manage social relations in more complex arenas in which it is unlikely that trust alone will suffice for very long, if at all. When there is no ground for trust, we can often establish reliability by demonstrating our commitment to take relevant actions. If we, whom you have no reason to trust, wish to convince you that we will be reliable in taking some action that will benefit you, we can try to establish a credible commitment. Thomas Schelling (2001) cites the example of the Greek leader Xenophon, who, pursued by the Persians, backed his army against an almost impassable ravine. To an objector, he argued, "I should like the enemy to think it easy going in every direction for him to retreat; but we ought to learn from the very position in which we are placed that there is no safety for us except in victory" (Thucydides 431 B.C.E./1972). The most important aspect of this commitment device was to get the Greek soldiers committed to each other in fighting energetically. They could not flee individually, so they had to stand together against the Persians, because they would otherwise suffer great personal costs.

There are at least three general ways to create credible commitments. First, we can use Xenophon's device of cutting off options.[6] Second, we can arrange to suffer losses from our failure to act cooperatively; for example, we might post a bond that is forfeited if we do not act as promised (a device sometimes called "hostage-taking" by economists; see Williamson 1993). And third, we can bring in a third party to oversee and even enforce the commitments we make to others. The last category includes the use of contract law, which is among the most common and standardized of all devices for creating credible commitments. All of these devices can be especially important in contexts of asymmetric power relations.

There is a surprisingly large literature, from both empirical studies and game experiments, on making credible commitments and on the value of such commitments.[7] Some of the results are mixed, perhaps especially in experimental work on posting a bond to secure another's expectation of one's reliability. In principle, posting a bond should facilitate cooperation in at least three ways. First, it should reduce the incentive to act uncooperatively. Second, by offering some potential compensation for losses, it should reduce the cost of uncooperative behavior. Finally, it should serve as a signal about characteristics of the poster that are perceived by others to be related to the poster's likely or even expected responses to opportunities to default and incentives to act uncooperatively (Raub and Weesie 2000).

To overcome a lack of trust, the amount of a bond (pledged to the second party if the first party defaults) should be large enough to compensate for a failure of reciprocal cooperation, or at least large enough to reduce the probability of such a failure. Compensating the truster is often more important than reducing the probability of abuse by the trustee. (The latter might be, in principle, harder to judge.) Moreover, the posting of a bond may itself give a positive signal (Snijders and Buskens 2001). Posting a bond may thus induce the other party to risk cooperation for two different reasons. The willingness to cooperate increases not only because the incentive structure changes in a favorable way but also because of the *mere fact* that the other has chosen to post a bond. Similarly, not posting a bond when one could do so produces a negative signal. Unfortunately, these signals are deceptive (see Bacharach and Gambetta 2001). Those who post a bond are not more likely to reciprocate cooperative behavior, and those who do not post a bond are not more likely to fail to reciprocate.

Beyond credible commitments, the range of devices that societies and individuals have developed to handle problems of potential untrustworthiness is remarkable, as the following chapters attest. These chapters focus explicitly on the wide variety of social and institutional devices available to facilitate cooperation when trust is absent or doubtful. Behind many of these devices are institutional arrangements that generally make it the interest of the trusted to behave in a trustworthy manner, but many of them work even in informal contexts without the possibility of substantial enforcement.

Concluding Remarks

We have examined several key aspects of trustworthiness based on a simple model of trust as a three-part relation (A trusts B with respect to matter x or matters x . . . z in situation S). First focusing on the psychological literature on trust, we discussed the positive relationship between trust and trustworthiness as well as the differences between high and low trusters. High trusters are not only more trustworthy but also more apt to take bigger risks on others; they are also better able to assess accurately the trustworthiness of others. Next we examined how individuals rely on their cognitive capacities to make social judgments of trustworthiness, especially when initially deciding whether to enter a relationship or engage in a transaction. Social psychologists have determined that, in the absence of other information, individuals often deem others with highly valued status characteristics and those who are similar to themselves as more trustworthy. The reliance on social cognitions to make these judgments of trustworthiness, however, is often flawed, and the judgments may not be very accurate. Given the precarious nature of these judgments, individuals seem to rely more often on their embeddedness in social relationships to reduce uncertainty about their potential partners and thus make a determination of their trustworthiness concerning the matter at hand.

Repeated interaction, reputation systems, and sanctioning and monitoring capacities are important features of the social context that affect our assessments of trustworthiness (or provide the backup for inaccurate assessments and thus the potential for handling failed trust). After discussing social cognition and the local social context, we mentioned some of the devices employed by organizations and other collective actors to ensure trusting relations or to enhance the capacity for trust. The irony is that reliance on organizational rules and institutional devices may increase over time and thereby undermine the capacity for trust in society or reduce the need for it. This dilemma is discussed in the chapters on organizations (chapter 7) and on state institutions (chapter 8).

Now that we have clarified the meaning of trust (chapter 1) and analyzed the bases for judgments of trustworthiness (chapter 2), we can specify when we rely on trust for producing cooperation and when we rely instead on functional alternatives (chapters 5 through 9). We can also identify some of the obstacles to trust (chapter 3) and specify the consequences, good or bad, of distrust (chapter 4). The final step in this process is to relate our findings to broad questions of institutional design, such as governance rules in organizations (chapter 7) and states (chapter 8), as well as in large-scale economic and political transitions (chapter 9).

The Hobbesian solution to problems of pervasive distrust is to impose incentives on people to behave as though they were trustworthy. In essence, this is the resolution of the problem of trust implicit in many social institutions, organizations, and even informal groups. Commonly, these devices enable us to avoid the worst of all possible outcomes in our dealings with others so that we may cooperate in achieving much better outcomes than the status quo. Sometimes these devices seem to tell the whole story of why people act more or less cooperatively, and we would not think that trust plays a major role. For example, strong police or military imposition can stop violent disorder. In other cases, such as contractual relations, the background of legal enforcement reduces the risks of undertaking many cooperative endeavors.

One may suppose that the best of all worlds is one in which we have legal or other enforcement mechanisms as well as trust relations. *Trust relations over lesser issues may well require strong enforcement on larger issues that sets the background conditions for trust by blocking especially devastating losses.* More generally, we wish to give a systematic descriptive account of available institutions and social practices, both historical and contemporary, for structuring interactions in ways that make cooperation and—sometimes—trust work when initially there is little or no ground for trust.

Chapter 3

Trust and Power

ONE OF the most important achievements of many societies, and especially of modern democratic societies, is the regulation of various kinds of organizational relations to make them less subject to the caprices of power. Such regulation is partly spontaneous rather than politically determined. People in ostensibly powerful positions often need cooperation from those under them if they are to succeed in their organization's purposes and in their own personal interests. When such regulation exists in the background, the less powerful might well be able to trust the more powerful. Even in the most sanguine cases, however, the one-sidedness of power relations must often cast doubt on the trustworthiness of the more powerful partner.

Even in democratic societies and organizations designed to give voice to the less powerful, great power differences can undercut the possibility of voluntary and uncoerced participation. Power inequalities are ubiquitous in modern societies; thus, any treatise on trust must take them seriously (Baier 1986; Hardin 2002b, ch. 4). They cannot be assumed away in any theory that deals with the world of social relations and social institutions. Power inequalities also create fertile ground for distrust (see chapter 4), especially when institutional constraints on abuses of power are weak or nonexistent.

In general, trust in the encapsulated interest model is more likely to occur in relationships in which there is not a marked power difference between the actors involved. Much of the trust literature assumes equal power relations, as would be typical among peers, friends, colleagues, and the subjects in standard experiments and surveys on trust. Although some of the research focuses on hierarchical relations and the possibility of trust emerging among parties of unequal power (see, for example, Kramer 1996), that literature largely ignores the potential impact of power differences.

The general view of the distinctive features of trust and power in relationships, however, is captured in Mark Granovetter's (2002, 36) statement that "horizontal relationships may involve trust and cooperation, and vertical relationships power and compliance."[1] Trust and power are typically viewed as orthogonal. In this chapter, we wish to present a more complex view of the links between power and trust. We discuss the ways in which power inequality serves primarily as an obstacle to building trust in relationships between actors who would often benefit from mutual exchange or cooperation. More generally, the management of power relations in a society is a key factor in determining the capacity for trust. If powerful actors have few constraints on the exercise of their power, our capacity for trust in them is limited. Later in the book, we identify organizational and institutional devices that constrain the unchecked use of power and create the social space for cooperative relations. In addition, we discuss some of the obstacles to building trust that are related to power differences, such as the lack of transparency and the failure of distributive or procedural justice. We begin with a discussion of power and then examine a number of cases in which the link between power and trust is important, including in physician-patient relations, employer-employee relations, and relations between representatives or agents of different firms.

Power, Dependence, and Trust

Power is commonly defined as if it were independent of the relationships in which it is exercised. In the political science literature, for example, power is often treated as an attribute or a resource of an actor or social unit rather than as a characteristic of a relationship between actors.[2] We treat both power and trust as relational constructs. Let us begin with a standard definition of power—based on the conception of power developed by Richard Emerson (1962, 1964, 1972)—that is especially useful in the analysis of personal relationships.

For Emerson, power in a relationship between actors is based on the degree of dependence of the actors on one another. Dependence is determined by two factors: the degree to which actor A values what B offers in the relation, and the degree to which A has access to these resources from sources other than B. High value and low access to alternatives mean that A is highly dependent on B, and thus that B has high power over A. In contrast, low value and high levels of access to alternative sources for A generate low dependence on B, and thus low levels of power for B in the relationship. The main power-dependence proposition is that *dependence is the basis of power in an exchange relation* (Emerson 1962, 1964; Cook and Emerson 1978). That is, the power of actor A over actor B in the A-B relation is a function of B's dependence on A.[3]

This general proposition relating power and dependence has been demonstrated to apply in many types of relations, including employer-employee relationships, marital relationships, friendship and dating relationships, and other social exchange relations involving mutual dependence that can be defined as relations of encapsulated interest. In addition, the power-dependence proposition applies to other types of social units, including relations between groups, organizations, and even nation-states (see Cook and Rice 2001). In this chapter, we examine the ways in which such power impedes the development of trust as encapsulated interest. And more generally, we examine the relationship between power and trust in society.

That we might not trust those who have power over us is not surprising. As Russell Hardin argues (2002b, 100): "The mutual trust that depends on reciprocal relations cannot easily develop in such unequal, nonreciprocal contexts."[4] In an iterated exchange between two relatively equal partners, both stand to lose more or less equally when one party fails to honor his part of the bargain. If a much more powerful partner defaults, however, she might be able to exact benefits without reciprocating. And the weaker party to a substantially unequal trusting relationship is at threat of seeing the interaction terminated at any time. In general, therefore, the weaker party cannot trust the more powerful much at all, especially in the initial stages of a relationship. Inequalities of power thus commonly block the possibility of trust. It would be unwise simply to assume that a more powerful actor is trustworthy in the sense that her interests *typically* encapsulate those over whom she has power.

There is a further interesting problem in power relations in which there are several or many subordinates. These subordinates may come to distrust one another over time. For example, courtiers are typically in contest with other courtiers over who has the greatest favor of the king (Hardin 2002b, ch. 4). And powerful actors often work hard to foster distrust among those over whom they have power, as captured in the phrase "divide and conquer" (see also chapter 7). As Emerson (1972) argues, thwarting coalitions of the less powerful is one of the ways in which powerful actors maintain and enhance their power over others. Power-disadvantaged actors, on the other hand, may coalesce to gain power if they can achieve mutual trust rather than succumb to mutual distrust (on "power-balancing" mechanisms, see Blau 1964; Emerson 1972).[5] Beginning with a discussion of power relations between individuals, we examine several cases in which the potential for trust has important consequences for the actors involved.

Interpersonal Power Relations and Trust

Experimental evidence indicates that trust emerges in ongoing relationships when both parties have an incentive to fulfill the trust (see, for example, Malhotra and Murnighan 2002; Molm, Takahashi, and Peterson 2000). One major source of this incentive is the implicit commitment to the relationship itself, based in part on a concern with maintaining future interaction opportunities. In a dyadic relation, both parties must have a desire to continue the relationship for it to remain viable. Over time mutual dependence on the relationship may emerge and secure some degree of commitment. However, in a relationship in which there is a power difference between the actors, the degree of commitment to the relationship may also be asymmetric. The less powerful actor in a relationship may even offer greater commitment as a way of "balancing" the power differential (Leik and Leik 1977). This is only one way in which power differences between actors affect commitment and the possibility for trust.

Trust may emerge in relationships characterized by power differences under some conditions, but such trust—if it occurs at all—is fragile for a number of reasons, including the fact that the individuals involved typically have different perceptions of the nature of the relationship based on their relative positions of power.[6] Both high- and low-power actors in social relations seem to recall more trust-increasing behaviors (such as efficiency, competency, and emotional support) than trust-reducing behaviors on the part of each party. Hence, there seems to be a general positive bias linked to trust per se. However, when asked to focus specifically on behaviors that decrease trust (such as failure to complete a task, "two-faced" behavior, lapses in attention or courtesy), low-power actors recall more trust-reducing actions by the high-power actor (Kramer 1996). We might infer that self-serving bias operates in the recall of trust-related behaviors in dyadic relationships involving significant power. In addition, the low-power actors recall more negative actions overall than do the high-power actors in the relationships, possibly reflecting actual behavioral differences.

Low-power actors ruminate over the relationship more than do high-power actors. The low-power actors believe the high-power actors focus on their relationship more than they actually do. A common finding in the relationship literature is that the low-power (more dependent) actors are more attentive to interaction nuances than are high-power actors. Those in powerful positions are generally less focused on the details of the relationship and less attentive to their own behaviors that might be perceived as inhibiting the development of a trusting relationship with "subordinates" (Kramer 1996).[7]

Evidence in the literature on physician-patient trust relations supports this conclusion as well. Patients are much more likely to ruminate over the relationship and to be attentive to the interaction details that sometimes inhibit the formation of trust than are the physicians (Cook, Kramer, et al. 2004). Evidence also suggests that, as a result of the perceived power differential in their interactions with physicians, patients frequently do not communicate important information that might be relevant to accurate diagnoses but is also embarrassing. Some of these power differences may be linked to discordant patient and physician statuses, including gender, race, ethnicity, and sometimes age. Lawrence S. Wissow and his colleagues (2003) found, for example, that compared to white mothers, black mothers bringing their infants for initial pediatric visits are less likely to disclose personal information to white doctors. Similarly, white mothers are less likely to disclose relevant information to a white male physician than to a white female physician. Over time black mothers disclose progressively more information, but only when they see a white female doctor, suggesting that the longitudinal relationship facilitates the development of trust. Patient-centered behaviors, which are more typical for female than for male doctors, also may contribute to the development of trust in racially discordant patient-physician dyads. Indeed, many patients prefer status-concordant physicians (that is, those of similar gender, race, ethnicity, language, and sometimes age) (Saha et al. 1998; LaVeist and Nuru-Jeter 2002; García et al. 2003). We expand on the example of power differentials in physician-patient relations since there is a substantial literature that has developed over the last decade on the topic of the role of trust in these relationships (see Cook et al. 2004).

In physician-patient relationships, mutual dependence can emerge between the parties to the exchange even though there is an inherent inequality in the relationship based on a clear power differential. Although this power differential derives in part from the differential competencies of the parties with respect to medical issues, both parties must rely on the other to some extent. Most physicians need patients as much as the patients need physicians, although market factors can alter this equation. In some rural areas, the number of physicians is so limited that the patients have very little choice of provider. This significantly reduces the dependence of the physicians on the patients, often making them less responsive to especially difficult or troublesome patients. Without a continuous supply of patients, however, the physician cannot practice her trade. And many physicians prefer to treat patients they can trust, since they are typically more compliant with medical regimens and less likely to resort to litigation. Patients generally receive better care in the context of an ongoing dyadic relationship in which the physician gets to know their health history and general life circumstances (Leisen and Hyman 2001; McWilliam, Brown, and Stewart 2000). Audiey Kao and his colleagues (1998), Dana Safran and her colleagues (1998), and David Thom and his colleagues (1999) show that patient trust increases with the number of visits to a single physician and with the length of the physician-patient relationship. Hence, maintaining relationships is an important factor in both the emergence of trust and the quality of care. If genuine encapsulated-interest-based trust emerges at all in physician-patient relationships, it does so in the context of a continuous relationship.

In contrast to rural areas, which are often underserved, competition among physicians for patients is more likely in urban areas, where there is often an oversupply of physicians, especially of specialists (McKinlay and Marceau 2002; Schwartz 1996). Competition may lead to greater efforts on the part of physicians to maintain their patient relationships and to limit what is referred to in the health services literature as "patient churning," most often caused by employers' decisions to switch insurance plans on an annual basis to reduce costs. This switching can throw patients into the market for new physicians continually, creating a high barrier to continuity of care and trust-building between patients and their physicians (for a discussion of the role of organizational factors, such as managed care, in the continuity of care, see Cook et al. 2004).

Physician-patient trust is most often based on the nature of their ongoing reciprocal relationship, but other, more macrolevel factors may impinge on this relationship. One such factor, noted earlier, is the supply and demand of both physicians and patients. Another factor is the power of physicians to control their practice conditions and the related power of patients, through consumer initiatives and collective action, to influence their treatment options (for example, treatment options for breast cancer). Traditionally it has been argued that physicians have dominance (Freidson 1986) because they are professionals who gained control of their working conditions through the formation of the American Medical Association.[8] In return for this power and autonomy, they have had to agree to police their own (see also chapter 6).

In the period (prior to the 1970s) in which physicians had greater power, they also seemed to enjoy relatively high trust as a profession (reversing the typical inverse relationship between power imbalance and trust). The most important difference between the earlier period, in which fee-for-service was dominant, and the current climate in health care service delivery is that physicians and patients typically had longer-term, ongoing relationships thirty or forty years ago. These ongoing relationships often induced trust in spite of the initial power differential between patients and their doctors. Ongoing dyadic relations typically become relations of high mutual dependence (Emerson 1972), reducing the power differential over time. There were still cases, of course, in which doctors abused their power. In fact, one of the reasons for the imposition of organizational controls over the practice of medicine (such as professional standards review organizations [PSROs] in the 1970s, as well as more effective internal hospital review committees) was the marked increase in malpractice suits and the highly publicized ineffectiveness of physician controls over other physicians.

Economic factors came into play as well. Over the past three decades, there has been a steady increase in the organizational control of the practice of medicine, including licensing, certification, financing, reimbursement, and even protocols for appropriate treatment. Thus, while there may have been a decrease in the autonomy and power of many physicians, there has also been an increase in the influence and power of patients through consumer movements and increased access to information (for example, WebMD). According to one national survey, about 40 percent of Americans who had Internet access used the Internet to search for information about health or health care in 2001 (Baker et al. 2003). Access to information and the consumer movement to some extent have muted the power differentials between physicians and their patients in contrast to the past, especially when fee-for-service was the dominant form of physician reimbursement.

Although it can be argued that there has been an increase in power equality in the typical physician-patient relation, at the same time other organizational-level factors have reduced the longevity of physician-patient relations; as a result, many interactions with physicians are not repeated. Furthermore, economic factors that constrain physician power by imposing limits on the freedom of their decisionmaking may also impinge on the development of trust, especially when ongoing physician-patient relations are not in place. Evidence shows that, compared to other physicians, physicians working for managed care organizations more commonly perceive the lack of clinical freedom (Sturm 2002) and often perceive the financial incentives for performing some procedures to be insufficient (Leider, Solberg, and Nesbitt 1997). Under such conditions, physicians may experience conflicts of interests between their desire to provide high-quality care and the financial incentives that health plans use to encourage cost-consciousness (Emanuel and Dubler 1995; Gould 1998; Kao et al. 1998; Mechanic and Schlesinger 1996; Pearson and Hyams 2002). Physicians have been cast into the role of a "double agent" who must serve the interests of both the patients and the medical care corporations (Shortell et al. 1998; see also chapter 6). The corporatization of medical care influences the experiences of "company doctors," who express a distressing conflict between their patients' medical care needs and corporate oversight. The conflicting demands of being both a corporate employee and an autonomous professional constitute a social and structural problem rather than a problem of individual ethics (Draper 2003). In addition, these sociostructural pressures may influence the power dynamics as well as the possibility for trust in physician-patient relationships.

David Mechanic and Marsha Rosenthal (1999) argue that the physician-patient relationship may be negatively affected if patients distrust their health maintenance organization (HMO) and worry that their physician's decisions are influenced by organizational constraints and incentives to limit services. When economic factors impinge on the development of trust by pitting the patient's and the physician's interests against each other and limiting relational continuity, trust is unlikely to emerge. There is evidence that compared to the patients of physicians paid on a fee-for-service basis, patients of physicians under managed care constraints and physicians who are paid by capitation are less likely to trust that their physicians put their health above keeping down the cost of care (Kao et al. 1998).

Surveys report that trust in professionals has been on the decline for some time (Blendon and Benson 2001; Hanlon 1998) as the media have publicized evidence of the lack of trustworthiness of some individuals in these professions. Interestingly, individuals tend to maintain belief in the honesty and trustworthiness of their own physicians even as their confidence in the profession of medicine at large and in the leaders in the field has declined. (This is also true of our evaluations of our local politicians in contrast to politicians in general.) Under such circumstances, *reliance on interpersonal mechanisms for maintaining trust gives way to organizational mechanisms that ensure trustworthiness through increased monitoring and sanctioning, ironically reducing the possibility for ongoing trust relations.*

Despite the rise of organizational mechanisms for ensuring trustworthiness, trust still has a role to play, especially in physician-patient relations, in which one party is more vulnerable than the other and monitoring cannot be fully effective. But the role of trust has clearly been diminished as the stakes for malpractice have risen and economic factors have driven a wedge between patients and their physicians. As a result, the continuity of these relations has been greatly diminished, and conflicts of interest have arisen that also undermine trust (Mechanic 1998a, 1998b). Similar issues arise in power relations between employers and their employees, another common relationship in which trust is often problematic.

Trust and Power in Organizations

In organizations, trust of those in power is often rare. Recent research indicates, however, that people become more concerned about trustworthiness when they have a relationship with the authorities on whom they depend than when they do not. Both the existence of a current relationship and the expectation of a continued future relationship heighten the centrality of trustworthiness in employees' judgments of their supervisors. When the supervisor is seen as a friend, trust judgments have an important influence on the acceptance of voluntary decisions, but when the supervisor is not perceived as a friend, such judgments have only a marginal influence. Similarly, trust significantly shapes the acceptance of decisions when a future relationship is expected, but it has much less influence if no future relationship is anticipated (Tyler and Degoey 1996). This evidence fits our theoretical framework in which trust is primarily an issue in ongoing relationships, not in brief, nonrecurring contacts with authorities.[9]

Because of the problems that power differences can cause in relationships, people frequently prefer to engage with their power equals when that is an alternative. For example, bankers have a tendency to use social ties or contacts in which power relations are more nearly equal, as is typical among close associates or friends, especially when there is uncertainty in the transaction environment (Mizruchi and Stearns 2001).[10] The drawback to this strategy is that being involved in transactions with close associates may create problems in the closure of deals. Information provided by close associates may prove to be redundant, and often such associates fail to subject the details of a financial transaction to the same degree of criticism or scrutiny that would be provided by external sources. It seems to be more difficult to finalize transactions when necessary in the context of strong relationships. Weak ties (Granovetter 1985) to actors whom you know but are not close to make it easier to deal with each other. Embeddedness in strongly connected networks, by contrast, seems to inhibit the closure of deals. This effect of strong ties may make it hard for bankers in such uncertain environments to be successful, and it seems to be an unintended consequence of the use of strong ties to provide some assurance that one has a trustworthy transaction partner. It appears that closeness also provides a sense of security that the relationship will not end if the deal is not closed in a satisfactory manner. The tendency for bankers to use ties in which the power relations are equal thus can limit their success in closing deals, although maintaining informality through the use of close ties may allow for greater flexibility under uncertainty and serve as a buffer against defaults in the long run.

The fact that trust appears to be easier to establish among power equals creates an additional "stickiness" to these relations. In this sense, there may be other costs to the preference for interactions with power equals and the avoidance of interactions characterized by power inequality. But relationships in which one party is more powerful than the other are likely to be unstable as trust relations since the trustworthiness of the one in power must be viewed as conditional. Later we discuss how institutional safeguards can help to resolve this problem. Interesting examples from the banking industry provide insights into the kinds of devices used to assess trustworthiness under conditions of risk and uncertainty.

To reduce uncertainty, some bankers and others in business environments deal only with their close associates, while others rely on reputation systems to extend the reach of their networks. For example, firms in the financial sector that base their commercial transactions on their social relations receive lower interest rates on their loans. Dealing with close associates under certain circumstances evidently pays off. But there is a trade-off. Hence, a mix of embedded network ties (social connections) and arm's-length (impersonal) ties is optimal, rather than the exclusive use of either, because such a mix provides access to both the private resources of relationships and public information about markets (Uzzi 1999, 502).

Given uncertainty, banks invest, as do many other organizations, in efforts to estimate their risks more precisely and to limit risk by dealing only with those who are deemed "creditworthy" (Ferrary 2003). When a bank grants loans, it takes the risk that the borrowers will default and not fully honor their debt. To reduce this uncertainty, banks and some other businesses have created instrumental evaluation methods to evaluate their potential risk more objectively. Banks frequently use statistical analysis to estimate the ability of the borrowers to repay their loans (usually based on estimates of their collateral). These methods are highly impersonal, and those doing the analysis often do not actually meet the potential borrowers. But these standard methods of risk assessment typically ignore the large amounts of information that can be gathered through informal networks.

The information that bankers gather through social ties can be invaluable in analyzing the capacity and motivation of the borrower to repay the loan (Ferrary 2003). This assessment process is especially important for small to medium-size business loans, for which personal information can reveal social ties that may have a great impact on the borrower's ability to repay. Through social ties, bankers can find out information that would be unavailable through standard instrumental methods, which focus on information such as whether a divorce is imminent or whether the borrower has a reliable customer base.

To investigate this thesis, Michel Ferrary (2003) studied the repayment of loans made to Parisian brasseries. He compared the loans made by two banks. One bank used only standard instrumental methods of risk assessment. The second bank used social networks to obtain background information on potential borrowers. Ferrary found that a majority of the brasseries were owned by Aveyronais (that is, people from Cardalez). In addition, all of the employees and suppliers were Aveyronais. The bank that used knowledge derived from social networks hired a banker from the same town so that he could obtain information on the reliability of potential borrowers. The bank that used only instrumental methods lost more than 200 million francs, while the other bank had many fewer defaults.

It is not bankers' accounting competence that often provides the correct risk evaluations, but the information obtained from their social networks. Thus, to obtain the information needed for financial risk evaluations and to reduce the information asymmetry between bankers and borrowers, these financial counselors often attempt to integrate their social networks, not only to build access to social capital in the form of a wide range of network ties but also to establish local bonds of trust. The quality of these social bonds determines the quality of the information that can be gathered and therefore the quality of the risk evaluation based on that information.

Bank management is often aware of the limits of information obtained through standard instrumental methods as the primary basis for their social risk assessments. Thus, to improve economic efficiency bank management often modifies its work organization and general management practices to facilitate access to social capital in the form of network ties by their financial counselors. Many such network ties are links between relative power equals. In the face of greater power inequalities, however, reputation systems become even more important, especially for those with less power to deal with the risk of exploitation or default. Reputations provide information on the trustworthiness and reliability of those in power. In addition, they provide incentives for actors to be reliable so as to protect future interaction opportunities.

In relations of unequal power, the more powerful party may use resources to monitor the less powerful, especially in the context of an employment relationship, but this can also happen in personal relations. A number of studies suggest that such monitoring reduces trust on the part of both parties. For example, supervisors are less likely to trust subordinates whom they have chosen to monitor, even when the act of monitoring is required in the experimental setting (Strickland 1958). Similarly, subjects are less likely to trust those whom they have to monitor and with whom they have explicit contracts (Malhotra and Murnighan 2002). The attribution of trustworthiness (or untrustworthiness) results from a consideration of the constraints posed by the contracts rather than from a consideration of their own earlier assessments of trustworthiness. These results suggest that the binding nature of the actual explicit contracts, including the possibility of monitoring, overjustifies the cooperation of the monitored party and thus negatively affects the subject's perceptions of that person's trustworthiness. The use of very explicit contracting can be a sign that one is not perceived as trustworthy. As a result, many business contracts are left incomplete, with many of the actual details left unspecified, and managed by handshakes, signaling trust.

Power inequalities in relationships are also problematic for those in power, who are as vulnerable to paranoid social cognition as are those who are the subjects of power use. Even though cognitive paranoia may also occur in relationships in which the parties are power equals, there is clearly less evaluative scrutiny and less need for hypervigilant processing of information in such relations (Kramer and Gavrieli 2004). There are devices for getting beyond the distrust that can arise in relations with power differences, including ways of altering the entrenched beliefs about the parties that hinder trust-building—and in some cases even the willingness to enter into negotiations.

One important device is the use of third parties as mediators or enablers. For example, the National Labor Relations Board (NLRB) serves as a mediator to help resolve conflicts between labor and management through complex multiparty negotiation. This is an interesting case in which the problems of trust and distrust reflect the shifting power relations between labor and management over time. The NLRB may be more active in periods when labor is less powerful in contrast to management, and less active in more equal power times. Hence, the NLRB may have been designed to "level the playing field between two unequal players" (Levi, Moe, and Buckley 2004b, 126), even though it has failed in this respect. Such third-party intervention or mediation is one general mechanism for managing problems of cooperation in the context of unequal power. Such intervention is more commonly used when trust breaks down or when the conflict is so great that resolution of the issues is unlikely without it. Institutions are often designed specifically to depersonalize the relationships involved in order to reach a compromise or successful conclusion and to standardize expectations. But even this may not work when the stakes are too high or the distrust between the partners is too entrenched (see chapter 4).

Power and Trust in Interorganizational Relationships

Beyond employer-employee relations and relations between sets of actors in a complex negotiating environment (such as labor and management), power and trust are also important factors in the relations between the agents or representatives of firms and other organizations. Here we comment on the various ways in which organizational representatives manage in the context of clear power differences when assessments of trustworthiness may be difficult to make. For example, groups such as trade associations serve to create shared norms among members and expectations that allow trust to form at the interpersonal level, thus facilitating vertical integration (Lane and Bachmann 1996). In a survey of 184 buyer-supplier relationships in the printing industry in the United Kingdom, Guido Mollering (2002) surprisingly does not find strong support for the popular notion that trust reduces transaction costs and thus the need for hierarchy. He finds greater support for the argument that markets, hierarchy, and trust represent alternative mechanisms for managing significant vertical relationships under varying conditions (Bradach and Eccles 1989). Trust can become a dominant mechanism for the management of vertical interfirm relations when neither price nor authority is available, especially in hybrid governance forms.

Trust is a pressing issue for joint ventures and other cooperative relationships—it may even enable their existence in the first place. This view is supported by data from the printing industry. Trust and trustworthiness are viewed as forces that influence the transaction process rather than the constitution of the transaction (a domain covered by price and authority). Flexible and reliable performance of transactions matters more than advance certainty about price and contractual obligations. Although federal laws prohibit contractual relationships between rail freight carriers and automobile shippers, these industries can overcome this restriction by engaging in informal, general, legally unenforceable agreements (Palay 1985). These agreements are intimately bound up with the identities of the individuals.

The perceived trustworthiness of the agents of firms in various types of economic exchanges is argued to have positive effects, creating greater flexibility, more sharing of information, and under some circumstances reduced transaction costs. Consider one indicative study. Jeffrey Dyer and Wujin Chu's (2003) study of the automobile industry in the United States, Japan, and Korea provides evidence of these effects in a sample of 344 supplier-automaker exchange relationships. They suggest that the value created for transactors through lowering transaction costs in these environments of high uncertainty and high interfirm specificity may be substantial. "The least-trusted automaker spent significantly more of its face-to-face interaction time with suppliers on contracting and haggling when compared to the most trusted automaker. This translated into procurement costs that were five times higher for the least trusted automaker" (Dyer and Chu 2003, 57). These authors also note that trust (that is, high perceived trustworthiness of the other party) not only reduces transaction costs but also has a mutually causal relationship with information-sharing, which creates additional value in the exchange relationship. Other governance devices (such as contracts) are necessary costs incurred to prevent opportunistic behavior, but they do not create value beyond reducing transaction costs, as suggested in this study. A number of industries fit the conditions specified by Dyer and Chu as conducive to significant transaction cost savings, especially when the firms are reciprocally interdependent, even if they are unequal in resources. These conditions include high expected transaction costs, due to factors such as environmental uncertainty and high interfirm asset specificity, and a particularly high value on information-sharing, due to product complexity and industry uncertainty (Dyer and Chu 2003, 67).

In markets, buyers rate reliability and flexibility as more important factors in maintaining an economic relationship in the long run, and they associate these factors with the trustworthiness of the key parties and the trust between them (Bradach and Eccles 1989). Especially under uncertainty, trustworthiness becomes an important determinant of transactions. In relational contracting (see chapter 5), parties seek continued partnerships in exchange for the lowering of the risks of defaulting (Macaulay 1963). This tendency sometimes comes with costs (see chapter 9).[11] In corporate alliances, repeat interactions increase trust, as implied by our encapsulated interest account of trust relations, and reduce the hierarchical elements of joint ventures, thus mitigating power differences (Gulati and Singh 1998). Trust is correlated with reduced power distance between the parties to the alliance, a fact that is corroborated in experimental evidence on the link between power inequality and trust at the interpersonal level (Lawler and Yoon 1998; Molm et al. 2000). Firms whose agents trust one another have fewer concerns about adverse selection and also have lower coordination costs (Gulati and Singh 1998).

Under some conditions, the presence of trust between partners to the alliance seems to promote fewer hierarchical controls in the alliance. Alliance members appear to rely instead on prior knowledge and the reduction in coordination costs that results from this prior knowledge about the parties involved. Thus, importantly, when it exists between potential partners to an alliance or joint venture, trust reduces the demand for more hierarchical governance structures. This finding implies that the type of power embedded in hierarchy is often antithetical to trust relations. Findings on the organizational level may be similar to the effects observed at the interpersonal level with respect to trust and a reduction in power distance between the parties involved. We discuss some of these issues in greater detail in chapters 5 and 7 (on physician-patient relations, see Cook et al. 2004).

In strategic alliances between organizations involved in the development of information technology, the greater dependence of one organization on another is negatively related to the emergence of trust in the relationship and also negatively related to the flexibility of the alliance (Young-Ybarra and Wiersema 1999). Such alliances include joint research pacts and various types of joint development agreements. The primary factors that facilitate the emergence of trust relations in this environment are high-quality communications and shared values among the parties to the alliance, given that the formation of a strategic alliance is in the best interests of the firms involved. Ironically, economic constraints on the alliance also seem to facilitate trust, a fact that Candace Young-Ybarra and Margarethe Wiersema suggest provides support for the significance of transaction cost economics in the study of organizational-level trust (but for negative evidence, see Mollering 2002). Trust, they argue, saves on transaction costs and thus may be more easily fostered in environments characterized by economic constraints, which often motivate cooperative efforts that might not otherwise take place, thus increasing interdependence.

Power asymmetries may not only block the emergence of trust relations but lead to distrust if the more powerful actors are not capable of making credible commitments (Farrell 2004; see also Lorenz 1988). In the absence of a credible commitment to the relationship, they may have incentives to renege on their commitments. In such situations, parties may find themselves in inefficient equilibriums, where the less powerful parties rationally refuse to be trustworthy because they perceive that the more powerful party may take advantage of their good faith without reciprocation. But trust can emerge between unequal power parties when the parties can and do make ongoing credible commitments.

Henry Farrell (forthcoming) examines three cases in industry: two in which credible commitments and trust exist and a third in which trust is not possible owing to the lack of such commitments from the more powerful parties. In the first case, final production firms that assemble parts from a variety of suppliers to produce goods in the Rhone-Alps consciously strive to make credible commitments to their subcontractors to ensure trust between the parties. In the second case, a reputation system has emerged among weavers and converters in the Japanese apparel industry to ensure credible commitments and hence foster trust among the parties involved in the chain of transactions. On the other hand, in the third case, the packaging machinery industry in northern Italy, a trend toward vertical integration has reduced the ability of high-power firms to make credible commitments to subcontractors, thus blocking the possibility of trust relationships in this industry.

Farrell's study provides a good example of the ways in which the analysis of power in exchange relations and the encapsulated interest view of trust are linked, and we expand on his arguments and evidence here. Farrell starts from the clear premise that if I have absolute power over you, there is no reason for me to take your interests into account. In such a relation, there is no interdependence and no reason for the less powerful to ever trust the powerful party in control. However, there is room for trust in the analysis of power relations when there is some degree of mutual dependence and thus the powerful must take the interests of the powerless into account, as implied in our relational analysis of power and trust. Farrell argues, as we do, that in such cases trust and power are closely related. If neither party to a relationship had any power to withdraw from the relationship, their necessary mutual reliance would be sufficient to explain their cooperation and neither would need to trust the other. This is not unlike the conditions of life in small, close communities whose members are subject to sanctions such as shunning from all others if they behave badly in their relationships (Cook and Hardin 2001).

On the other hand, if one party has many alternative partners or little need of the other party's continued cooperation, that party's power typically disrupts the possibility of trust and trustworthiness and may even instill distrust. Hence, modest power inequality entails the possibility of trust, while great power asymmetry commonly entails active distrust (see chapter 4). Moreover, if there is moderate power inequality, the more powerful party may be able to trust the less powerful party more (and over a wider array of issues) than the less powerful can trust the more powerful. Indeed, this is an important way in which power is advantageous. It is useful not only in coercive relationships but also in fairly straightforward exchange relationships.

In general, *the relationship between power and the possibility of trust relations is curvilinear.* In a two-party relationship, if I have no power to withdraw from our relationship, you do not need to trust me. You can use coercion without the risk that the relationship will terminate. If I have some power to withdraw, you may hope to develop a trust relationship. And if I can withdraw at will without cost to myself and you know this, you cannot trust me. Indeed, in this last case, my interest does not encapsulate yours at all, so that the encapsulated interest account of trust cannot apply. There is no mutual interdependence. Farrell investigates this general conception of the relationship between power and trust empirically.

Farrell's measure of power in a relationship is essentially the level of cost I incur if I unilaterally withdraw from the relationship. Low cost of withdrawal implies high power; high cost of withdrawal implies low power. The cost of withdrawal in Farrell's analysis is analogous to the level of relational dependence in Emerson's view that power is based on dependence. High dependence implies a high cost of withdrawal from the relationship; low dependence implies a low cost of withdrawal.

One party to a potential cooperative relationship may have such great power over the relationship that he can withdraw at will, while the other party can withdraw only at great cost. Still, as Farrell argues, the more powerful party may be able to convince the other party that he will be trustworthy if he can bind himself with credible commitments. Farrell defines these as commitments that the less powerful party knows it is in the more powerful party's interest to fulfill once he has made them.

Clearly, different strategies for managing power differences have important consequences, not only for the development of trust relations but also for economic efficiency. We return in our concluding section to the discussion of the role of institutions in managing power relations and the possibilities for relational trust.

Farrell's study also emphasizes the fact that trust relations are often sealed by a handshake, not a formal contract. Contracts generally facilitate exchanges by reducing risk and uncertainty, thus making it possible for "risk-averse parties to create mutually beneficial relationships" (Malhotra and Murnighan 2002, 534). Formal structures or institutions that require binding contracts may limit the development of trust since the parties involved do not need to attribute trustworthiness to their partners if the contracts are binding. Experimental research suggests that only if exchanges are secured by informal and nonbinding mechanisms of cooperation do they yield attributions of trustworthiness and thus lead to the emergence of trust relations. Hence, *overuse of contracts can block the emergence of trust in social relations* (Molm et al. 2000).

In much of the literature, trust and contracts are viewed as substitutes rather than as complementary mechanisms for managing transactions under uncertainty (Zucker 1986). The fear of exploitation makes parties more comfortable if they have binding contracts. Without institutional backing, however, contracts may be meaningless. Perhaps only in the face of strong and reliable institutions can trust and contracts be viewed as alternative modes of transaction. "The bottom line," Deepak Malhotra and Keith Murnighan (2002, 556) claim, "is that the creation of confident expectations for the behavior of powerful others (people who are in a position to exploit vulnerability) requires tremendously careful action."

Power differences between parties are often accompanied by other factors that create obstacles to trust-building and are typically correlated with power inequalities. These factors include lack of transparency, secrecy (on the part of the powerful actor), the failure of procedural justice, and often the related lack of fairness in outcomes, in addition to negative histories of interaction (or past actions that have generated distrust). These factors can be independent of power asymmetry, or they can be exacerbated by it.[12] The power asymmetry in a relationship (or an organizational or network setting) can create conditions that foster secrecy, lack of transparency or fairness, and even a failure of procedural justice. Power provides the more powerful actor in the situation not only with the capacity for some of these actions but sometimes with the motivation as well. Power corrupts, and it may do so precisely in ways that destroy the trustworthiness of the powerful actor and hence the possibility for trust. Examples of this principle exist at all levels of analysis in social systems and are discussed throughout the following chapters on principals and their agents, on institutions, on government and its actions, and on the role of the state more broadly. The management of power relations is central in law and politics. Informal social devices (see chapter 5) also work to restrict the exploitation of the powerless, but often they are only as good as their backing in the law and legitimate institutions.

Power is often correlated with lack of transparency and secrecy (Currall and Epstein 2003; Garcia 2002). In chapter 9, we discuss how this tendency hinders the development of trust under conditions of uncertainty and risk. Under some conditions, opening up the decisionmaking processes of powerful actors to public scrutiny fosters transparency, and it may increase the extent to which those in power are viewed as reliable. But this may be highly contingent on the nature of those decisionmaking processes and what is at stake. In an increasingly complex information-based society, the provision of more information and increased transparency may even obscure public understanding and undermine trust through information overload (Tsoukas 1997).

In addition, transparently biased, unfair, or particularistic decisions and processes may undermine trust in ways that make it hard to recover. Some such decisions are even illegal, and their transparency creates scandals, as in the Enron affair in the United States, which destroyed the company as well as those who violated the trust of the employees and investors, and even Arthur Andersen, the main auditing firm associated with the scandal. Enron executives used their power to give themselves phenomenally lucrative benefits by looting the firm and its stockholders. To do this they depended on secrecy, dishonesty, and a lack of transparency. The collapse of Enron clearly reveals inadequate scrutiny and monitoring by the stakeholders, who were not in a position to know what was really going on (Currall and Epstein 2003). To some extent, the Enron tale is also a story of a closed community with high internal cohesion that fostered secrecy and trust among the insiders (for a discussion of the possible negative externalities of closed trust networks, see Cook, Rice, and Gerbasi 2004).

Generally, however, those in power can increase the probability that those over whom they have power will view them as trustworthy if they try hard to create conditions that foster trust. Such conditions include honesty and fairness (see Kramer and Cook 2004) and a decisionmaking process that is transparent enough to those dependent on them to reveal clearly that their actions are in the best interest of those over whom they have power.

The transparency of transactions in the context of relationships characterized by trust, honesty, and sincerity can also contribute to the success of economic development. From macrolevel research, Alexius Pereira (2000) argues that these factors clearly contributed to rapid and successful industrial transformation in Singapore, especially after the decision to restructure the economy post-1980. On the other hand, in many post-Communist societies the transition to democratic institutions and market economies has been problematic owing to the legacies of autocratic regimes that operated under the shroud of secrecy, fear, ineptitude, and often corruption (Rose-Ackerman 2001). Even at the interpersonal level, secrecy most often protects the interests of the powerful (Richardson 1988).

Piotr Sztompka (1998) hypothesizes that the key to rebuilding civil society in the post-Communist countries is restoring the trustworthiness (or what we refer to as the reliability) of public institutions. Accountability, fairness, representativeness, and benevolence are of great importance in accomplishing this complex task, Sztompka emphasizes. These and related issues are taken up in greater detail in chapter 9.

Procedural and distributive fairness are also clearly associated with the increased legitimacy of decision outcomes and the perceived trustworthiness of the relevant decisionmakers, especially when there is a power difference between the actors involved, as in the case of employers and their employees.[13] Procedures that are perceived to be fair are said to engender trust—meaning confidence—in the "system," as well as in the decisionmakers (Brockner and Siegel 1996). A lack of procedural fairness, on the other hand, elicits low levels of such confidence. In addition, those with highly positive expectations based on past treatment tend to be less influenced by the fairness of any specific current outcome. But past treatment sets expectations that can be problematic when violated. Two broad dimensions of trust that we identified in earlier chapters—competence and motivation—are clearly differentiated in evaluations of procedural justice issues (Brockner and Siegel 1996). Procedural justice is more closely associated with the perceived intent (and incentive) of decisionmakers to be trustworthy than with their competence or ability to act in trustworthy ways. Both factors are significant predictors of the acceptance of decisions regarding allocations, but integrity, because it reflects motivational intent, is a stronger predictor of decision acceptance than is perceived competence (Brockner and Siegel 1996).

Concluding Remarks

The major way we constrain the exercise of power in our lives is through institutional constraints. Trust relations may thus depend heavily on stable legal, political, and social institutions, especially if there are power differences between the actors involved. For example, an analysis of the relationships between buyer and seller firms in Great Britain and Germany suggests that trust-based vertical interfirm relations rarely evolve spontaneously on the level of individual interaction but are highly dependent on stable institutions (Lane and Bachmann 1996). In Russia, where contract enforcement in the legal system is of limited effectiveness (Radaev 2002, 2004b), businessmen have only very weak power to make credible commitments to secure trust relations in their business transactions.

Against this fairly standard view, the role of contract law in economic development may be overstated. Arguably, it is the growth of commerce that produces good law, not the reverse (Mueller 1999). In support of this thesis, we might look to the contemporary Chinese experience of a booming economy before the development of relevant legal institutions, or to Adam Smith's (1776/1976) views on the development of the English economy. Increased reliance on laws seems not to have displaced the system of economic organization based on social connections, or guanxi, according to preliminary evidence produced by the World Bank (1993) in *The East Asian Miracle* (see also Ginsburg 2000, 830). All of these cases raise doubts about the indispensability of the rule of law (see Davis 1998).[14] In this debate, consideration of informal alternatives to law and the role of the state are paramount (Tamanaha 1995; Ginsburg 2000). Other debates center on the management of conflicts of interest and the effectiveness of various devices for managing such conflicts.

A central issue in medical care, for example, is the difficulty of the complications that commonly arise in principal-agent relations involving power differences when the agent (the doctor) has expert knowledge or access to resources that the principal (the patient) needs but cannot obtain except through the offices of the agent. The potential for exploitation of the principal by the agent is great in many such relationships. In another example, financial agents can often act in their own interest in ways that are against the interests of the principal. Clearly, when there is such a conflict of interests, especially when the principal is at a power disadvantage, the principal should not trust the agent. Indeed, if the principal knows of the conflict of interests, then the principal cannot trust the agent in the sense of supposing that the agent encapsulates the principal's interests enough to motivate trustworthy action. This problem is at the core of many of the issues discussed in subsequent chapters. Before examining the many ways in which cooperation is secured by various devices in the absence of trust, we next investigate distrust, which is often the natural consequence of power differences.

Chapter 4

Distrust

I N THE burgeoning field of trust research, there are far more studies of trust and the role it plays in society and in social relations than of distrust and the role it plays (but see contributions to Hardin 2004a). Yet we probably learn as much about trust from the analysis of distrust as we do in analyzing the role of trust in society.[1] Distrust can be an active state, not just a passive state. When it prevails, it often creates a real problem for those involved—at any level of analysis. It is a problem to be solved. But it is also a correct stance in many contexts; when this is the case, misplaced trust might be deeply problematic. Lack of trust is a more passive state and does not have this problematic character. This is an important distinction that commends deliberate attention to the nature and implications of active distrust (see Hardin 2002b, 90; Levi 2000, 140–44; Ullmann-Margalit 2004).

When we take a serious look at distrust and its role in our lives, we immediately realize that much of the hand-wringing about the lack or decline of trust in some societies is overwrought. Distrust is not necessarily bad or destructive; indeed, it can be good and protective when it is well directed. Moreover, relying on another's trustworthiness is not the only or often even a good way to accomplish our goals. We can get people to cooperate with us even without trust between them and us. People who live in a city of even moderate scale pass many days with far more encounters with and reliance on people they are in no position to trust than with people whom they do trust. Moreover, in some fundamentally important aspects of life, distrust is a very healthy fact of our condition. For example, James Madison believed that, because no government can be trusted, a decent government must be substantially restricted in its powers. He would have even greater cause to worry today than in his own day of exceedingly weak and resourceless government, when the share of government in the national budget was 10 to 15 percent of what it is today and when government's capacity to intervene in individual lives was radically weaker than it is today.

Much of the point of this book is to make sense of life without trust. In subsequent chapters, we analyze ways in which we manage cooperative relationships even when we do not trust those with whom we interact. Sometimes we are merely neutral—we have no reason either to trust or to distrust another person or group or institution. Sometimes we distrust, but even so we can manage cooperation and prosper in our lives and in our dealings with others. It is part of the magic of a modern economic and political order that we can prosper through dealings with millions of people whom we do not know and whose motives toward us are essentially uncaring at best. Most of these millions, if they held stock in some firm on the verge of collapse, would happily sell the stock to us so that we might take the loss. Yet we can coordinate our lives with these others so that we and they enhance our lives through our interactions, however anonymous these might be. The change in the scale of our interactions from earlier eras to the present day in modern nations is astonishing (see Leijonhufvud 1995). Hence, the range and number of our social relations in contemporary industrial societies are vastly greater than in past centuries.

Contemporary writing on trust is often afflicted with reasoning from the fallacy of composition. That literature seems to assume that we would all be better off if we were more trusting, and therefore we should all trust more. If we found a society in which distrust was endemic, we might readily conclude that almost all its members would be better off if we could somehow lead them to be more trusting, perhaps by creating institutions that substituted for trust while educating them through positive experience to be trusting. Yet we might have to recognize that it would not be in the interest of individuals in that society to simply start trusting—if that were even possible conceptually[2]—because their pervasive distrust might be well grounded in the untrustworthiness of their fellow citizens.

It is commonplace to say that we need more trust (Luhmann 1980), that trust is good, or that supposed declines in, say, trust in others generally or in government are bad. In many contexts, however, distrust is clearly justified and it would be a mistake to trust. Indeed, even the most trusting person would grant that it is naive to trust many people in many contexts. We wish to consider when and why one might find distrust justified. This question is important, of course, because *a lack of trust reduces the likelihood of entering into cooperative interactions unless we have other devices to secure reliability.* In some contexts, the best response to this loss is to risk cooperation enough to begin to build a relationship of at least limited trust. In others, the best response is to use institutions to safeguard one's interests while working, through an institutional intermediary or overseer, with an otherwise distrusted person or group (as discussed in chapters 5 through 7). In still others, the best response is to walk away from an untrustworthy relationship. Finally, trust relationships may develop in one arena in response to distrust in another. For example, if the larger society or the government is a source of threat, we may develop stronger local relationships to protect ourselves against intrusions by the larger society or government, and vice versa.

In this chapter, we canvass various devices for managing relationships pervaded by distrust. Then we turn, in later chapters, to alternatives to trust in contexts in which distrust is warranted or in which at the very best there is a lack of trust. We note some conceptual issues in the differences between trust and distrust and then survey issues at the macro level of society and government after turning to more nearly micro or small-group levels. Distrust can be pervasive, and it can block possibilities for social cooperation and even for social order. It can also be constructive by preventing reliance on institutions and individuals who would abuse us if we acted as though we trusted them (Levi 2000).

The single best developed literature on distrust as a general problem is in liberal political theory, in which distrust in government is a fundamental stance (Hardin 2002a; see also Ely 1980; Warren 1999). Oddly, against the current worry about declining trust in government, distrust was advocated by early liberal theorists, and fairly deep distrust of government explains much of the structure of the U.S. government under the constitution of 1787. Barriers to government power were primarily designed by James Madison—perhaps the greatest of all constitutional thinkers, not least because Madison was not merely a theorist of constitutionalism but was concerned with the pragmatic task of actually designing a working constitution. There is probably little hope that our arguments will block the continued worry about distrust in American and some other governments, but we are convinced that those worries are substantially misguided.

Note that from the very definition of trust as encapsulated interest and from the fact that your trust in someone depends on the knowledge you have of that person's interests, two realizations immediately follow. First, even though someone encapsulates your interests to some extent, she may still have other interests that finally trump the weight she gives to your interests. Therefore, a central problem in distrust is *conflict of interest* between a supposedly trustworthy person's other interests and the weight that person gives to your interests. Conflict of interest therefore underlies much of the discussion throughout the remainder of this book (for example, in the interaction between an agent's and a principal's interests, as discussed in chapters 6 and 7). Second, because the degree of someone's trust in you turns on the knowledge she has of your commitments, it follows as an analytical matter and not merely an empirical fact that secrecy, deceit, and lack of transparency on your part, if intuited by or known to her, will undercut any chance that she trusts you and will make instead for distrust. These two issues—the transparency of your commitments and the conflict of interest between your own commitments and any commitment you might have to give special consideration to someone else's interests—are logically implicit in the definition of trust as cognitive and as a matter of encapsulated interest.

Asymmetries of Distrust and Trust

In its definition, distrust is the negative of trust. A's trust of B entails that A's interests be encapsulated in B's interests to some extent. *A is likely to distrust B if there is a dominant conflict of B's interests with A's.* Despite this similarity of definitions, there can be causal differences in the likelihoods of trust and distrust. First, it may take less knowledge to establish distrust than to establish trust. If you betray someone a single time, she is likely to distrust you thereafter, although she still might choose—or even be forced by lack of alternatives—to take a risk on you again. Even if you are cooperative and therefore seemingly trustworthy in an interaction, however, she may still not trust you in her next interaction with you.

Second, the potential losses from cooperating over a particular range of payoffs with a person who proves to be untrustworthy are typically much larger than the potential gains from cooperating with a person who proves to be trustworthy. For example, in the prisoner's dilemma of game 1 (see figure 4.1), the row player's loss from cooperating while the column player cheats is greater than the gain to the row player when both cooperate. It would therefore take more than one successful cooperation to make up for a single instance of mistakenly cooperating while the other defects. In game 1, the combination of two successful cooperations (two payoffs of 15 for a total of 30) plus one play in which the other defects (a payoff of –25) is barely better than not entering the interaction at all. In many contexts, it may take many successful cooperative interactions to outweigh the losses from a single defection against one's cooperative play. Indeed, in normal economic contexts, in which the profits from successful exchange are typically a fairly small fraction of the values at stake (profits are often said to be 1 to 3 percent in grocery stores, for instance), it would take many profitable sales to overcome the loss of having one customer take merchandise without paying. For example, just to break even and be as well off as if one had never opened a shop, it would take twenty successes for each loss if the margin of profit from a typical sale is 5 percent.

Historically, the most important argument on this issue is the central tenet of Hobbes's political philosophy. Hobbes argued that, when there is no serious political power to regulate relations between people, it is reasonable for everyone to distrust virtually everyone else; as a result, there is pervasive distrust and a failure to enjoy the benefits of cooperative interactions. His solution to this problem, famously, is not to try

Figure 4.1   Game 1: Prisoner's Dilemma or Exchange Payoff Matrix

Column Player

		Cooperate	Not Cooperate
Row Player	Cooperate	15, 15	−25, 40
	Not Cooperate	40, −25	0, 0

Source: Authors' figure.

to engender trust and trustworthiness but to put a powerful sovereign in place to enforce order and secure ownership so that people's investments in their own productive capacity will be beneficial to them (Hobbes (1651/1968, 188). Hence, we will be safe in our efforts to prosper, and our own production and exchange with others for their production can make us all better off; without government, there is no such production (186). Hobbes does not suppose that we are bereft without trust and trustworthiness toward our fellow citizens, but only that we need alternative devices for securing order and cooperation. He is right on this fundamental issue, and dozens of contemporary writers are not.

Third, if someone trusts you, that means, on the encapsulated interest view, that she thinks you take her interests into account *because they are her interests.* She could think that you do not care at all about her interests per se but that your own interests conflict with hers. Hence, *she would distrust you, but she would not say that you specifically wish to harm her interests as hers.* Distrust is therefore not the exact converse of trust. Someone who wishes to harm another person's interests just because they are that person's would be vicious as well as worthy of distrust by him or her. One might sometimes imagine that certain of one's colleagues are vicious in this way, but such viciousness surely would require an unusual motivation that is relatively rare in our lives (although not completely foreign to many of us). Typically, we do not have to suppose that someone is vicious in this way to distrust them.

As we noted in chapter 1, trust has two conditions: belief in the other's competence to do what she is entrusted to do, and belief that her motivations are to tend to one's interests in the relevant matter. For distrust, we can add to competence and motivation the concern with conflict of interests. If we have the same interests, those same interests do not by themselves ground trust. But if we have contrary interests, those opposing interests do ground distrust.

Hence, there are practical asymmetries in both the knowledge and the motivational elements of trust and distrust. The former comes from the asymmetry of the weight of knowledge necessary to establish that someone is relatively trustworthy versus the slight bit of knowledge that establishes untrustworthiness. The latter comes from the commonplace asymmetry between gains and losses in successful versus failed exchanges. We can see this latter asymmetry very clearly in the analysis of the prisoner's dilemma or exchange matrix of game 1 (figure 4.1). On the motivational side, there is also the possibility that conflicting interests will block you from encapsulating my interests or that will trump my concern with your interests. There is a sad but elegant example of such a conflict in the story of the Chinese woman, Mrs. Chen, who loses her investment in a credit circle, as reported in chapter 5.

The first of these asymmetries suggests that it may make sense to distrust government even in a context in which it would be implausible to have relationships and knowledge adequate to ground trust. The second suggests that we tend to stop trying to cooperate with people who once fail our trust, so that those who occasionally cheat might lose substantially from lost opportunities. It might not genuinely be true that the number of observations of trustworthy and untrustworthy behaviors needed to establish the one or the other differs. In a context in which we typically have many potential partners in trust, however, we may tend fairly quickly to drop those who fail when we entrust anything to them. We may tend to start all relationships at a low level of stakes at risk, drop those who fail our trust at that low level, and develop our relationships with those who fulfill our trust at a low level by escalating our interaction to higher stakes (see Cook et al., forthcoming). Hence, although those who cheat us early gain substantially more in their single cheating move than they would have from a single cooperation, they may lose the opportunity to do far better in escalated interactions thereafter. The implicit prospect of the escalation of stakes helps us justify the risks of initial cooperation despite the logic that says offsetting one attempt at cooperation that goes wrong requires many successes.

More generally, we might suppose that there is psychological reason for doubt to be more insidiously effective in its workings than even great confidence, as exemplified by the power of Iago's weak circumstantial evidence of Desdemona's unfaithfulness to mislead Othello, whose evidence of her faithfulness up until then was substantial (on the general problem, see Gambetta 1988, 234). Indeed, when the evidence is merely that there is no evidence, there are often tendencies toward paranoid cognition (Kramer 1994, 1998) or negative assessments of the other's attitude, which can provoke distrust that is essentially ungrounded in any evidence except the seeming implication of lack of any sign. That might also be true not as the result of a strange psychological motor but even as the result of merely rational assessment of one's interests. In some contexts, because the losses from misplaced trust outweigh the gains from well-placed trust, as argued earlier, having no information leaves us not in a neutral state but on the negative side of the calculus. We need positive evidence of trustworthiness or other assurances, such as legal protections, to counter the asymmetry of potential losses over gains. Hence, the knowledge and motivational conditions of the trusting (or distrusting) relationship interact to exacerbate distrust.

When we merely doubt another's trustworthiness, we may invest in efforts to test the other or to discover the other's malfeasance while still relying on the other to a substantial extent. If we actively distrust someone, we may sooner restrict our interactions with that person to block the risks of failed cooperation. Our costs then are merely the costs of finding others for needed interactions of cooperation. While we are in doubt, we may hang on to a relationship and thereby run not only the risk of betrayal but also the risk of damaging the relationship if our doubt turns out to have been ill founded.

Such boundaries between trust and distrust define personal relationships and explain their development through certain kinds of crisis. They also determine, however, many aspects of social and group structure. We wish to extrapolate from the microstructure of individual trust relationships grounded in the encapsulated interest model to understand phenomena at the group and societal levels. We address these social effects of trust, and especially of distrust, beginning with a quick survey of the social contexts of distrust and then turning to the liberal political theory of Madison, with its grounding in distrust of government. We then reverse the focus to look at the effects of government on interpersonal distrust. Finally, we consider problems of breakdowns of trust, societies rife with distrust, contexts in which risks are so grievous that distrust virtually follows from the enormous scale of the conflict between the potentially trusted's interests and the interests of the potential truster.

If trust and distrust are analogous in relevant ways, then some theories and discussions of trust do not make compelling sense, because they must treat distrust as *not* analogous to trust. In particular, it seems especially sensible to treat distrust as directed at specific individuals in response to their conflicts of interest with us. *Distrust therefore cannot be purely grounded in the moral commitments or psychological character of the distrusted person.* This does not fit a conception of trust that makes trust not a function of the potentially trusted person's interests in fulfilling a trust (we expand on this argument in chapter 10). When you have compelling reasons to distrust A that many of us do not have, we can sensibly trust the person whom you sensibly distrust.

Social Contexts of Distrust

In general, we are likely to deal more with those whom we trust. Hence, we tend to narrow our associations to certain networks, such as a neighborhood group or an ethnic group. If others in the same context do the same, we have effectively defined a group from which others are de facto largely excluded for many of our relationships. They may soon enough become excluded deliberately and not merely de facto, so that we begin to define them as actively foreign. In a sense, then, distrust defines the boundaries of our group (Brewer 2000; Hardin 1995, ch. 4; Hewstone, Rubin, and Willis 2002). It does so in two senses. First, it is those in the group who are plausibly to be trusted while those outside are to be distrusted. Second, just because someone is outside the group, we distrust that person. Hence, the boundary may become reinforced and reified, and our group may become exclusionary. As a result, relations between those inside and those outside our group may become indifferent or even hostile. At the worst, deliberately hostile acts toward members of the outside group may even be rewarded within our group.

Once the group boundary is established, you may not be able as an individual to have a trusting relationship with anyone outside your group—or at least not with those in the immediate outsider group—because they will define you as hostile just as much as your fellow group members will define them as hostile. You may be identified by your group membership rather than as an individual. Once we have defined our groups as merely separate and not interacting, we set up the likelihood that they will become actively hostile, because we structure our relationships to have few or no opportunities to test the trustworthiness of any of the members of the other group. Paranoid cognition might be our central stance toward those in the out group.

Even if we establish trusting relationships that include people from another group that differs in some way from our own group, those relationships might be at risk if the larger relationship between the two groups changes. For example, there were many marriages across ethnic lines in Sarajevo (and other Yugoslav urban communities) before 1990. Many of those marriages were broken by the gruesome conflicts, especially those between Serbs and Muslims in the battle for supremacy in Bosnia. Similarly, in Rwanda there were reports of Hutus who murdered their own Tutsi wives and half-Tutsi children during the extraordinarily murderous violence of 1994. In both these instances, the interpersonal relationships within marriages of mixed ethnicity may well have been as good as those within marriages of single ethnicities in the same communities until the sudden efflorescence of violent intergroup conflict. Individuals face daunting difficulties in constructing relationships that go against the general norms of their own groups when identity with those groups is potentially in question. Social context both enables and constrains trust relationships.

If we have need of relationships with people outside our group, we are more likely to engage with them and therefore to develop trusting relationships with them. This is more likely to happen if we have complementary capacities. But if we are essentially identical in our capacities, so that we have no specific need of each other, then we may have no occasion to work together and therefore no occasion to overcome our distrust. In the extreme case, we might be like Edward Banfield's (1958) amoral familists, who trust and cooperate only with their own family members and treat virtually everyone else as potentially hostile.

Social cohesion, by providing the conditions for it, makes trust possible. Distrust undercuts cohesion. Many social theorists have supposed that cohesion in the sense of widely shared values of a whole society is required for social stability (Parsons 1937/1968, 89–94). But this is even possible only for small, relatively homogeneous communities. It is not clear just what the shared values of a whole modern society could be. One can imagine social order that is based on some fairly general interests in having order, a legal regime to help enforce contracts, some provision of collective goods, and so forth. Beyond such limited interests, there may be no widely shared values in any large modern society. Concentration on so-called values was politically deeply divisive in the U.S. presidential election of 2004. The idyll of bringing us together by focusing on "shared" values seems likely to be hopeless. And those things are generally means rather than values. You and I are able to fulfill our values—which may be quite different— because we have social order, a reasonably good legal regime, and so forth. Even the collective goods that we all (or almost all) want—such as highways, harbors, and a tax system—are themselves often means.

It is true that in our various limited contexts of family, neighborhood, work group, and so forth, we depend on some shared values and probably prosper much better in these relationships if we have relatively good trust relations. That is because being able to rely on each other enables us to benefit from cooperative endeavors more readily and at lower costs (of transactions, monitoring, and so forth). It is hard to say what could be the cooperative endeavors that a whole society wishes to share in—perhaps winning a war. Hence, some of the concern with so-called social or generalized trust—meaning universal trust in the random other person in our society—is surely misplaced. It would be pointless for us even to assess the trustworthiness of most people, and it often clearly would not benefit us to trust the general other. It is only beneficial for us to trust those who are trustworthy in their interactions with us, and these people constitute nowhere near all of the society. They are perhaps a very large fraction of the people we know, but they are a minuscule fraction of all Americans, let alone all humans.

One might say that social order is somehow a federation of such trust networks, and maybe one could give a constructive account of such a federation. Generally, however, that sounds too formal. There may be overlapping networks, all of which are piecemeal in the sense that any one of them serves only some of our needs. Each of us is a member of many such networks. A trust network analysis of a whole modern society would be extremely complex. For example, in a society of nearly 300 million people, the overwhelming majority of Americans would be outside each of one's networks; indeed, the overwhelming majority are even outside *all* of one's networks.[3]

Many of those outside our networks might readily be includable without much risk if ever we had reason to deal with them. But until they are included, we can generally say that we do not trust them—in the very limited sense of saying, not that we distrust them, but that we are agnostic about their potential trustworthiness toward us. Such others have no reason to act specifically in our interests just because these are our interests and generally cannot be assumed to do so. Some of them might act in ways that serve our interests, as when they drive properly according to the rules of the road when we are on the same roads with them. But that is because acting in those ways directly serves their own interests independently of any benefit to us, whom they generally do not know. For some of these people, we might actually be able to say that we distrust them because their interests conflict with ours. Indeed, it is likely that most of us do distrust large numbers of our fellow citizens, much the way Hume thinks we should distrust or at least be wary of agents of government.

Liberal Distrust of Government

In the view of Hume, Montesquieu, Madison, and other pragmatic liberal theorists, government should be distrusted by its citizens (Hardin 2002a). As Hume (1752/1985, 42) says, "Political writers have established it as a maxim, that, in contriving any system of government, and fixing the several checks and controuls of the constitution, every man ought to be supposed a knave, and to have no other end, in all his actions, than private interest." Hence, we should design government institutions so that they will work well even if they are staffed by knaves.

Madison fairly clearly thinks government is at risk of falling into the hands of knaves. He therefore makes positive uses of distrust in governance in the constitution he designed for the United States. In one of the most cited passages of the *Federalist Papers*, in number 51, Madison says, "If men were angels, no government would be necessary. If angels were to govern men, neither external nor internal controls on government would be necessary. In framing a government which is to be administered by men over men, the great difficulty lies in this: you must first enable the government to control the governed; and in the next place oblige it to control itself" (Hamilton, Jay, and Madison 1787/2001, 269).

In *Federalist* number 10, Madison argues for the relatively weak new national government to block the capricious powers of the states, which were the source of an "increasing distrust of public engagements, and alarm for private rights, which are echoed from one end of the continent to the other" (Hamilton, Jay, and Madison 1787/2001, 43). In the final *Federalist*, number 85, Alexander Hamilton repeats this thesis that the new national government will block "those practices on the part of the state governments, which have . . . planted mutual distrust in the breasts of all classes of citizens" (453). The generation of Madison and Hamilton was particularly horrified by the star-chamber holding of individuals without charge for long periods of time at the whim of the king. At Guantanamo, the United States has recently engaged in a similar practice with captives from Afghanistan.

Hume is not as misanthropic as his injunction seems to imply to many readers. But he grasps the essential fact that it is government's performance *at the extreme* that we have to fear. Hence, we should design government to be safe against extreme performance. His claim is one of risk aversion, not of misanthropy. Hence, for Hume it is occasional agents of the government whom we must distrust. (Hobbes also holds that there need be only some bad apples in a society without government for that society to descend to his awful state of nature. He further supposes, from his experience of the ugliness of the English Civil War, that such bad apples are always available.)

Well before Hume, however, this view of wariness toward government is already well stated by Locke (1690/1988, sect. 143), who opposes lodging too much power in a single branch of government (as Hobbes wishes to do) because "it may be too great a temptation to human frailty apt to grasp at power." He also notes the tendency of people to seek their own advantage and to use the powers of government to serve themselves. Indeed, he supposes that "the properest way to prevent the evil, is to show them the danger and injustice of it, who are under the greatest temptation to run into it" (sect. 226). The people show their leaders by rebelling.

Why would we distrust a government official whom we do not even know? We might instead simply neither trust nor distrust that official. If, however, we have any sense of the possibility that the official will use her office to benefit herself substantially, then we have some reason to suppose her interests substantially conflict with ours on various issues. Her interest could be nothing more than to get reelected, and still that interest might trump ours in her view. We might also simply worry that government agents' attentions will flag. Arguably, therefore, citizens should be wary and distrustful of government agents who are in charge of providing various goods and regulations (such as those governing fire safety in building codes). They should develop "healthy" distrust to ensure that regulations are dynamic and responsive to technical and other changes of the conditions that call for regulation (Troy 2004).

From a Humean or Madisonian view of the corrupting influence of having power with some discretion, we can distrust government officials *in principle* for being likely on occasion to use their offices for personal benefit in ways that conflict with the "public interest" or the interests of their own electorates (Hardin 2002a). It is not easy to imagine a converse general claim that such officials are likely *in principle* to serve our interest. Hence, at the level of mere theoretical understanding, we can justify distrust in some contexts in which we could not justify trust, even though the relevant party might be trustworthy. Hence, trust and distrust of government are asymmetric (but see Quirk 1990 and Kelman 1990). We can have what might be called generalized distrust of government, but not generalized trust of it.

There is a massive and growing literature on the claim that trust in government is declining in at least some democracies, especially the United States (see contributions to Pharr and Putnam 2000). As noted in chapter 1, much of that literature supposes that such a decline is bad in that it is harmful to the working of government. That is a surprising supposition for the United States, whose Constitution was framed by liberals such as James Madison who assumed that government cannot and should not be trusted and therefore explicitly designed a set of institutions to block government power as much as possible. The framers thought that a good government is one with extremely limited power to intervene in our lives. Sometimes this concern is said to be a peculiarly American worry, a bit of American exceptionalism (King 2000). But it is a standard worry in English thought as well, and it is central to Hume's political theory (for example, Hume 1752/1985) and to John Stuart Mill's (1859/1977) and Wilhelm von Humboldt's (1854/1969) libertarianism. One might suppose that the real issue of the era that saw the rise of such libertarian thinking was the parallel rise of the modern state, though the libertarian vision ran ahead of the political developments.

Liberal political theory is largely founded on distrust of government, which David Hume, James Madison, and to a lesser extent John Locke think is the only intelligent stance for citizens to take toward government (Bailyn 1967; Hardin 2002a; Morgan 1999; but see Wills 1999). Theirs is a theory of liberal distrust. As Edmund Morgan (1999, 39) quips, "Between 1776 and 1789 Americans replaced a government over them with a government under them." Under great stress (from the Civil War, the two world wars, and the current war on terrorism), that government has managed to climb out from under American citizens and threaten their civil liberties. One could generally distrust government in many ways and still hold that the presence of the government to help back up various inter- actions, such as legal contracts, enhances the possibilities of developing trust relationships between the relevant parties. That is to say, even a gov- ernment we should not trust might make it easier for us to trust each other.

Not only might we generally distrust government, but we might have relatively generalized distrust of particular groups, even though we would not claim generally to trust everyone in any group. Hence, we could have group-generalized distrust but not group-generalized trust for any substantial group. For example, those of one ethnic group might be generally distrusted by members of another group. Many women may generally distrust men in certain contexts. Children are taught to be wary and distrustful of adults, perhaps especially men, whom they do not know. Many Americans and Germans generally distrust scientists. Many people distrust business people of more or less all ranks. All of these might be no more than probabilistic judgments, but if the probabilities are high enough, the distrust might come naturally (Hardin 2004c). Indeed, if it makes sense to say that one can choose to distrust, the distrust in such cases might even seem wise. In general, however, it does not make sense to say that one chooses to trust or distrust, because these are both merely degrees of knowledge of the other's trustworthiness or lack of it. In gen- eral, we presumably make only probabilistic or relative assessments of how trustworthy another person is. For example, we might say that we trust Mary more than Bill, or even a lot more than Bill.

In the encapsulated interest view of trust, you take my interests to heart in part *because they are my interests.* A politician can do this, but it is complex for her to do it because of the complexity of issues that she is apt to face in office in a modern democratic state. Moreover, the elected offi- cial might suppose that it is only her supporters in the election to whom she owes accountability and not the entire polity that she represents (Hardin 2000).

Can the general theory that officials are relatively self-interested be trumped by an expectation that a particular official will take my interests seriously enough to act in my interests rather than against them? Consider one kind of case: the charismatic leader. Such a leader mobilizes a fol- lowing on some issue or on some relatively grand interest. If that issue or interest is also ours, we may be among her followers. Just because her sup- port comes from such charismatic appeal, we can probably expect her to stick with that commitment, and to this extent we can rely on her. We might not be able to rely on her or even trust her on many of the other issues that she will face in office, but we can rely on her for the range of issues that define her charismatic appeal because she has to perform on those issues or lose her charisma.

Typically, this device is available to politicians only when the issues are relatively simple and few, without crosscutting complications. That is to say, the device is more likely to be available to politicians in straitened circumstances than in times of general prosperity because our interests are not so readily focused on some narrow range of issues when we are prosperous. And this device is also more likely to be useful to a candidate who takes a strong stand on some moral issue that is more nearly ideological than interest-based.

In the case of a charismatic leader—or, more accurately in many contexts, an issue candidate—the leader and we just happen to share interests. The leader may share that interest only indirectly through the fact that pushing the relevant issues wins her votes. Hence, a wealthy man such as Senator Ted Kennedy of Massachusetts can be a charismatic leader of the poor, who may vote for him with relatively great confidence that he will take their interests seriously. In many cases, however, we might suppose that someone actually shares the interest of the group she represents. Hence, it is possible that a candidate would directly serve her own interests while being a charismatic leader to others. For example, David Duke perhaps sees himself as a victim of supposed racial preferences for blacks and has therefore been a credible leader for other white supremacists in Louisiana. Often, however, anyone able to marshal resources for waging an electoral campaign may be too prosperous to genuinely represent certain interests in this direct way—for example, the interests of the poor and unemployed.

The general problem of politicians' complicated array of interests can be exemplified even for ordinary citizens in the complex context of civil liberties. We may all agree in principle that individuals should be protected against certain kinds of action by government. But we know that we may be tempted by our own interests to override the principle in particular instances, such as when the civil liberties of some other or others offend us or even run counter to our interests in some ways. We therefore want to tie our hands in advance of knowing what the issues will be and who the relevant people will be. Even more, of course, we want to tie the hands of others to protect our own liberties, and the price of doing that is to tie our own hands as well. This is a principle that may be more naturally understood in a nation whose people have diverse religious affiliations, and it is perhaps only natural that the first body of civil liberties protections was codified in the U.S. Constitution and early amendments to it. That constitution was written for a nation of religious diversity, and various religious groups were more concerned with protecting their own religious freedoms than with imposing religious restrictions on others. But we might often expect people to understand the principle even in contexts other than those of religious conflict, and modern constitutions generally include protections of civil liberties.[4]

Government and Interpersonal Distrust

A commonly accepted conclusion of the anthropological literature is that centralized states sometimes destroy the social cohesion of traditional communities, undermine cooperation, and destroy trust among individuals (Taylor 1982; Gellner 1988). If so, then the state is arguably a major source of distrust in society. There is little real question about the first thesis (that the state can destroy the social cohesion of a traditional community), although other forces may be more important. From Hobbes on, there are compelling arguments for how social order, which virtually requires a state in modern circumstances, is necessary for social cooperation. Hence, the anthropological claim that the state undermines cooperation is miscast. It is hard to imagine the nature of the evidence that would test the third claim (that the state destroys trust among individuals) in moderately benign states, as opposed, say, to Argentina under the generals, the Soviet Union under Stalin, or much of Europe under Hitler. It must certainly be the case that government agencies, depending on their nature and their personnel, are at times among the major forces for destroying interpersonal trust, either directly or by destroying other institutions that support trust. For example, modern governments have often literally destroyed communities that were in the path of major highways or urban renewal or major dams, such as the dam currently destroying communities in China in the Three Gorges Project (see Hessler 2003).

But the lakes and electrical power grid created by the Tennessee Valley Authority (TVA) in the 1930s provided electricity to an impoverished region that prospered thereafter. The farming families in Tennessee and Kentucky who lived in extreme poverty and isolation before the TVA developments must have been much less cooperatively engaged with each other than were people in the communities that grew up around those developments. Moreover, government may sometimes help citizens to understand and even trust each other by creating forums in which they can address political issues (Gutmann and Thompson 1996). Perversely, through such forums citizens can even come to mobilize against the government that sponsors their existence. Any conclusive claim that the state is inherently likely to destroy rather than occasionally create the conditions for cooperative endeavors therefore seems implausible. The centralized state can drive out the spontaneous coordination that depends on small groups and thick networks of interaction (Taylor 1982), but there can also be a strong positive correlation between precisely these kinds of organizations and the strength of the government of a large state (Fukuyama 1995, 62–63 and passim).

The French government, after military defeat in the Franco-German War of 1870–71, set out on a program of educating children in French, with the eventual effect of destroying dozens of regional languages (Weber 1976). There must have been pain and anguish as older generations were linguistically cut off from their own grandchildren. There may even have been loss of cooperative energies in many communities. At the same time, however, opportunities improved for the younger generations to enter more varied employments and to migrate more easily to other areas of France, especially to the Île-de-France.

These changes must have wrecked some previous patterns of social organization and cooperation. But they may have opened other very attractive possibilities. As with the TVA, the French effort to make Frenchmen out of millions of French peasants must have had mixed effects. Surely it did destroy some particular communities. But did it destroy or reduce community overall? This is no trivial question, and it is not easily answered without a kind of research that may be exceedingly difficult to carry out retrospectively. Was the French government misguided? That too is a hard question. Many nations of Africa might benefit future generations by educating their children into a single national language. If the claims for community turn on preserving particular communities as though in aspic, then community is a grim value. It may require the destruction of some forms and instances of trust to create others.

Normative communitarians tend to overlook the destructively oppressive norms that can exist within families, villages, and small towns. Women are often victimized by patriarchal social orders in traditional communities. Feuds within families and between families suggest that intimate knowledge does not always produce either trust or cooperation and in fact can produce the opposite. Marital conflict can induce many forms of distrust, even in societies in which the state is extremely weak at best (Brown 2004). Banfield's (1958) amoral familism seems more likely the result of neglect by the state than of state intrusion. In such cases, a government that reduces personal dependencies and resolves conflicts may actually enhance familial trust. By protecting social rights, the state plays an important role in reducing risky personal reliance on others. For example, government-provided welfare or health care reduces the range of services that the needy must otherwise depend on their families or community to provide.

Finally, however, if the state has a major impact on wrecking old patterns of trust, that impact may primarily be felt through the indirect effects of the economic changes that are partially enabled—and sometimes deliberately planned, as in the Communist world—by a state that oversees contract relations and provides infrastructures. Urbanization and later suburbanization were chiefly economic and social movements built out of individual and family decisions to migrate to where the economic and social opportunities seemed better. Urban society lacks the traditional structures of small farming communities, and it has been the mostly spontaneous movement to such societies—not the state—that has wrecked small-town communal ways of living together. Rural towns are generally abandoned by their residents, not bulldozed by the state. Reverence for such communities is particularly odd if life in them has been as hard as sometimes described.

Karl Marx (1852/1963, 123–25) seems to have understood very well how stultifying rural societies can be. They must often have more in common with the societies of endemic distrust discussed earlier than with the idylls of communitarians. If we all lived in such communities, we would today have dismal life prospects. If they once spawned trust that has been lost as they have disappeared, then perhaps the price of trust is too high. It seems likely, however, that they often maintained their order through oppressive norms rather than through trust (Amato 1993; Cook and Hardin 2001; Fischer 1982).

Breakdowns of Trust and Trustworthiness

It is argued that many of the fundamental problems facing the contemporary world are grounded in a lack or breakdown of trust: between individuals, between groups, between individuals and the state, between groups and the state, and between states themselves. For example, without some level of trust between trading partners, markets would be less efficient. Trust is widely thought to be an essential component of effective government, economic performance, and relative peace and stability within and among nations. Where there is trust, there are more likely to be contributions in time and money to community enterprises, from cleanup campaigns to the construction of public works to provisions for the helpless and the homeless. Trust evidently lubricates exchange relationships, resolutions of common resource problems, and, in the view of many, the efficacy of representative government. Some writers hold that trusting impersonal institutions, such as government or corporations, resolves many problems that incentive structures do not handle as well. Studies of management commonly show the importance of trust in corporate leadership in enhancing productivity.

Although the story is not yet fully told, consider the particularly grim example of failed trust in the ongoing saga of Ford Motor Company's SUVs, which rolled over when their Firestone tires failed, often killing someone in the SUV. Initially, the received wisdom seems to have been that Ford was at fault in using tires that were inadequate to handle such large vehicles, which are top-heavy and therefore prone to rolling over with any tire failure. Ford, of course, accused Firestone of producing poor-quality tires. The problem may largely have been poor-quality workmanship by workers angry at Firestone during a period of labor unrest after Firestone was taken over by Bridgestone (Krueger and Mas 2003).

Because tires are marked with the plant and week in which they were manufactured, the origins of tires whose treads separated and caused rollovers could be traced (Krueger and Mas 2003, 14). Tires for Ford's Explorer SUVs were manufactured in several plants, but those made in the Decatur, Illinois, plant during labor unrest were fifteen times more likely to lead to claims of tire failure than tires made in other plants, and they were also substantially more likely to lead to such claims than were tires made there in other years (17).[5] About forty people died as a result of poor workmanship, and the number would have been about twice that had the remaining tires not been recalled (34).

An internal Bridgestone document reportedly states that, "while it was nice to share a good relationship [with the union], it would no longer be in the company's interest" (Krueger and Mas 2003, 34). Against this claim, the stock market value of the company fell from $16.7 billion to $7.5 billion within four months of the tire recall. Top management was replaced, the Decatur plant was closed in 2001, and Bridgestone considered dropping the grand Firestone name. Workers have great discretion in the handmade process of manufacturing tires (11), and their goodwill on the job is evidently very important to the interests of the firm, as well as to the lives of the firm's customers. Since the plant closing presumably cost many of the restive workers their jobs, they paid severely for their grudging work during the period of unrest.

Despite such a case, many of the claims for the benefits or even necessity of trust are far from being demonstrated, and some of them might not be demonstrable at all. Ordinary exchange in the market, for example, seems likely to be made workable even without trust, as discussed more fully in chapters 6 and 9. Indeed, John Wanamaker changed retail practices and became the dominant force in Philadelphia department store retailing when he backed his wares with money-back guarantees to enhance his sales (Mueller 1999).[6] Similarly, some of the claims that trust is now in decline and we are therefore worse off are almost entirely ungrounded in any evidence other than subjective assessments. These seem to be clouded by the golden-age fallacy of believing that the past was better than the present. One should probably not tell women of the North Atlantic nations or African Americans that the 1950s were a golden age of harmony and cooperation.

Societies Rife with Distrust

Various studies of peasant communities in southern Italy, Mexico, and Peru suggest that people in such communities sometimes develop amoral familism (Banfield 1958; see also Aguilar 1984; Westacott and Williams 1976). Family members stick together and both lie to and distrust others. The societies in these studies are more accurately characterized as subsistence societies, experiencing as they do daunting levels of poverty and hunger. People in these societies seem to see life as a zero-sum competition with others. There are at least four reasons for this.[7]

First, these societies, with their economy of agricultural subsistence, are overwhelmingly dependent on land. Land is essentially zero-sum: if my family has more land, some other family has less. Second, if we are all producing the same things (food for our families), there are few opportunities for division of labor outside the family. Some of the opportunities for exchange or cooperative behavior in more complex societies are therefore not available in some subsistence societies. Third, the form of agricultural production in these societies does not depend on joint efforts, so that there is no natural reason to have a system of broadly cooperative agricultural effort that might spill over into other realms. And fourth, in a subsistence system it is natural, because sensible, to be highly risk-averse and to develop practices that are least likely to result in especially bad years, when many would starve, rather than more likely to produce a surplus in the average year.

People in these societies therefore fail to cooperate in part because it would do no good in many contexts and in part because they naturally focus on the competitive, zero-sum aspects of their lives. If there is no point in cooperation, there may even be advantage in deceit, secrecy, and cheating, as there typically is in a zero-sum conflict, such as poker. If everyone outside our family is likely to cheat us, we have good reason not to trust them. One would like to see what Julian Rotter's (1980) studies would have concluded if they had been undertaken in such zero-sum societies. In such a society, it may be the most adamant distruster who prospers most and is happiest with life. In Rotter's studies of relatively affluent American college students, the most trusting—or the most optimistic—students were also the happiest, perhaps because they were the most prosperous and had happy family backgrounds.

At an intermediate level of distrust, consider the destructive effects of the corruption of the judiciary in the Philippines (Montinola 2004). Corruption in the justice system leads to low levels of perceived trustworthiness not only of the government officials (and hence government in general) but also of citizens. A result is the deterioration of the rule of law that undercuts the prospects for development. The generally low opinion of the judiciary may have led to violent responses to politicized decisions, such as the ouster of the democratically elected president Joseph Estrada. Here the asymmetric nature of trust and distrust seems to be evident. Knowledge of a government agency's corruption is enough for citizens to distrust the agency, because its corruption is clearly against the interests of most citizens (those not bribing the agency). A common argument about trust is that it can spill over from one arena to another, although there is virtually no evidence of this in the literature. With distrust, however, there might be such spillover. If we know that the government is corrupt over certain issues, we may suppose that it is generally corrupt. In particular, if we know of corruption, we can be sure that top personnel of the government know of it too. If they are not corrupt, they should take action against those who are. If corruption continues without hindrance, we may generally conclude that the government is generally corrupt. There is no parallel argument for the generalization of trust (Hardin 2004b).

More generally, we can say that in many contexts what we can trust you to do cannot far exceed what others in like circumstances could be trusted to do (as noted earlier for Hutus, Serbs, and others in groups that are in conflict). You might have to do something extraordinary to show your commitment to going beyond usual expectations. If the general communal context is one of distrust over the range of issues with respect to which we might wish we could trust you, you will have to make such a commitment, and it will have to be credible, or we will not trust you. In Madagascar, there is widespread distrust of marital partners that comes from the fragility of marital relations (Brown 2004). Extramarital affairs and divorce are common. Hence, spouses distrust each other, and the children of mixed parentage distrust each other over property inheritance. An errant husband establishes an unusually strong commitment by exceeding the demands of the community's norms governing food taboos, which differ by family. Although this is not expected under prevailing norms, he takes on his wife's taboos to show that he is really committed to her despite his bad behavior. In this case, it is striking that the shared value system of the villagers does not lead to strong trust. "In fact, it signals to both parties the limits of their trustworthiness" (Brown 2004, 178). That is, they cannot reliably be expected to go beyond prevailing norms.

It is a commonplace view that relations within families are grounded in moral commitments rather than rational or calculative commitments. They would therefore seem to be a poor context for the development of trust as encapsulated interest. Margaret Brown (2004) argues, on the contrary, that distrust can pervade family relationships and that the devices to overcome distrust in families are not unlike those for overcoming distrust in other contexts. She focuses on three kinds of intrafamilial relationships, all of which are essentially economic: handling joint income in a marriage, buying property, and jockeying for inheritance. In her community, market institutions are weak or nonexistent, so that there are few alternatives to kin ties for economic opportunity, and formal institutions for handling relevant conflicts are weak. Brown argues that people expend energy and resources to stabilize weak but important ties. In general, in her cases the less trustworthy party typically must find informal devices to establish a commitment to being fair within the relationship. In the end, Brown supposes, her villagers have to expend so much effort on securing familial ties that they have relatively little room to work on trust relations with nonkin. Hence, contrary to the view that the strength of family ties gets in the way of extending networks beyond the family (see Banfield 1958), it is the weakness of even very important family ties that forces all resources into maintaining them, so that there is little time or energy to develop other relationships or networks.

High-Risk Contexts

In contexts in which too much is at stake to rely on trust—as in game 2 (figure 4.2), where the potential benefits to the trusted of cheating and the concomitant losses to the truster are massive—we generally want to have powerful institutions to block cheating. We are able to enter into ordinary exchange relations on a daily basis in large part because we have police protection against some kinds of massive cheating and because we have such legal protections as the law of contracts to protect us in other extremely important areas. In such areas, to recommend that people merely trust each other would be irresponsible. Distrust is clearly the rational and generally beneficial stance because it is correctly grounded in a reading of the facts. One does not have to be Hobbesian to argue for the enormous benefit of having a powerful enough state in the background to maintain social order in the face of such grievous risks.

If potentially awful outcomes can be prevented or at least made far less likely, people will be more open to risk-taking over smaller issues. They need not initially trust potential partners to various exchanges; they need merely take the risk of cooperating at a level of modest commitment of resources and time. Even if they are wary and perhaps even tend to distrust, they must take such risks or lose out on life altogether. The same is generally not true for very high-stakes risks. We are generally likely to distrust virtually everyone when the stakes are high, and rightly so. Distrust even of close friends is only right in such matters. We do not want to wreck our friendships by putting claims on them that are too great. We therefore take care of such matters with legal and institutional assistance that substantially reduces the likelihood of losing and the likelihood of damaging personal trust relationships.

If we have been cooperating on various matters for a long time and quite extensively, the escalation of the stakes we face can essentially change our interaction into a very different one—from game 1 to game 2, for example. If we trust you with respect to x but now we risk losing far more than merely x if you default, we may not trust you with respect to the new stakes and might even distrust you. Indeed, the newly higher stakes may change our interaction into one that is at endgame, so that each of us wishes not to be the first to cooperate for fear that the other will then defect by taking the high stakes and not reciprocating our cooperation.

Figure 4.2   Game 2: Prisoner's Dilemma Payoff Matrix with Very High Risk

		Column Player	
		Cooperate	Not Cooperate
Row Player	Cooperate	1, 1	−10,000, 10,001
	Not Cooperate	10,001, −10,000	0, 0

Source: Authors' figure.

We might continue our low-level cooperation and pass on the opportunity to engage over higher stakes, or we might see our relationship as somehow polluted by the introduction of large-scale opportunities that we do not wish to risk. Increasing our stakes slowly might lead us eventually to cooperation at a very high level, but we might not be willing to jump to that high level immediately, any more than we would enter a new relationship at a high level of risk. We know from our own experience that high stakes and low stakes are different in the incentives they evoke. Your friend might instantly forget the cost of the cup of coffee she buys for you today, but she might never forget the thousand-dollar loan she makes to you. (Perhaps we all have friends who would not forget the cost of the cup of coffee either.)

Concluding Remarks

Asymmetries of information, power, resources, and alternative opportunities can all induce distrust. If I discover that you, my partner in some enterprise, have another person as a potential fallback in the event that we do not successfully cooperate in our joint venture, I must immediately think that you do not trust me or that you even distrust me, and I must immediately therefore also distrust you somewhat. In such a relationship, it may be true that trust must be mutual or distrust will be mutual.

Again note that distrust and lack of trust are not generally devastating to our lives. They are commonly the correct assessment of the competences and motivations of others, and they therefore help us to negotiate our way through efforts to cooperate with and rely on others when doing so serves our interest. In the five chapters that follow, we discuss numerous devices for managing relationships when trust would not be warranted. These run from the very small scale of interpersonal relations to the large scale of dealings with big institutions and government. In general, we argue in the following chapters, one can say that an institution that cannot be trusted might nevertheless be used to handle relationships in which trust is lacking. The same might even sometimes be true of individuals.

One can also suggest that the actual structures of many institutions and even their very existence are justified and may have been motivated by problems of lack of trustworthiness on the part of many. The most trivially obvious general instance of this is contract law, without which our societies would be impoverished but which would not have been necessary if others were sufficiently trustworthy. A more particular example is the initial design, by Madison and others, of the U.S. government in the constitution of 1787. Contract law and the U.S. government have been among the greatest social inventions in human history. Hence, if we wish to understand our own societies and their institutions, we might sensibly begin with an account of the justified ubiquity of distrust and how we manage despite it. It is often far less useful to start from an account of trust.

Chapter 5

Cooperation Without Law or Trust

N OW WE turn to the heart of our enterprise, which is to explain how people manage their lives in the absence of trust and largely in the absence of legal or state enforcement of cooperative arrangements, all despite sometime inequality of power and often solid grounds for distrust. As is prima facie evident, the existence of the state and a legal system to govern many relationships can substitute for trust and other spontaneous motivations for cooperation in joint ventures of various kinds. In the role of providing law and stability, the state does not generally provoke cooperation but only enables it. Indeed, this fact is the rationale of the Hobbesian vision of order under an all-powerful sovereign (Hobbes 1651/1968).

The failure or limits of state regulation or legal devices often leads to the creative development of informal devices. For example, the informal economies of the Third World arise in the context of weak states.[1] But such informal "contractual" dealings permeate First World contexts as well, in part because law is too imprecise and too costly to cover the details of ordinary commercial agreements (Macauley 1963; Portes and Sassen-Koob 1987). There is evidence that strong informal institutions can thrive locally when central government is weak.[2] Contrary to the more nearly standard view, we might argue that, historically, commerce seems to have stimulated the growth of law and legal institutions, which were not necessary for the early development of commerce (Mueller 1999, 95–98). Adam Smith (1776/1976, 412), crediting David Hume with the original insight, remarks that with the rise of towns, "commerce and manufactures gradually introduced order and good government, and with them, the liberty and security of individuals." Robert Ellickson (1991, 1998) argues that, in the face of potentially prohibitive conflict more generally, local norms commonly handle many economic issues of cooperation that the law could not handle as efficiently or as well. In many of his cases, there is an ongoing relationship, which suggests the likelihood of developing a trust relationship that makes cooperation relatively easy. Ellickson's work and even the title of his 1991 book are forerunners to the present book, although he addresses cooperation without law and we are concerned with the supposedly even harder problem of cooperation with neither law nor trust. We may conclude that many activities are best regulated by norms and that the law itself requires norms to enable its own working (Hetcher 2004, ch. 2).

In analyzing cooperation without trust, we begin in this chapter at the individual level and with largely spontaneous interactions. Then we turn to relatively systematic patterns of interaction, but still at the level of individuals rather than of institutions. Many social practices can readily be seen de facto as devices for managing and motivating cooperative behavior in the absence of adequate trust, or even in the presence of substantial distrust. Often we need to be able to cooperate with some of those whom we do not trust. In fact, of course, we are in no position to trust the vast majority of people in our society, and possibly we cannot trust even the vast majority of those with whom we have to deal, both directly and indirectly. If we could handle these relationships through the law, we might not need to worry about the lack of trust. But many of the cooperative relations we would like to enter cannot be regulated by law. Even for many of those that could be brought under law, the costs of appealing to legal institutions might dwarf the benefits of the relationships. Ideally we might wish we could find people whom we could trust. In the large number of cases in which that is not possible, we would like to have some less formal social devices available to give potentially useful partners the incentive to be cooperative.

The state may lurk in the background for most of the interactions discussed here, but often the scale or the specificity (sometimes to the point of idiosyncrasy) of an interaction makes it not a good candidate for legal oversight. Even then, the general order that the state provides is usually the essential background on which all of these devices play out. If there were no stable order, we would not be so heavily engaged in cooperative interactions because we would be more focused on self-protection than on marginal improvements in our lives. All of the interactions discussed here are outside the law, although they are not necessarily illegal.[3] They may sometimes even be pre-law. For example, communal norms must have worked even in many communities in which there was no powerful legal authority.

Many of the alternative devices rely on reputational effects, both of individual cooperators and of institutional agencies (short of government) and other formal institutions that back reputations with some degree of sanctioning for failure to live up to them. The force of reputation here is not that it carries information on past behavior (which would be of central importance for a dispositional theory of trustworthiness). Rather, the value of a reputation is that it can give others reason to believe one wishes to maintain the reputation *in order to enter into cooperative relations with others in the future.* Hence, when we refer to reputational effects here, we always mean their future-oriented effects. In this sense, the value of a reputation for trustworthiness is that it gives one incentive actually to be trustworthy, and it therefore gives others incentive to take the risk of assuming that one will be trustworthy, as in the encapsulated interest theory.

Institutional devices, ranging from informal to formal, are discussed in chapters 6 through 8, and we do not address them here. Nevertheless, it should be clear that many of the devices we discuss in this chapter could not work entirely well without the background protections of various institutions, especially government. Indeed, one of the strongest claims to make for (good) government is that it enables us to rely on such informal devices. These are especially useful in contexts in which, for example, standard contract law would be too expensive to handle the interaction, which would therefore simply fail in many instances if there were no workable informal devices. Many of the repressive governments of Africa, the Middle East, the former Communist world, and many other places impede interactions between citizens and produce dreadful economic results in addition to their antilibertarian abuses of individuals. Benign government is often a necessary background for spontaneous successes of social cooperation.

The chief categories of informal devices for controlling social behavior—that is, those not formally backed by an organization—are norms that are backed essentially by moral commitments; norms that are backed by sanctions strong enough to make it typically one's interest to adhere to them; and interest-based interactions, such as those within networks of individuals who rely on each other for certain activities. We begin the discussion with an account of social capital, which gives a very general explanation of why and how informal relations work in many contexts. Then we turn to various devices many or all of which depend on social capital to some extent, beginning with norms and going on to social devices that are largely embedded in interests, especially in exchange relations. Both of these, but especially exchange-based devices, are often enabled by well-developed social capital. First we compare norms and exchange-based devices in a pair that might each work on its own but that commonly define alternative structures for communal organizations: communal norms of cooperativeness versus networks that enable trust.

In general, we do not discuss norms that are backed essentially by moral commitments. Such norms can produce trust that is grounded in an assessment or expectation of the moral commitments of the trusted. Such norms are therefore not in need of separate discussion here because they are subsumed under trust as grounded in the moral commitment of the trusted to be trustworthy. In all three standard theories of trust, trust is justified by the apparent trustworthiness of the other, whether from encapsulated interest, disposition of character, or moral commitment of some kind. Norms that are backed by moral commitments therefore are not alternatives to trust, because if you adhere to such a norm, then I can trust you with respect to relevant matters.

In this chapter, we address interactions that commonly have the form of A somehow inducing B to motivate C to do something A wants (or, in some cases, the shorter form of B motivating C to do something A wants or would value). For example, in Muhammad Yunus's Grameen Bank, it is groups of neighbors (usually women) who induce each other to repay their loans so that others in the group might also have access to loans. Yunus and his bank, A, do not need to be assiduous in chasing after repayment from a customer, C, because they have, in a sense, delegated the incentive for doing this to the neighbors, B. The loans from the Grameen Bank are too small for the bank to use legal devices to enforce repayment; in any case, in many of the societies in which such banks operate the legal system is not capable of enforcing repayment of any loans, large or small. In essence, the Grameen turns clusters of neighbors into network (social) capital.

When we turn to institutional devices for managing cooperation without trust, B in this formula is the nongovernmental institution, such as a professional membership organization, a formal organization, or an organ of the state, all of which can directly motivate C to do something that A wants or values. The cooperation of role holders with their organization can be secured strictly through the use of incentives to align behavior with organizational goals, but it can also be aided by rich relationships of trust among organizational members. Only if we first succeed in aligning individual behavior with organizational goals can we then expect reliability from formal organizations in inducing us and our potential partners to be cooperative under the aegis of the relevant organizations.

This formula de facto captures the idea of social capital in one of its forms, as we argue later. In this particular form, *individuals can have access to social capital*. For you (A) to call on social capital is to have access to a facilitator (B) who can motivate the relevant provider (C) to act on your behalf. In an advanced society, the relevant C is usually an institution of some kind, often government. B might also be an institution, but B is more likely to be a role holder in an institution. Social capital is a vague, not to say murky, concept that takes on many meanings. Many scholars include trust in the bag of many unrelated things that they say constitute social capital (for example, Putnam 1995a, 1995b, 2000; Brehm and Rahn 1997).[4] As we conceive the idea of social capital that takes the form of individuals having access to it (Cook 2005), trust can play a small initiating role, but it does not have to do so.

It can happen that because a particular facilitator, B, trusts you, A, to some extent to reciprocate favors, B is induced to try to motivate a relevant C to act on your behalf. But the facilitator can do this even without trust because A and B can simply enter an exchange in which A pays for B's effort to motivate the provider C. As a crass but evidently very common example in American politics, you give money to B's campaign for political office, and B gets government agency C to do what you want. We spell out the implications of this general view later. Social capital enables us to get things done by people with whom we do not have a substantial trust relationship—indeed, people whom we need not even know. That is commonly why we want access to social capital—because it is the only form of access we might have to accomplish our purposes, although vernacular vocabulary would not put the case that way. Hence, although trust might be important in calling on social capital, social capital is not constituted by trust.

Some of the practices for motivating cooperative behavior develop to such a stable and forceful degree that they begin to seem almost governmental. For example, trade before the rise of international legal institutions to regulate it must have taken on such aura that the informal institutions for regulating it may have seemed statelike at the time (see chapter 9). More generally, the range of devices for securing cooperative trade relations even in the absence of state enforcement is impressive and attests to the great value of trade to those who invest so much effort to make it work.

Cooperative behavior across a wide array of issues can also be motivated by communal norms so that almost every member of the community plays the role of facilitator in motivating individuals' cooperation (see, for example, Cook and Hardin 2001; Hardin 1995, chs. 4 and 5). We impose our communal norms on C, and C has no hope of refusing to comply without suffering great costs from our sanctions. Finally, even within markets governed by extensive legal systems, there are commonly issues of quality and reliance that cannot be adequately written into contracts or enforced by courts, so that other, often informal devices are necessary for governing these (Macauley 1963; Macneil 1980). There are even whole contracts, often quite complex, that can be virtually self-enforcing (Klein 1985). Contract and regulatory law are often too clumsy and costly to regulate details of behavior, which must therefore be spontaneously regulated. For example, as we discuss in chapter 6, the detailed regulation of professionals and scientists is accomplished largely without legal intervention, which has been relatively rare except for the rise of malpractice suits through the tort law.[5]

Social Capital

Although recent work on the social underpinnings of government often starts from claims about the nature or decline of social capital, the main role of social capital in our lives is in enabling us to accomplish things at the level of individuals and groups. There have been many different attempts to define social capital, but here we restrict the term to two forms. The first—and for present purposes the more important—of these takes the form of the various networks on which certain people can call to get things done. Again, many writers include trust in the category of social capital, although that is a mistake. Your trusting does not do much for you when you need to call on a network of associates to help you resolve some family or broader social problem, such as how to protect your child within the educational system. That there are people in your networks who trust you, however, may be very useful. Hence, as seems to be pervasive in discussions of trust, what—if anything—is really at stake here is trustworthiness rather than trust. The fact that you have found me trustworthy in some prior dealings makes it likely that you will now let me rely on you to get something done. If you have previously found me to be untrustworthy, you are likely to see no future in cooperating with me for my benefit because you would not expect me to reciprocate. Even to mention reciprocity here suggests the possibility of exchange, which need not be grounded in trust. Hence, our understanding of social capital is not yet complete.

The second form that social capital takes in the literature is the capacity of a group to act together in certain ways. Here we can meaningfully say that groups can have social capital. This capital inheres in the connections within groups. For example, if we all trust each other, we might all take the risk of investing in some collective enterprise at a cost to each of us as individuals, although we could not be a large group because we could not have thick enough relationships with a large number of people to be able meaningfully to trust them or judge their trustworthiness. Those who worry about declining social capital must have larger-scale issues in mind.

We should note that not all group actions are dependent on such social capital. Some groups act from spontaneous coordination in which no one's actions entail individual costs. For example, one day in October 1969 an enormous number of mostly young people marched from Cambridge Common and other venues to Boston for a rally against the war in Vietnam. That day was a glorious day to be out of doors, and many of the people in the marches were unconnected individuals, couples, or small groups of friends who did not know many, if any, other people in the entire demonstration of tens of thousands. The occasion was so pleasing that even people in favor of the war joined the activities. For many people, participation in the event was a consumption good, similar to going to a concert or a theater performance, and its only cost was the opportunity cost of other activities that might have been available to them (see Hardin 1982b, ch. 7). The organizers may have relied on the social capital of their group to elicit cooperation in the tedious tasks of organizing the event, but the participants did not need to have any such social capital to induce their participation. It is inconceivable that any of the participants could have trusted all of the others, and indeed, apart from the organizers, none need have trusted any others in any meaningful sense with respect to the collective endeavor.

Very few writers are clear about the difference between individuals *having access to social capital* and groups *actually having social capital*. James Coleman (1988, 100–2; 1990, 302–4) makes the distinction (but sometimes blurs it) and gives examples of groups that have social capital that enables them to act collectively. We might similarly include many organizations in the list of "groups" that have social capital. Such group or organizational capital is explicitly the form of social capital that is of central interest to several writers (see, for example, Cohen and Prusak 2001). And it may be what is at issue in the recent literature about Tocqueville's claims for the import of group activity in the democratic politics of the early United States (as in Putnam 2000). He supposed that group organization was a laboratory for learning democracy (see chapter 8). Here we focus, however, on the first of these forms of social capital: individuals having access to social capital that can help them accomplish their goals. Again, individual access to social capital has the form of A getting B to motivate C to act on A's behalf.[6]

Note that your individual access to social capital turns on the interaction between two things. First is the potential usefulness of some network in getting done what you want done. Second is the likely commitment of those in the network to be motivated to take actions on your behalf. In your ordinary life, there are probably many people in many networks with whom you deal, and those networks are much of the social capital that is, in some sense, available to you. Many of these people—but probably not all—would say they trust you in certain matters.

In this view of it, the social capital to which an individual might have access is analogous to physical capital, such as machinery. Any bit of physical capital enables you to do various things. It enables you more if you are especially talented at using it, so that the value of that capital to you is not identical to the value that same capital has to others. For example, you might be able to produce the sounds of a wonderful Mozart sonata from a violin while many others could produce only unpleasant screeches from it. Social capital is similar, but rather than a talent for making the violin or some machine do its tricks, you have relationships that enable you to get the network capital that is available to you to do its tricks. Your relationships might differ enough that you get different results from calling on the same networks for the same kind of issue. However, one could imagine using the same networks in a very different way. There might be professional enablers who can tap into the networks to get things done for those who pay for the service. This is essentially the story of how many contributors to politicians' election campaigns get things done. They have paid up front and can be expected to pay again at the next election, and they receive entrée to relevant networks to solve various problems. Similarly, some might be able to call on social capital because they reciprocate in some way; you can call on it because you have paid for access.

When we see social capital in this way, we can see two somewhat contrary effects. On the one hand, many of the problems of ordinary life can be resolved through its use, and this makes it sound like a generally beneficent thing. On the other hand, some people have access to networks—especially networks that connect with government—that far surpasses the access of the rest of us, although the government might formally be democratic and also supposedly egalitarian with respect to many policy implementations. These individuals' greater access to social capital distorts outcomes, because they have access to government personnel who might have substantial power to use public funds or political influence. This does not sound so clearly beneficent. But this general conclusion should come as no surprise because, in essence, social capital is merely a means to do things, and there is no reason to suppose that it can only be put to work to accomplish good or egalitarian things. It can also be put to work to accomplish generally bad or inegalitarian things. The machine in a factory may be used to produce weapons or consumer goods. Similarly, social capital can produce both awful policies and good policies. The Ku Klux Klan can have access to social capital as great as that of the NAACP.

All of these networks depend on social order and technological access to people. In the past our networks were far more likely to have been face to face, although not exclusively. Now our networks cover far more ground, but perhaps they cover it more thinly (Leijonhufvud 1995; Hardin 1999b). Yet Robert Putnam (1995a, 1995b, 2000) and many others argue that social capital in some advanced democracies is in decline. For Putnam, this is worrisome because he supposes that citizens' access to social capital makes government perform better. Differential access, as noted earlier, seems likely to make it perform especially well for some people and much less well for others.

In general, the claim in many recent discussions of declining social capital must be wrong. *Individual access to social capital in general is increasing for many people in modern societies, not decreasing.* People in advanced nations have many connections through their workplaces, their neighborhoods, their extended families, their fellow university alums, and numerous other groups. And they have various talents for figuring out which of these can best help them in various contexts. As evidence of how connected we are, every year many of us receive especially targeted solicitations for help of various kinds, usually for donations of money. These come through networks with which we have been long associated as well as from those we have joined very recently. It seems that every time we respond to one of these, we get several more, almost as though by return mail. For example, contributions to any police or hospital benefit, no matter how good the cause, are an invitation to be hassled incessantly by telephone solicitations, usually at dinnertime, for years to come. These are networks that commonly use us; we cannot so readily use them. But they are an indicator of our connectedness and our general level of access to varied networks. Changes in our degrees of connectedness over time are a worthy subject for investigation (see Watts 2003; for a relatively popular account of connectedness and its value, see Gladwell 1999).

Having individual access to social capital seems to be an important part of our lives for accomplishing many things at the personal or family level. Here we consider various social devices for accomplishing cooperative results even when there is little trust. In some of these cases, there might be some trust that gets things going, but the devices are not primarily exercises of trust and trustworthiness, and trust is not necessary for them to work. As usual, when there is trust, things may be easier, but trust is not a sine qua non. The devices considered here are exercises in applying individual pressure to individuals to get them to behave in certain ways. These exercises range from the imposition of strong communal norms, including even outrageous norms such as that of the duel, to the device of fictive kinship to give someone the incentive to act as a reliable agent for another, and on to various devices to secure communal lending.

All of these spontaneous social devices, which take place outside the coverage of the law, regulate life when trust would be inadequate for the simple reason that there might not be much trust in many of these contexts because *there are conflicts of interest great enough to trump individual encapsulation of another's interests.* The greatest challenge to trust as encapsulated interest in many relationships is often such conflicts of interest. If law stood in the background for these interactions, trust between the relevant parties would also not be necessary. But these are cases in which law is not sufficient—because it is too poorly developed or because the stakes are too low to call on such heavy, expensive machinery. One of the devices discussed here is the duel, which has often been called pre-law. In fact, many of the devices here are pre-law, although, again, most of them depend on some degree of social order without which marginal issues could not be important in our lives.

Communal Norms of Cooperativeness and Responsibility

There is virtually always a larger context in which trust relations play out. A somewhat stylized social history of trust relations is as follows (Cook and Hardin 2001). In relatively small-scale communal organization of life, trust is generally not at issue, and indeed there is no term for trust in English before about the twelfth century, and still none today in many languages of the world (Hardin 2002b, 76). When everyone in a community knows everyone else and when everyone oversees everyone else's interactions, reliability can be enforced by norms that are backed by the sanctions the community would apply. Your default in an interaction with me commonly brings down sanctions from all of us, not merely from me. This fits the paradigm of social capital: A induces B to motivate C to do something for A. If C has been derelict in some dealing with A, A can induce the whole community, B, to motivate C to behave better toward A, or even to make some kind of restitution to A.

The stylized history of trust appears to be mirrored in systematic differences in the nature of helping and cooperative relations in contemporary small towns and large cities (Cook and Hardin 2001). Helping behavior in small towns is in fact not a matter of reciprocity but of helping or communal norms, whereas seemingly similar behavior in urban areas is typically a matter of reciprocity (Amato 1993). Moreover, in small communities behavior under communal norms is generalized to cover everyone in the community, whereas in cities the reciprocity governs behavior within particular networks. You reciprocate helping behavior toward those in your network who would help you in similar circumstances (and who may have helped you already). In small towns, the social networks are multiplex, membership is stable, and the norms for responsibility are relatively generalized. In urban settings, the networks tend to be more specialized, less multiplex, more sparsely connected (instead of almost wholly overlapping), and more numerous. They are multiple instead of multiplex (Fischer 1982), although there may be certain subcommunities within urban settings that approximate the character of small-town life.

An apparent implication of these differences in the nature of cooperation in small communities and in urban settings is that trust and trustworthiness help to ground, or grow out of, reciprocal exchange relations in cities. To examine this thesis we draw on theories of generalized exchange in networks and groups (Cook and Hardin 2001; Yamagishi and Cook 1993). Trustworthy behavior can be based on interests, on psychological dispositions, or on moral commitments. Trust must therefore be grounded in knowledge of the interests, the dispositional character, or the moral commitments of the trusted.

If helping behavior is based on norms, as in small communities, the relevant norms could have grown by socioevolution out of reciprocal exchange relations within groups. This could be a natural development for teaching a child, whom it might be much easier to teach a simple rule (as in a norm) than an understanding of the complexities of the interests of others and how these strategically relate to the child's own interests, especially long-run interests. Indeed, many adults appear to be unable to grasp even the logic of the interests embedded in iterated prisoner's dilemma (exchange) interactions (Hardin 1982a) or the logic of collective action (Hardin 1982b; Olson 1965). Communal norms can govern relatively little beyond some degree of cooperativeness, or they might be quite extensive, in which case they are likely to be imposed on some more heavily than on others. If they are grounded in strenuous religious principles, for instance, they can be very extensive and even draconian. We are concerned primarily with cooperativeness and how it is motivated in the absence of state power. Hence, we are not concerned with the full panoply of norms that might govern relations in some community, but only with norms of cooperativeness.

That a communal norm might commonly be enforced by interests could well help it to survive and to motivate people. A communal norm of helping or of trustworthiness might arise out of reciprocal exchange relations and then be transformed into a more generalized norm, albeit one that is still reinforced most strongly only as a within-group norm. The urban norms may be less normatively conceived and more openly grounded in reciprocal relations within ongoing networks, and they might almost never be generalized beyond their initial contexts. These differences have important implications for intergroup relations in both urban and small-community contexts.

Communal norms of cooperativeness and other positive matters are commonly backed by more onerous norms of exclusion. Such norms commonly work to keep members of various groups loyal to the group. They do this by using sanctions against those who are weakly committed or who violate expected practices within the group. The sanctions can range from mild reprimands to total exclusion from the group, with moderate shunning somewhere in between these extremes. There is often a supposition that efforts to control members of a group must be costly and therefore must commonly fail. For several reasons, this is often not true. Behavior that runs against a group's practices can actually be discomfiting to other members of the group, so that any costs of sanctioning can be offset with immediate gains. For example, some Indian tribes in the United States have recently revived the use of banishment of offensive members of the tribe from tribal lands. Banishment of some serves the interests of those who remain behind by protecting them from drug addiction and other offenses (Sarah Kershaw and Monica Davey, "Plagued by Drugs, Tribes Revive Ancient Penalty," *New York Times,* January 18, 2004, pp. 1, 26). Among the offenses for which a member can be banished from the Chippewa tribe of Grand Portage, Michigan, are "being in a gang, selling drugs, harming the [tribe's] cultural items, disrupting a religious ceremony, unauthorized hunting or fishing, and being banished from another reservation." The chair of the tribal council says,

"We see ourselves here as kind of a big family, and so we needed to be part of the solution" (26).[7]

In sum, small-community and urban contexts are strategically different in ways that lead to different modal ways of resolving the problem of mutual assistance. The small community commonly works through norms that are quasi-universal for the community and cover many aspects of potential cooperativeness. The urban society works through networks of ongoing relationships that are embedded within the much larger context. Any one of these networks is partial in that it covers only a particular realm of potential cooperation, so that each urbanite is involved in many quite different networks. In the urban setting, trust and trustworthiness might play a very large role in motivating behavior, while in the small community norms play the central role and trust might not even be cited.

Note that social capital takes two different forms in these two cases. In the communal norm of cooperativeness, the social capital on which you can call is that of mobilizing others in the community behind your sanctioning of a violator of your norm. Without a norm of exclusion, you could only renege from further cooperative ventures with the miscreant. That might be a real opportunity cost to the miscreant, but it would usually have a trivial effect in comparison to shunning by most of your fellow community members. Complete shunning or banishment could be devastating.

In the social networks of urban societies, we can affect your reputation among other participants in our network, and that might lead to your de facto exclusion from the network. That would, of course, affect only a small part of your social existence. Perversely, however, if your value to others is much higher than ours, our effort to degrade your reputation might lead to our own exclusion, even though it was you who violated our trust. Sadly, one can be excluded from a group or network for being injured by an especially important member of the group. Social networks are commonly valuable to their members only for what they can help provide to those members through enabling cooperation with others. Because the value of cooperation with one member can be substantially greater than that of cooperation with another member, network relations can be distorted by the problems of power inequality (see Cook and Emerson 1978; Farrell, forthcoming). But when the network works positively, broadcasting someone's violation of a network member's trust on a relevant matter (the matter for which the network is organized) can work well because the network provides or is a form of enabling capital to its members.

In some of the discussion in the next section, social capital can be put to work forcefully to make the devices of various norms and networks benefit those among their members who are reliable.

Honor, the Duel, and Vengeance

The historical invention of the law of murder can arguably be explained as a device to control the systems of vengeance that had governed relations before the growth or creation of legal institutions that could control certain kinds of sometimes especially violent conflict. The story of interpersonal relationships in medieval nations that were largely outside the control of the Catholic Church—such as Iceland (Miller 1990); the pastoral communities of the Berbers in North Africa (Stewart 1994); the nineteenth-century South of the United States (Nisbett and Cohen 1993; Schwartz, Baxter, and Ryan 1984); Albania still today (Hasluck 1954, 219–60; Anderson 1999);[8] Montenegro (Boehm 1987); other isolated areas of Europe; and to a lesser extent even in England—is largely a story of varied systems of feud and vengeance. The feud in Albania, or kunun, is a blood feud similar to that of Corsica in Prosper Mérimée's (1840/1989) tale *Colomba*. It allows vendetta transversale, or revenge directed at a relative of the party to be punished.

Later, in an odd "refinement" of such practices, the code of honor among aristocrats in otherwise quite civilized nations such as France, Italy, and Germany led to the duel, which, to most cultural outsiders, seems boorish (Kiernan 1986). The oldest written law in Europe is the law code of Crete (circa 600 B.C.E.). Already by then Crete had moved to a legal code under which harms were to be addressed by the courts, not by feuds or acts of vengeance (Chapman 1984, 28–30). A similar turn was made in England when the law of murder was created to deal with what otherwise would be very destructive sequential acts of vengeance (Fuller 1981, 231–32). Law displaced norms and made for more orderly societies.

There are many dueling manuals from various times and places to instruct duelists and their seconds in proper behavior for the sake of honor. John Lyde Wilson, a onetime governor of South Carolina, published "The Code of Honor: or, Rules for the Government of Principals and Seconds in Duelling" in 1858.[9] In the time it took to read all the finer points of this manual, the ardor of the duelists might have died and their lives might have been spared. Wilson's manual had no status in the law, and presumably it governed at all only if the duelists were of a mind to abide by it. Because the issue was one of honor, it is likely that, once such a manual was commonly used in some locale, it would have been dishonorable to refuse to follow it. Moreover, failure to follow the code might have led to a charge of mere murder. The paraphernalia of seconds and the punctilious following of codified procedures establish that both parties know what they are doing and give each party the honorable prospect of simply walking away once all the rules have been followed—if they have not been killed or severely injured. The code would be like *Robert's Rules of Order* in a vast range of decisionmaking bodies, including quite informal bodies. The force of Wilson's code or *Robert's Rules* depends on their acceptance: if enough people accept them, virtually everyone is pressed to accept them, and anyone who does not accept them stands to suffer embarrassment. The result is a form of social order with very stable expectations about behavior in certain contexts, all maintained by spontaneous adherence to the norm, with a need for neither trust nor law to back the norm.

We could characterize all of these practices as norms that are enforceable from within the relevant communities and that enable the relevant communities to achieve a particular cooperative social order. Hence, they are communal norms. Indeed, they are powerful norms of exclusion (Hardin 1995, ch. 4). That is, violators of the norms are subject to exclusion from the community through killing, shunning, or banishment. The force of shunning might seem minor in comparison to killing or banishment. But in close societies without great resources, shunning can be devastating because individuals cannot readily find a new community in which to live. Even a South Carolina gentleman—some of the most violent men in history were called gentlemen and would kill to prove it—would lose face in his own society if he violated Wilson's code and would not be able to find an alternative society in which to live as well.

In its early manifestations, law was relatively open and unformalized. A miscreant could be judged according to communal sentiments rather than according to a law that could be shown to have been breached. Indeed, in its original meaning in medieval England, a jury of one's peers was a jury of one's communal peers, who could be expected to know enough about one's character and likely motivations to judge whether one had committed some crime (Green 1985). Proof was merely agreement by such people, and proof could follow without any evidence that would convince anyone not already familiar with the community and the accused. Anthropological accounts of law suggest a similar understanding of communal determination by communal norms (see, for example, Moore 1978).

In the societies in which it prevailed, the custom of the duel must have been a strong force for eliciting relevant kinds of behavior. Any man of honor could be "trusted" to have strong incentive to live up to the norms that were enforced by the challenge to a duel. That the duel and vendetta were communal norms is shown by the fact that those who failed to act on them were sometimes ostracized for their lack of character. Mérimée's *Colomba*, for instance, pressured her brother, long since civilized by life in, of all things, Napoleon's army, to overcome his reluctance and live up to his moral duty to kill the Barricini brothers (for intracommunal sanction of those who were too cowardly to engage in a duel, see Kiernan 1986, 14–15, 137, 156, 328). That the norms perhaps served positive social functions, especially before the rise of law, is argued by Max Gluckman (1956,

18), who refers to "the peace in the feud" in African settings, in which the threat of a disastrous feud kept people orderly. In Europe the duel served to reinforce the distinction between aristocrats and lesser mortals (Hardin 1995, 91–100). The cost of doing anything that might provoke others to want a duel or vendetta may often have been a massive deterrent to certain behaviors.[10]

Fictive Kinship

Supplementary to the social networks that form among family members, close friends, and fellow workers, fictive kin binds those not related by blood and establishes mutual obligations. Although the fictive kin relationship is commonly not recognized and upheld by courts, it can be a very strong relationship, enforced by the religious or social group. Some form of fictive kinship exists in a wide variety of countries, and it takes a wide variety of forms. It can range from the honorific title of "uncle" and "aunt" bestowed on the friends of one's parents to extensive and reciprocal responsibilities. It includes the "blood brothers" of gangs and the "godfathers" of the Mafia.[11]

Let us summarize one case study of an elaborate fictive kinship role. The Orma of northwestern Kenya traditionally made a living from herding but have now become more sedentary. They therefore have a much harder time monitoring their herds, which cannot be sedentary but must move seasonally to where the grazing is good (Ensminger 2001, 186). Wealthy families choose to educate their sons rather than to make them herders; therefore they use hired herders. This entails principal-agent problems. We need agents when we cannot do certain things ourselves, and what the Orma need are herders to manage their far-flung herds. Unfortunately, cooperative behavior cannot be enforced on the herder, and there is little ground for a trusting relationship. Fictive kin is the device of choice to overcome these liabilities.

Traditionally, sons could be expected to protect the herd well because the cattle would eventually be theirs. Similar care is wanted from hired herders, but hired herders face a severe moral hazard or conflict of interest (Ensminger 2001, 191, 196). They can sell cattle and then report that the cattle have died, or they can herd badly and put stock at risk from bandits and wild animals. Such agency problems would seem to get in the way of a cooperative relationship between herders and owners. To prevent agency failures, Orma cattle owners publicly adopt certain of their herders and promise social protection and other rewards in return for high-quality effort while the agent is away with the cattle. They do so by marrying the herders to their own daughters. The "adopted" herders do not inherit through bequest, but they inherit de facto through gifts during the lifetime of their adopter (195).

Fictive kinship works here because it gives the adopted herders a future-orientation that aligns their incentives with the interests of the adoptive father. The relationship may develop into one of trust, but it need not do so for the device to work in motivating the fictive son to manage the herd in his own and his adoptive father's interest, because there is a strong future-oriented incentive to motivate reliability. If trust does develop, it is built up through small steps, with heavy supervision at first and less and less suspicion as time passes (Ensminger 2001, 198; Cook et al., forthcoming). Indeed, in the end there may be a suspension of account-keeping as the interests of the owners and the adopted herders become virtually aligned.[12]

Communal Lending

Informal economic devices have been used to enable cooperative inter-actions in contexts that at first seem implausible: making loans that are unsecured to actors who have virtually no resources to use as collateral. Among the varied devices that have been used for securing such loans, two are especially noteworthy: practices that integrate new immigrants into an ethnic community through the work of those who have already succeeded and are no longer without resources; and organizations that are organized by sponsors or sponsoring institutions and that make small loans to poor entrepreneurs. With neither of these devices is there necessarily or even often any trust in the sense of encapsulated interest, because there is virtually no relationship between the lender and the recipient of the loan.

We begin the discussion with the seemingly similar practice of rotating credit associations. Such associations form among the poor and include no partner who is not also poor, and they seem to be governed by strong communal norms and therefore need not involve conscious trust. As we did in comparing multiplex communal norms and more focused networks earlier, we then turn to cases in which the relationships are more complex—for example, with third-party lenders in the cases of Cuban character loans and the Grameen Bank. The character loans are from established Cuban immigrants in Florida to newly arriving Cuban immigrants, who arrive with no resources other than their own human capital and perhaps some family connections. Both character loans and Grameen loans are made without collateral, and both are made plausible for the lending banks by the use of social capital to force repayment.

Rotating Credit Associations

Rotating credit associations typically have a small number of participants who all make regular contributions to a fund that is then given to one after another participant, in rotation. Although there are variations in the basis of associational membership (Ardener 1964; Light 1972; Velez-Ibanez 1983), these associations share some common features that distinguish them from other kinds of cooperative activity, including mutual benefit clubs. There is evidence of such associations throughout the centuries and in a wide variety of countries. They offer a solution to the lack of credit-worthiness with banks and other formal institutions and to problems created by discrimination against even those who do possess some collateral. They exemplify a form of relational commitment that offers the promise of economic advancement.

Such associations also suffer from a very real threat of default and theft of funds (Besley, Coate, and Loury 1994; Hechter 1987), even by friends. In Kellee Tsai's (1998) study, Mrs. Chen, a middle-aged bean curd vendor, tells of the failure of her rotating credit association, which was organized by her friend. "Every month each of the ten members would contribute two hundred yuan to a collective pool and then one person would take the pot of two thousand yuan." Mrs. Chen wanted to rent a regular market stall rather than sell out of the back of her bicycle cart. Four months "after she joined the credit association, her friend did not show up to claim her usual space in the market place. 'I worried that she was sick,' " recalls Mrs. Chen. But in fact her friend had disappeared, and Mrs. Chen lost eight hundred yuan—the equivalent of one month's earnings (Tsai 1998). There is always a danger of default and always a problem of reliability, even among those who believe themselves to be friends, as Mrs. Chen's woeful story shows.

An irony of such an outcome is that the reason for creating this kind of association may be simply to help individuals overcome their own weakness of will in saving money for larger purposes. Each member requires of all other members that they contribute weekly or on some schedule. And each of them eventually gets a sum of money equal to what they contribute over time. As a matter of simple logic, each member could as easily save that much money individually. The joint effort offers them a bit of psychological trickery to get themselves to do the saving by invoking the power of communal sanction. As a Dominican says of his sociedade, "It forces us to save because we're committing ourselves to other people" (Sasha Abramsky, "Newcomers Savings and Loan," *New York Times*, October 22, 2000, p. 14-4).

If we suffer from such weakness of will, we might wonder about how safe our money is when held by others like ourselves. It surely will not be very safe if ours is not an extremely stable, close society in which we can expect everyone to remain in it into the distant future. In such a close society, it is probably not so much trust that motivates us as communal norms. If you might soon leave the community, those norms are likely to have little sway over you. Rotating credit associations' members attempt to select out those who might be unreliable. This effort may be generally less successful than severe and effective penalties, generally enforced within a community (Hechter 1987, 107–11; Hardin 1995, ch. 4). These associations almost always form among those with little mobility and with strong ties to each other, such as exist among certain ethnic groups or within traditional societies.

In the rotating credit association, the form of incentives is that B, who are most of the rest of the members of the association and maybe other members of the society, motivate C to play fair with the communal holdings. B can do this only if there is a long enough future in which to sanction C effectively for default. Hence, such an association can work without trust among its members, although some of them might trust each other.[13]

Character Loans

A kind of lending when neither trust nor ordinary market incentives governs is the so-called character loan. This is a seemingly complex but perhaps commonplace device through which immigrant communities enable new immigrants to get established in their new community when the standard banking system will not help them. One of the most highly developed of these systems was used in Miami for arriving Cuban immigrants who had been in business in Cuba before Castro's revolution. Cubans who had already succeeded in Miami, especially in creating small banks that served the Cuban population, made what came to be called character loans to these new arrivals (Portes and Sensenbrenner 1993).

There are two natural criteria for making a business loan. First, the loan will be productive so that it can be repaid, and second, that the person or business receiving the loan be taken as committed to repay, commonly by putting up collateral to cover any default. Having successfully run a business in Cuba was evidence that an immigrant could run such a business in Florida. For commitment to repay the loan, the Cuban bankers in Miami could not expect collateral backing of their loans, but they could count on the borrowers' strong incentives to use the loans well and to repay them. There was also little chance that they could acquire loans from any other source. They lacked the kind of collateral that a standard bank would require as backing for a traditional loan. Hence, if they failed to repay their character loans, they might be out of business forever.

In this interaction, A, the lender, expects B, the larger world of those who would be reluctant to lend to C if C defaults, to motivate C to repay the loan to A. Here B is in an entirely passive role and can be invoked without knowing it. And yet B is de facto part of the social capital that the bank A, but not the loan recipient C, can call on. A's interest, of course, is in profitable banking through charging interest on loans. A's business is enhanced when it helps competent immigrants get established. In this relationship, A can virtually trust C to repay (unless C's business fails) both because C is in a relationship that C values highly and because *C has no other options* if she does not repay the loan to A. C is in a strongly power-dependent role. With most bank loans, the bank relies on legal incentives for repayment. For character loans, the Florida banks had to rely on the social capital of the larger banking community to enforce repayment.

Because she has no other options, C wants her relationship with A to continue in the sense that she wants to repay her loan. C does not strictly encapsulate A's interests in her own, however, because she might prefer that A go bankrupt before she has to repay the loan. Once C's business succeeds and she has repaid her loan, she has collateral to secure loans from any one of numerous banks, so that C does not necessarily value an ongoing relationship with A. Hence, trust as encapsulated interest is not necessary for the system of character loans to work, and A need not trust C for this loan system to work well.

In the Cuban case, the lenders did not rely on past reputation for reliability in repaying the loan but only for credibility that the person had the experience and ability to handle an entrepreneurial undertaking. When the character loans ended in 1973, a principal reason was that newly arriving refugees from Cuba had not had recent experience as entrepreneurs. Hence, there was no basis on which to suppose that any of them could successfully run a business. If they had been given character loans, new arrivals would have had the right incentives but not the relevant capacities. The label "character loans" was apt in that the loans were made to those with the character to be entrepreneurial; once that character could no longer be assessed, the loans lost their point.

Microlending and the Grameen Bank

Another kind of lending when neither trust nor ordinary market incentives govern is the Grameen and similar banks. Like the Cuban banks in Florida, these banks make what are essentially business loans, often to start up new small businesses. Beginning in 1977, Muhammad Yunus (1999, 62–63) organized the Grameen Bank in Bangladesh. The way the Grameen Bank usually works today is that a collection of friends—typically five, and usually all women—come as a group to present their individual proposals for small loans to help them in their businesses. Typically two of the group are then picked to receive small loans (very small, maybe a few dollars). Others in the group are eligible to reapply after the initial recipients have at least seriously begun to repay their loans with weekly payments for at least six weeks. The periodic repayment is similar to mortgage loans but unlike many loans that require a lump-sum repayment at the end; Yunus thinks that the latter is a daunting and unreasonable expectation.

This system creates group responsibility that gives the others in the group strong incentive to make sure the first recipients are faithful in how they expend their funds, work to produce an income from those funds, and begin to make repayment. This is virtually holistic monitoring well beyond what would happen with ordinary bank loans. Not all of this was seen clearly at the outset of Yunus's program or noted fully by him in his account of how the system works. The use of what he calls support groups was a later discovery. But it is clear that the whole system offers a sophisticated set of incentives to enhance productivity through solidarity among those funded by Grameen and through competition between them in trying to succeed with their small businesses. As with Cuban character loans, there is no collateral to back these loans. But there is also not even law, because the smallness of the loans makes legal recourse too expensive to be worthwhile, whereas the Florida banks had law as a recourse against anyone whose business succeeded but who did not repay according to contract. The Grameen must rely entirely on social capital to induce repayment.

As noted at the beginning of this chapter, the Grameen Bank (A) does not need to be assiduous in chasing after repayment from a customer (C) because it has, in a sense, delegated the incentive for doing this to the group of neighborhood friends (B). Those friends become, by a bit of clever management, part of the bank's social capital, which it puts to work in the community to make life better for more or less all. The bank does this by relying on the social pressures within the neighborhood groups that apply for loans. Trust might play a role in some of these groups, but it need not, and it need not play any role in making the system work. In the end, however, the entrepreneurial successes among the recipients of Grameen loans might begin to develop trust relationships that enable them to enter into mutually beneficial but risky cooperative ventures. The result can be a thriving market economy that eventually displaces communal norms as the mobilizer of productive activities and exchange.

There is substantial disagreement on just how ideally the Grameen has worked. Yunus's account suggests that it has an astonishing repayment rate (Yunus 1998; 1999, 70; Holloway and Wallich 1992). Critics think it absorbs a lot of money from donors to cover for the defaults of many of its loan recipients (see, for example, some contributions to Bardhan 1999, especially Morduch 1999). There is also little compelling evidence that the social pressures from joint liability or "peer monitoring" are the main reason for what successes such banks have (for a general survey of the issues, see Ghatak and Guinnane 1999). Even if the Grameen's default rate is high, however, that does not mean it has failed. Some of the defaults must happen not because the incentive system for eliciting repayment fails to work but because some of the entrepreneurial activities fail, as is always true in all societies. The Grameen model may be brilliantly effective even though it cannot guarantee entrepreneurial success.

Incidentally, the Grameen Bank is itself the result of mobilizing social capital. As Yunus (1999, 117) says, "Though Bangladesh has a population of 120 million, it is run entirely by a handful of people, most of whom are college or university friends. Time and again, this unfortunate feature of Bangladesh society and politics has helped the Grameen overcome otherwise impossible bureaucratic hurdles." For the success of Grameen, Yunus is happily a member of this small club of people who can make things happen. He repeatedly tells of chance or deliberate meetings with people whom he has long known and who oversee national banking policy (89–91, 117). And repeatedly the results of his invoking their friendship is help for Grameen, either in the form of financial help or of easing cumbersome bureaucratic regulations that would make microloans expensive and unfeasible.

All of these devices—rotating credit associations, character loans, and the Grameen Bank—are spontaneously created in the face of the failure or limits of state regulation or legal devices for enabling people in straitened circumstances to obtain the funds to improve their lives. It is striking to see how well and how creatively people manage their lives in the absence of trust and largely in the absence of legal or state enforcement of cooperative arrangements, all despite sometime inequality of power and often solid grounds for distrust.

Concluding Remarks

It is sometimes said that social capital is like money (Portes and Sensenbrenner 1993, 1324). It is more nearly analogous to human capital in that using it can increase it, because its development is simply the result of the kinds of activities that create networks that then constitute social capital. Similarly, your use of your human capital in a craft further enhances your human capital because it gives you practice that hones the relevant abilities.

James Coleman (1990, 180–88) writes of the role of third-party mediators who bring people together for cooperative ventures (see also Hardin 2002b, 140–42). Throughout this chapter, B has been the third-party mediator or facilitator, or, even more strongly, the third party who can motivate C to act on A's behalf. Third-party mediation might also work merely to bring two parties together so that they might develop a cooperative, trusting relationship. Most of us have probably benefited from the services of such a mediator, who is more nearly a matchmaker than a mere mediator. Nevertheless, on the account here, it is clear that the focus on mediators is fundamentally important for understanding cooperative relationships in some contexts of little or no trust. All of us occasionally need Bs on whom we can rely to get the cranky, distracted, and hostile Cs of the world to act. We need assistance from many and varied others with whom we do not have trust relationships. People in many times and places have invented a remarkable array of devices to substitute for trust where it is lacking in getting others to cooperate.

Chapter 6

Institutional Alternatives to Trust

S PONTANEOUS DEVICES to secure cooperation, such as those discussed in chapter 5, and direct oversight by government (chapter 8) might not work well in some contexts of great importance to us. We need intermediate devices. To secure certain goals that require reliable behavior from particular people in many contexts, we often rely on nongovernmental institutions to regulate them. We might need only the sporadic services of professionals, business representatives, scientists, and many others, but these are people whom we could not trust in the sense of encapsulated interest because we cannot monitor them and do not have repeated interactions with them. A principal reason for our inability to monitor many of them properly is that we do not know enough to judge the quality of their behavior, even though in some sense we might observe it fully. We want to be able to rely on these actors because, if they are reliable, they can do important things for us—things that we very much want done, but things that we could not do for ourselves. The task we often face is not to make them encapsulate our interests because they are ours—an unfeasible task—*but to align their interests with ours.* Hence, we want devices that are de facto alternatives to trustworthiness to align their interests with our own.

We can generally characterize such actors as our agents. Our agency relation with them is commonly fraught with the usual problem of principal-agent relations: *conflict of interest.* Often our agents can serve their own interests best by violating ours, in particular by violating the very interest that makes us put an agent in charge of securing our interests. We focus throughout this chapter on conflicts of interests between agents of various kinds and their clienteles. This is centrally of concern here because in the encapsulated interest model of trust, the interests of another encapsulate our own or include our own as part of theirs, usually from the desire of the trusted agent to maintain a good relationship with us. *Their interest in being reliable comes from within their relationship with us.* Trust is relational, as noted in chapter 1, in the strong sense that it arises in relationships that we value. What we need for the agents whose actions we cannot readily judge or even oversee and whose interests do not so strongly encapsulate our own is to impose sanctions or some other form of interests on the agents to constrain their behavior so that they act in our interest. When we do this, *their interest in being reliable comes from outside their relationship with us.*

We consider three major institutional structures for getting our agents to be reliable: professional regulation, competitive self-regulation by scientists, and the market regulation of business. In the next two chapters, we treat organizational structures and government. In sum, our concern is with the form that interests can be made to take to give these agents incentives to behave in ways that we might call reliable but without our being able to say that the agents encapsulate our interests, as would be required for trust relations.

It is difficult for an individual to trust government or a large institution on the grounds for trustworthiness in any of the standard views: encapsulated interest, psychological disposition to be of a certain character, or moral commitment to behave in certain ways. It is difficult because an ordinary individual cannot have the knowledge to judge a large institution or its role holders to be trustworthy for any of these reasons. Indeed, that level of ignorance applies already in smaller-scale contexts in which we have to rely on professionals, scientists, or business managers or firms. All of these agents have specialized competencies that make them valuable to us just because we do not have those competencies and commonly cannot judge them. There is a further obstacle to our ability to judge business managers and firms: they keep much of what they do secret because such secrecy serves their interests in the competitive market.

Hence, for all three groups, we as ordinary individuals, such as patients, clients, and customers, are in no position to judge their trustworthiness—either their competence or their commitments—but we have great need of their services. Therefore, we have great interest in creating devices and institutions that can secure reliable conduct from these specialized people. All of these people sometimes act as our agents, and we expect them then to act in our interest, and yet their interests often conflict with our own. This is the central problem of the conduct of these people: they often have good reasons of self-interest to be untrustworthy because their own interests trump and do not encapsulate ours.

Managing Conflicts of Interest

With respect both to intraorganizational and extraorganizational relations, there are at least four possibilities for controlling the individual behavior of those in professional and organizational roles to align their interests with the interests of their principals: simple self-interest; organizationally induced self-interest; legally backed enforcement, such as through a regulatory agency; and individual commitment to trustworthiness. The last of these fits some standard visions of trust as grounded in the moral or character commitments of the trusted. Virtually all professions seem to seek the high ground of claiming that they are motivated by such a commitment. The second and third of these devices are readily seen as alternatives to simple trusting and trustworthiness on any of the standard visions of trust, especially the encapsulated interest view. The second of the devices is discussed further in chapter 7, because it applies generally to intraorganizational problems in all kinds of organization.

Simple Self-Interest

Simple self-interest successfully governs an enormous fraction of relevant behaviors, although we may have grown so accustomed to its working that we often take little note of it. In Adam Smith's (1776/1976, bk. 1, ch. 2, sect. 2, pp. 26–27) claim, "It is not from the benevolence of the butcher, the brewer, or the baker, that we expect our dinner, but from their regard to their own interest." Smith's constraint of mere self-interest might often work for a local shop owner or for many other individuals in business. It is most obviously ineffective in inducing proper behavior in business when individual incentives for gain conflict with organizational gain or with client interests, as in various professional conflicts of interest. For example, consider accounts of questionable practices in recent decades of some mutual fund managers who enriched themselves at investors' expense (Diana B. Henriques, "Questions of Conflict Sting Mutual Funds," *New York Times*, August 7, 1994, pp. I-1, 41; Dwyer 2003).

Simple self-interest is also often ineffective when organizational interests conflict with broader social concerns, such as gender and racial equality and environmental protection. Addressing these concerns may undercut the productivity of organizations as varied as universities and industrial corporations. Organizations can often therefore be expected to attempt to skirt these issues and to avoid bearing the burden of implementing social policies.

Organizationally Induced Self-Interest

Organizations are commonly designed with internal incentive systems to induce role holders in various parts of the organization to be reliable, even if not strictly trustworthy, so as to contribute to the goals of the organization. Such systems are perhaps most transparent and effective in certain assembly-line production organizations, in which no worker can expect to shirk without being discovered and likely sanctioned. But analogous systems are necessary for all kinds of organizations. For example, hierarchical reward structures can give incentives to employees to perform well in order to rise and be rewarded more generously. Certain sales organizations can directly reward effectiveness in the job. Other kinds of organization must design roles that in some way give incentive to do what is required of the role holders to make the organization succeed. The core problem in organizational design is creating roles that virtually entail the right incentives to act according to the definitions or purposes of the roles.

Legally Backed Enforcement

Legal sanctions are, of course, a major device from ancient times, and they can be used in many business contexts, as in governmentally imposed conflict-of-interest standards for the securities industry. For three reasons, however, law is apt to be a clumsy device for securing organizational commitments in general. First, it is too expensive and cumbersome to bring into play for minor matters, which are common and aggregatively important. To be efficient, organizations must therefore find ways to handle most of their own problems of trustworthiness.

Second, law typically lags the state of the art in problem creation. For example, many of the problems of organizational behavior in causing harms with various externalities that we know best were problems that taught us what the law should be. The law of corporations was invented to deal with the rise of new corporate forms only after they were coming to dominate U.S. economic life (Berle and Means 1932). The idea of conflict of interest arose in American law only in 1949 (Luebke 1987; see also Davis 1982), and it must have entered law just because it was already a major problem. In the development of law, problems typically come first and then law follows.

Third, and arguably most important, law runs up against the problem of complex causation within organizations. Let us discuss this problem more extensively because the legal notion of responsibility does not readily transfer to other contexts. The usual causal model for determining responsibility in the law works reasonably well for the criminal law.[1] In this model, for the purposes of assigning responsibility, the cause is what seems anomalous in the series of actions and conditions that lead to a perverse result, such as a death or an organizational wrong. The model takes for granted that many actions and conditions are likely to contribute to any result of significance and that therefore we do not literally want a full causal account—we want only an account that somehow is relevantly focused.

The legal model of causation does not work for managing trustworthiness for the trivial reason that there is no enforcement agency analogous to the legal system (Hardin 1988, 155–60). Hence, in many professional and corporate applications the legal model lacks a value that strongly commends it to legal use: the law tends to get definitive results despite the fact that its application is highly conventionalized. This is important in the law because we want order and finality in order to make our plans and investments. We want the legal system to settle things and let us move on. The law usually tells us in advance what will determine culpability and thereby gives us incentive to act well in our own longer-run interest. A corporate analogue without a credible, stable enforcer cannot do this.

Despite its specifically legal peculiarities, the model of legal responsibility has a compelling feature: it sidesteps the problem of the fallacy of composition that undercuts simplistic causal accounts of such responsibility. If we are to get anywhere, we must get past this problem. Hence, we turn from the fallacious composition to a full causal model of our organization. Unfortunately, a full causal account of a significant organization's actions would require massive understanding far beyond what is possible for any individual agent. But if this is true, then the agent can hardly be held accountable for fitting her actions precisely to the organization's goals. In lieu of this, the agent must fit her actions to standard routines and even rules that have been designed with the hope of fitting them to the desired result. Some of these, such as accounting practices, can be overseen by outside agencies.

Individual Commitment to Trustworthiness

Much of the writing on organizations, and especially popular writing on business, focuses on inculcating commitments of trustworthiness or relevant moral principles. It is probably for psychologists to say whether this can be expected to be successful, but it seems prima facie the least likely of the four devices to motivate actions on behalf of organizations. Even if we could inculcate various values, it is not obvious that doing so could resolve the complex problems that organizations typically face.

The crudest theory of the relationship of individual to organizational behavior would be one of mere aggregation from individual to organizational results. Unfortunately, such a theory typically fails for at least two general reasons. First, it is a fallacy of composition to suppose that a cluster of people individually aiming at some organizational goal, such as delivering a particular quality of service to the organization's clientele, will collectively achieve that goal (Hardin 1982b; Olson 1965). Rather, each may have to act strategically in ways that seem superficially unrelated to the organization's goals. For example, my actions may contribute to those goals only in interaction with your very different actions. Second, for many purposes we wish to control individuals' behavior for stochastic, not directly individual, reasons. For example, we might have far greater success in reducing road accidents by arresting those who test as drunk to some standard and getting them off the road, than by merely punishing those who are in fact personally responsible for accidents. On some moral theories, obtaining the result of reducing fatalities among innocent others is good reason to commend punishing a driver who drives drunk independently of whether she has actually caused harm (Hardin 1989).

A very important special case of attempting to inculcate organizationally or otherwise mandated principles of behavior that would override the incentive of self-interest is the effort to get certain professionals to act according to a code of behavior. Accountants, auditors, and other agents of corporations may typically be in positions in which their interests and the interests of the corporation or of its owners, stockholders, or managers are in conflict. There is an enormous literature on such professionals, and this is too big and tangential an issue to address here. It is plausible, however, that this is the most important unresolved area of conflict between individual interest and intraorganizational role requirements in all of public life, as suggested by recent massive accounting frauds at Enron, Tyco, WorldCom, and other corporations. One way to resolve this conflict, at least in certain piecemeal cases, is to eliminate it by changing the form of, say, the audit function to make it much more a matter of public record and to make it easier to hold individuals liable for wrongdoing.

Note that to suppose we can simply aggregate universally good individual actions to produce good collective organizational results is to suppose that there is nothing distinctive about the ethics of business people, professionals, or public officials. It is to suppose that such ethics have exactly the same content as ordinary personal ethics or to suppose that all professional codes of behavior should be the same.[2] It is also to suppose that there is nothing distinctively effective about introducing complex organizational structures to accomplish various tasks. All of this might be a correct view. But we should probably assume the contrary—that the structure of roles for various purposes entails distinctive principles for action in those roles (Bovens 1998; Hardin 1991a, 1996a, 1998a). The whole point of institutional design seems to be to define roles and the actions appropriate to them to fit the institution's purposes.

We discuss the regulation of professionals relatively briefly and then turn to the partially analogous problems of scientists and businesses in the context of the institutional arrangements that substantially govern their reliability, insofar as this can be overseen. We are brief in the discussion of professionalism and more expansive for the other two major social institutions because professionalism has been extensively discussed in this context already.[3] It is a good preliminary model for institutional regulation in general, however, and we can make better sense of the limits of oversight of other institutions by comparison to the regulation of the behavior of professionals. We discuss science most extensively— in part because regulation of the practice of science is currently at issue as a relatively new concern. When American doctors and lawyers formed the early versions of the American Medical Association (AMA) and the American Bar Association (ABA) well over a century ago, they were relatively weak organizations, and they faced alternative groups that wanted to compete with them. Scientists have managed to be massively successful with little reason of their own to organize as self-regulating professionals. But now, under threat of government regulation, they are attempting to govern their own behavior to preempt government control. Indeed, even the threat of international terrorism has put American biologists on the defensive in trying to ward off government intrusion and regulation of their research (Malakoff and Enserink 2003).

Professionals

The best studied of nongovernmental institutions for securing trustworthiness are the organizations for the regulation of professional behaviors in many contexts, especially in law and medicine. The problem of securing the trustworthiness of such professionals in their dealings with us is the topic of one of the earliest and most important studies of trust in recent decades, Bernard Barber's *The Logic and Limits of Trust* (1983). Although, like most writers, Barber almost invariably speaks of trust rather than trustworthiness, his account is primarily about the latter in that it is about devices for controlling the behavior of the agent who has to be reliable in performing a professional service. Barber (1983, 14) notes two issues in the conception of trustworthiness: competence to do what one is entrusted to do and the proper commitment to doing it. The former involves "expert knowledge, technical facility, or everyday routine performance." The latter "concerns expectations of fiduciary obligation and responsibility, that is, the expectation that some others in our social relationships have moral obligations and responsibility to demonstrate a special concern for other's interests above their own."

Those who have defended the creation of such agencies as the AMA and the ABA have commonly argued, somewhat loosely, that these agencies secure moral commitments from their practitioners (see, for example, Berlant 1975; Larson 1977). John Bell, one of the drafters of the first AMA code of 1847, called it "medical deontology"—implying that it is a collection of deducible rules for moral behavior, as though the actions of the relevant professional agent and not the consequences of those actions were at issue (Chapman 1984, 106). The reason for a specific code of behavior might more sensibly be characterized as moral simply because there is often a conflict of interest, perhaps especially clearly in legal practice, between the professional and the clientele. But this was also a serious concern in the traditional practice of medicine before the rise of big organizations to deliver health care. Individual doctors could de facto determine their own income to a substantial degree by determining what medical care they delivered. Hence, in acting as agents of their patients, they also faced a major conflict of interest of a kind commonly labeled as a moral hazard. Today large health maintenance organizations (HMOs) can determine their own costs by setting levels of care, so that they have a conflict of interest and their own peculiar moral hazard, although their incentive is likely to underprovide rather than to overprovide. Such conflicts are, again, a central problem of virtually all agency relations. They are a major concern of, for example, the "Code of Medical Ethics" of the AMA.[4]

To many people, it must be surprising to hear that lawyers are *primarily* motivated by moral concern for their clients, and for almost as many it must be nearly as surprising to hear that doctors are. One could more readily suppose that the ABA and AMA have their chief function in inculcating competence through the regulation of professional education. These professional organizations not only set standards for medical and law schools, however, but also officially define their role as somehow to inculcate moral commitment to following professional norms in dealings with clients or patients. Implicitly, therefore, the advocates of these associations subscribe to a view of trust that is based on the moral commitments of the trusted. Such commitments might be inculcated through education—except that, until recently, few law or medical schools in the United States taught ethics or professional responsibility. Hence, the implicit view is not matched by relevant actions.

The chief tasks of the professional organizations seem, rather, to be some slight degree of oversight of actual practice and much more assiduous oversight of laws that might affect the professionals. Even if some doctors and lawyers are morally motivated to serve their patients and clients well, the typical patient or client cannot easily know that, and many of us would want to know our doctors and lawyers have strong incentives for proper behavior in addition to any possible moral commitment. Malpractice suits do give incentive, and even very limited regulatory oversight gives some incentive for proper behavior. For the public, the most important role of the professional associations is probably in their oversight of the education and training of future professionals. Their motive for such oversight was originally perhaps to help establish their own monopoly control over the realms in which they worked through legal authority to determine accreditation to serve as professionals (Berlant 1975; on medicine, see Chapman 1984, 105–12; Scott 1965). Their oversight of training was a rationale for the state to give them special powers that were virtually backed by the state (Larson 1977).

Professional codes of behavior were once conceived as regulating the one-on-one interactions between individual professionals and their individual clients or patients so as to make the professionals reliable agents despite the fact that the clients or patients would typically be unable to judge the competence and commitment of the professional.[5] Because the public—and public officials—cannot adequately monitor or police professional behavior, the professionals, who have the requisite knowledge, themselves claim to take on much of the task. Professional codes in conjunction with regulated educational requirements can arguably be considered fairly successful at securing the *competence* of professionals. They may be less successful at securing the *commitments* of professionals. We wish here to focus on this latter concern, which is the core element in trust as encapsulated interest. Of course, it is largely because the medical and legal professions seem to be relatively competent in their domains that we are concerned with them at all.

The so-called ethics codes of the medical and legal professions shifted during the latter part of the twentieth century from an individual professional focus to an institutional focus.[6] In David Hume's (1739–40/1978, bk. 3) terms, the duties of professionals are increasingly seen as artificial. That is to say, they are not natural duties to do particular things that, if done, would have generally good effects. Rather, their good effects turn on the way in which they are related to the actions of others, especially others in institutions such as complex hospitals, health maintenance organizations, and insurers (see also Hardin 1991a). The changes in their codes of behavior mirror, belatedly, the changing structures of these professions, which are increasingly involved in large institutional settings with care delivered by teams of specialists rather than in private, one-on-one relations. Doctors and lawyers may be said to have natural duties, just as everyone does, but these are not duties specifically related to their professional function. The Hippocratic Oath proscribed having sex with patients (see appendix to this chapter). However, that is not exclusively or even distinctively an issue for doctors.

Doctors and lawyers have no justification if not to benefit patients and clients. Hence, it is sensible to treat doctors and lawyers as having agency roles—with patients and clients as principals—and therefore to see their primary professional norms as derived not merely from medical or legal principles but also from organizational and institutional constraints. The provisions of the early codes of medicine and law were typically directed at what an individual doctor or lawyer in general should do, as though the practice of medicine or law were a universal, not a particular or contingent, matter. Revisions of the AMA and ABA codes—adopted in 1980 and 1983, respectively—have eliminated much of that discourse to focus instead on how professionals should fit within a large organization or firm.

What is the form of self-policing by professionals? The focus of professional oversight is often on the procedures rather than on the substance of professional efforts, and on the general character of the professional.

A lawyer may be sanctioned for having a conflict of interest with a client rather than directly for failing the client. Failures in representing the client are used as evidence of the influence of the conflict of interest. But the conflict of interest is taken to be wrong tout court unless it has been fully revealed to the client. Consider a current example in law. The singer Michael Bolton is suing Weil Gotshal & Manges, a law firm that represented him in a copyright infringement suit even while it also represented his recording company and his publisher in that suit. Such multiple representations in a single case are not uncommon. But Bolton contends that his publisher had a deal with its insurance company that protected it only in the event of a trial judgment and not in the event of a negotiated settlement. Bolton contends that he wound up liable for the full judgment only because a Weil Gotshal partner hid opportunities for settlement. In such a case, Bolton should have been required to sign a "waiver indicating he understood the conflicting interests" (Karen Donovan, "When Big Law Firms Trip over Their Own Clients," *New York Times*, October 3, 2004, p. 3-5).

At the core of professional codes of behavior are rules requiring some behaviors and proscribing others. Superficially, therefore, the codes appear to be deontological, as asserted for the initial AMA code. But the reason a profession is desirable is that it benefits potential clients. Its focus must be on service to patients, not on the medical professional. Moreover, modern revisions of the two oldest codes of professional behavior cannot be understood without reference to the consequential tendencies of the sanctioned actions.

It would commonly be prohibitively difficult for the ABA to assess whether a lawyer did an honorable job in handling a client's case. But in the face of ordinary human nature, especially the tendency to take one's own interests into account, it makes generally good consequential sense insofar as possible to block behaviors that tend to have bad consequences for clients. Still, a lawyer might handle a client's case very well despite a conflict of interest (for example, the lawyer has substantial stock holdings in a firm the client is suing or represents that firm in other legal matters).[7] The ABA "Model Rules" merely require that the lawyer reveal any such conflict of interest so that the client can choose whether to use the lawyer's services.[8] Of course, it is generally in the collective interest of lawyers to have a code that sanctions certain kinds of behavior, because lawyers will generally be used more if they can be confidently expected to act on behalf of their clients without serving other interests instead (Barber 1983). This is a collective good for the class of lawyers, and an individual lawyer may be better off having such a code in place while violating it or free-riding on it. And the fact of the collective good gives reason to create an enforcement mechanism to secure it against free-riding, which would undercut it.

Science

Professional self-regulation by scientists, if it is strictly analogous to the self-regulation of lawyers or doctors, would similarly focus on procedures and character (see Hardin 1999a). This might be the correct focus for such matters as fraud in science. Consider the problems of David Baltimore, who, with a coworker, Thereza Imanishi-Kari, was accused of falsifying data in an extremely important paper,[9] and Robert Gallo, who was accused essentially of stealing viral samples of HIV from a French colleague and claiming them as his own discovery.[10] Such cases could come under procedural rules on record-keeping and handling competing work by other researchers. Unlike in law or medicine, however, these problems seem to be primarily the concern of scientists generally, or of particular scientists in competitive research programs, and *much less urgently a matter of fiduciary responsibility to a nameable client.* Historically, some part of the concern over codes of behavior within professions has been about such intraprofessional problems, but the more central part has been about fiduciary responsibilities. In particular, the putatively moral argument in defense of self-regulation was that doctors and lawyers must be inculcated with the relevant norms of service to their clientele.

The corrective for scientists who might have succumbed to conflict of interest may not be to address their motivations but only to address flaws in their science: poor research methods, bad statistical tests, apparently falsified data, and so forth. Such flaws can be motivated by anything from venality to sloppy character traits and may affect the work of any researcher, not only that of researchers working against a background of conflict of interest. Is my messy desk a sign of unethical professional practice? Is your cavalier record-keeping on the backs of envelopes unethical? Going after such practices as these may not be an efficient or sensible device for controlling conflicts of interest, because the number of scientists caught up in claims of sloppy practice might grossly swamp the plausible number of those who are genuinely guilty of succumbing to conflict of interest to distort their findings. Conflicts of interest might not correlate at all with sloppy practices.

Truth as the Ideal of Science

Among scientists, it is commonly claimed that truth is their only judge. They would agree with Charles Sanders Peirce (1935, 3), who writes that "the scientific man is above all things desirous of learning the truth and, in order to do so, ardently desires to have his present provisional beliefs (and all his beliefs are merely provisional) swept away, and will work hard to accomplish that object."[11] If we put their claim into the language of this book, we can say that scientists are reliable just to the extent that they are bound by truth. The scientific truth is typically a good guide to what a scientist should say. For example, in debates on regimes for controlling severe pollution, scientists often take a universalist stance and speak about the regulations that would be desirable for the world. Their models and assumptions are relatively apolitical. Political leaders often take a nationalist stance and oppose standards and methods of measurement that might put the burdens of controlling pollution on their nations. Politicians often play as though to win against other nations. The ideal-typical scientist would speak for a truth around which all nations might coordinate their efforts.

In discussions of the commitments of scientists, their commitment to truth is often treated as normative, as though scientists were an odd breed of human driven primarily by values rather than by interests. This is the apparent intent of Peirce's claim. But the claim that scientists are motivated to seek the truth is not merely a normative claim, and indeed, normative commitments might be relatively minor in the concern for truth. In many contexts, scientists care deeply about truth because *finding the truth is virtually a matter of self-interest.* Ambition and truth can be strongly allied. It is in the interest of any given scientist to find the truth because other scientists are likely to show them wrong if they do not, at least on issues of great importance. For example, consider the case of claims made for cold fusion, which would be of enormous commercial significance as a source of cheap energy if it were possible. With so much at stake, many scientists challenged the claims when they could not be replicated by others.

Scientists themselves can commonly judge who among them is reliable, and they can even suppose that virtually all are reliable in contexts of pure research in which there is likely to be no conflict of interest. To see just how strong the tie is between self-interest and the truth, consider the recent cases of Jan Hendrik Schön of Bell Laboratories and Viktor Ninov of Lawrence Berkeley National Laboratory. Their careers have been destroyed after they reported results that could not be replicated. Schön reported high-temperature superconductivity and molecule-level switching in thin films of organic material. Ninov claimed to have seen evidence of the brief life of the nuclei of elements 116 and 118. Their cases are especially disturbing because they both worked with several collaborators, who might have been expected to notice fraud (Minkel 2002). Their failure may cause nonscientists to wonder whether other high-powered scientists are reliable. Still, it was other scientists who found flaws in their work. Physicists who have since reported the (exceedingly brief) existence of elements 113 and 115 have cautioned that their discoveries cannot be fully accepted until other laboratories have confirmed them (Weiss 2004).

Career prospects for scientists tend to turn on getting it right, and it is hard to imagine a more forceful incentive structure being generally developed. In science, truth, interest, and passion must often be aligned.

Perhaps, as Dennis Flanagan (1992) says, abuse in major scientific contexts is therefore typically a matter of pathology. Unfortunately, a scientist often experiences internal conflict between his interest in the future knowledge acquired by others (who may find, for example that his own work was wrong) and his interest in his current status and income. Quick publication of flawed science might, for example, lead immediately to tenure. That is to say, scientists' *current interests may conflict with their future interests.* In this respect, the tenure system in U.S. and many other universities can have perverse consequences, and not only in the physical and biological sciences.

Physicists have long argued against regulation of their behavior on the ground that the incentives in place are sufficient to deter fraud, although not necessarily to deter mere error. Some physicists now wonder whether this view is naive.[12] Whatever the case for physicists, who generally do not stand to make massive profits from their work, biologists must often face strong temptations to work for the bottom line rather than for abstract science. A survey of German scientists finds that personal experience of misconduct is a major problem in clinical research (80 percent) and the life sciences (59 percent), but that it is not a great problem in physics (4 percent) (*Nature* 2003). There are vast fortunes to be made in biology, and the lure of money often corrupts.

Corporate Science

Unfortunately, many issues are divisive for scientists, who may firmly disagree about causal effects or the facts on which explanatory models are based. Politicians, public interest groups, and corporations may naturally choose those scientists whose science is most congruent with their interests. For example, the tobacco industry was once good at ferreting out and hiring scientists who said there was no proven association between smoking and cancer. Hence, scientists may appear to be aligned with interests, as though their science were determined by their association with particular interests. As a result, the public may come to suspect scientific expertise that supports any policy position. Perhaps this is one reason why the public often says it does not "trust" scientists. One thousand scientists may agree with an analysis that recommends regulating or labeling substance X, but if one is found who disagrees, that one may be given a platform by an affected interest.

There is a perhaps worse problem in the public's inability to assess the expertise of conflicting experts or typically even to know that the experts on one side may overwhelmingly outnumber those on the other side or have far greater scientific prestige. It is now a fairly popular assertion that science is as divided as, say, history or sociology. This may be a sad implication of the news media's frequent practice of giving seemingly equal time to opposite views, even though science itself does not give equal time to the views of the small, sometimes disreputable groups of scientists who are advocates of commercial interests such as the tobacco industry or the lead industry.

Hence, a major reason for developing canons of professional conduct is that relevant publics cannot know enough to judge the reliability of professionals. Because the public—and public officials—very often cannot adequately monitor or police professional behavior, the professionals themselves take on much of the task. Or perhaps the correct causal claim is that scientists take on the task to keep the public from doing so—as seems to be the history of some professional self-regulation. For scientists to do this spontaneously would require a grand success of collective action. Of course, it is not merely spontaneous action by scientists but action by their professional organizations, such as the American Physical Society (APS), that can mobilize political action.

If truth worked its influence without fail, so that every false finding was immediately discovered to be false, there might be no debates over malfeasance in science today. But this is not how truth works, and science may now be on the way to professional self-regulation without any tradition to build on—or perhaps more likely, on the way to regulation by public agencies that would trump professional self-regulation. Professional codes are a novelty in much of science, although not in engineering. Civil engineers long ago recognized their role as substantially that of public service because they typically have worked for a public client under massive public supervision (Bella 1987). The American Chemical Society (ACS) adopted "The Chemist's Creed" in 1965. This was superseded by "The Chemist's Code of Conduct" in 1994. Both documents are very short.[13] Chemists are vaguely exhorted to note that "conflicts of interest and scientific misconduct, such as fabrication, falsification, and plagiarism, [are] incompatible with this Code." The APS "Guidelines for Professional Conduct" are similarly brief and vague.

Scientists might argue, with some force, that public regulation by the hearings of Congressman John Dingell (D-MI), with his politicized crusades against particular supposed miscreants, was a travesty, while regulation by other physicists stopped the fraudulent careers of Schön and Ninov.[14] Moreover, they did not need "Guidelines for Professional Conduct" to do so. The core problem in the threat of a transition to greater public oversight has probably been conflict of interest rather than the seemingly pathological behaviors of Schön and Ninov. Conflict of interest has been an issue in medical practice, but among the traditional professions it has been most important in the practice of law and therefore in legal ethics.[15] Legal practice, however, may be a bad analogue for science.

It is true, of course, that corporate scientists are in some respects not unlike lawyers. American lawyers have long gone through the U.S.

Justice Department and on to major law firms or to corporate legal staffs. Critics of this practice suppose that lawyers seeking a comfortable home after a few years in, say, the Antitrust Division of the Justice Department will be careful not to hurt future employers too badly. But future employers have no financial interest in merely rewarding those who have been kind to them in the past but who are no longer in a position to be kind. They are interested in hiring those lawyers who have demonstrated the most inventive competence in the antitrust laws. Other things being equal, the lawyer who does best after leaving the Department of Justice is therefore likely to be the lawyer whose talent has been demonstrated in serving that department first. Here the analogy between corporate lawyers and scientists breaks down. It is the scientist's views that might help win a corporate job, but the lawyer's talents at arguing from the law. A lawyer can change substantive positions without losing face; a scientist cannot readily do so.

Conflict of Interest

A scientist has a direct interest in being on the side of scientific truth when career and opportunities depend on the quality of her past scientific judgments. In the era of corporate science, this interest could be overridden by support from an interest that wants the science to be other than what the scientist thinks it is. But this problem is not parallel to that of the lawyer with a conflict of interest. The lawyer's conflict is directly *with respect to the lawyer's client*. A scientist's questionable practice is to join in *supporting a client's interest even against the science* (Marshall 1990). The scientist's conflict, metaphorically speaking, is with what she should believe to be the truth.

Unfortunately, we cannot stipulate or identify the truth in the trivial way we might identify a lawyer's stock holdings. It is through debate and disagreement that we are likely to achieve better understanding of the science. Hence, we must often expect that there will be divergence of views on a scientific matter. If scientists function to produce knowledge for the collective benefit, that fact recommends a form of competition between ideas. We would not generally want to have a formal structure of scientific opinion to rule on what arguments or approaches meet some ethic of truth and which ones must be ruled out, as the medieval Catholic Church did until long after medieval times had passed in other realms.

Scientists working for industry in developing profitable technology are partially subject to control by truth through standard market forces at least with respect to whether the technology works as advertised. *It is only when the technology has unaccounted external effects or hidden direct effects that the role of scientists begins to affect the larger public in ways that may involve conflict of interest.* The hidden direct effects are analogous to the harms that lawyers and doctors may inflict on their clients without their clients knowing; if known, those harms would undermine trust relations. Doctors and biological researchers who work for relevant industries may tell us that tobacco does not cause lung cancer, that low-level exposure to lead does not cause mental and other deficits in children, or that a very expensive patented drug is better than an equally effective but cheap generic drug. But we cannot say definitively that a scientist supported by a particular partisan interest must have let her research be influenced by that interest. An independent scientist with a dissident view might well become supported by an interest that finds her views congenial. For example, Claire B. Ernhart and Sandra Scarr were early critics of the work of Herbert L. Needleman showing harm to children from low levels of lead exposure. The dispute became vitriolic (see Palca 1992). Ernhart and Scarr subsequently were supported by the lead industry in their further research and even directly paid for consulting. The issue continues to be politicized.[16]

In 1998, a U.S. federal court recently ruled that gifts given by lobbyists to public office holders cannot prima facie be considered illegal (Joan Biskupic, "High Court to Review Espy Probe Conviction: Law Covering Gifts to Officials at Issue," *Washington Post*, November 3, 1998, pp. A1, A4). Rather, it must be shown that a gift resulted in a favor. The court's proposed standard is hopelessly rigid and will effectively overrule the point of legislation to block conflict of interest itself, as the code of ethics for the city of Chicago and many other similar codes do. We might grandly want to bar all support of scientists that might entail a conflict of interest. In science, however, the immediate consequence of such a stringent policy against conflict of interest might be a severe reduction in funding for science and a radical decline in the quality of technological change. No scientist could work for industry, perhaps not even for government. All research would have to be funded by individual scientists themselves or by disinterested foundations, including universities. This consequence of a strong rule against conflict of interest argues against such a rule. Hence, it seems likely that we would not choose to have scientists treat conflicts of interest the way we would want lawyers to treat them. If we went through many other specific principles in the code for lawyers, we might similarly think that they do not apply to scientists. The more general principle behind the conflict-of-interest rule for lawyers is to enhance the prospects that lawyers will serve the interests of clients. The role of some scientists at least is in this limited sense quite similar to that of lawyers: their activities are supported only because it is supposed that they will benefit a relevant clientele. This clientele may be the relatively grand public at large rather than a particular party to a suit or a criminal trial.

There is a further conflict of interest that may be of major significance in some scientists' lives: the conflict of interest of employers, such as universities and perhaps corporations, which may find it *in their interest* to sanction scientists to protect themselves. It is very difficult for an outsider to judge such cases. In a notorious case that was eventually reported by the *Wall Street Journal,* the pharmaceutical firm Boots funded research at the University of California at San Francisco (UCSF) to compare its expensive drug Synthroid to much cheaper generic versions. The researcher, Betty Dong, found that the drugs were interchangeable, a result that jeopardized Boots's $600 million annual revenues from Synthroid. Boots sued UCSF, the university backed down, refused legal support to Dong, and let Boots force Dong to withdraw publication of her findings (Zinberg 1996; Ralph T. King, "Bitter Pill: How a Drug Firm Paid for University Study, Then Undermined It," *Wall Street Journal,* April 25, 1996, pp. A1, A3).[17] In this case, the scientist was forced into a conflict of interest between truth and commerce in the form of expensive litigation that, even if she won, might have bankrupted her.[18] In response to many such cases, the editors of thirteen leading biomedical journals "no longer publish articles based on studies done under contracts in which the investigators did not have the unfettered right to publish the findings" (Michaels and Wagner 2003). There is also evidence of a funding effect: funders now get results that they want (Krimsky 2003). Dong did not suffer from that effect.

Science as Collective Enterprise

The central concern with science is how to make it reliable. Historically, this was not apparently a major issue, in large part because science did not have direct effects on policy until the Manhattan Project, which created the atomic bomb, and the twentieth-century development of high-tech medical science. Both of these have entailed massive public support. Perhaps the most striking feature of public support of science is the remarkable change in the structure of scientific practice as so-called big science has developed. A popular image of science in earlier times is of the individual researcher seeking truth and perhaps fame, especially including recognition by peers. P. W. Bridgman, who won the Nobel Prize in Physics in 1946, did almost all the work for his 230 substantial scientific papers with the assistance of only one long-term assistant (Holton 1996, 75–76). Science became big in the Manhattan Project only shortly before Bridgman's Nobel Prize. The Manhattan Project signaled dramatically how different the contemporary reality is. The bulk of science is now done by big research teams, working with large sums of money, and housed in large institutional infrastructures. Important papers can have hundreds of authors from many institutions around the world.[19] And prominent scientists now spend very little time actually doing lab work. Indeed, in a recent survey by the Howard Hughes Medical Institute, 55 percent of respondents said they spend *no time at the bench,* and most of the remainder spend less than five hours a week on lab work (Papon 2003).

In a sense well beyond the contemporary fact that much of science is increasingly carried out by large teams, most scientific work historically has been and continues to be inherently a collective or social enterprise (Hardin 2003; Holton 1996, 71–75). What David Bella (1987, 117–18), a civil engineer, writes of engineers, we may say more generally of all scientists. *They depend on socially created knowledge, most of which they are not individually able to test or confirm.* Hence, Bella writes, "professional integrity involves more than personal integrity" (see also contributions to Schmitt 1994). There must be institutions or social processes that have integrity if individual scientists are to have any integrity in the eyes of those unable to judge the science directly, and even in the eyes of the scientists themselves. *Such collective enterprises require trustworthiness—either from encapsulated interest, moral commitment, or character—within the collective or some incentive system to enforce reliability.*

Bridgman's long-term association with his research assistant must have produced a high level of trustworthiness between them. Collaboration with hundreds of others, none of whom is competent to have oversight of the entire typical experiment in contemporary science—as in much of high-energy particle physics or in the mammoth project that mapped the genome for humans—rules out reliance on the well-founded assessment of the trustworthiness of one's collaborators. Holton's (1996) "evolution of trust" in big science is therefore essentially the evolution *away from trust relationships and toward externally regulated behavior.* This change might imply changes in the degree to which outsiders, such as ordinary citizens, can be confident of the findings of science. But it might be even more detrimental to trust within science, because big science involves teams of specialists who differ so much from each other that they are not likely to be able to oversee each other's work, as seems to have been true in the recent cases of the team players Schön and Ninov.

Self-Regulation and Public Regulation

Regulation of scientists' trustworthiness or reliability could take three quite different forms or some combination of these: public regulation by an independent public body with some policing and sanctioning power; professional self-regulation by a professional organization of scientists themselves (perhaps no institutions could be designed to handle either of these first two forms very well); and nothing more than individual self-regulation by the scientist and by spontaneous competitive claims from other individual scientists. If the third regime were self-enforcing—as scientists commonly suppose it to be—there might be no urge to pursue either of the other two regimes.

Is the search for truth self-enforcing? To a large extent we must suppose that it is, as argued earlier in the claim that it fits scientists' self-interest because no scientist will want to be shown wrong, perhaps especially not deceitfully wrong. Hence, scientists should generally be reliable with respect to their scientific findings. *Their own interest typically secures their reliability.* In the long-held official view of the American Physical Society, this incentive is sufficient, but recent cases have somewhat upset this view, because this incentive does not seem to be conclusive in every case (Service 2002). Generally, we know of far too many cases of scientists who were willing to be wrong in order to serve a particular master. During the Nazi era, some German scientists were willing to discount the scientific findings of Jews just because they came from Jews. But for particular scientists who are firmly committed to scientific reputation, it may not matter very much that they are found wrong only years later rather than immediately. They wish not to be found wrong at all.

Why is truth not self-enforcing for scientists in commercial firms? They depend for their income on buyer expectations and understandings. When there is uncertainty in buyers' minds about the claims of a manufacturer and the manufacturer's critics, at least some of these scientists may conclude in favor of the manufacturer. In this case, the scientists who advise a firm to pursue its interest may be pursuing their own interests rather than the scientific truth. Much of current research is focused on matters of great uncertainty, so that the criterion of truth is indeterminate, especially to the larger public. Hence, there is room for honest disagreement and *therefore incentive for dishonest disagreement.* For a firm such as a cigarette producer, the difference between letting the public record assume an association of smoking and lung cancer and contesting such an assumption might well involve billions of dollars in earnings in a few years even if truth eventually will out.

Although public regulation may well grow in breadth and significance in the immediate future, much of the regulation of responsible behavior by scientists is likely to remain subject to little more than self-regulation by individual scientists and their individual detractors. It seems obvious that we cannot sensibly establish an agency that would replicate all or many important scientific findings. Historically, such replication was commonly possible, as any student in a university physics or chemistry lab course knows. The Millikan oil-drop experiment from a century ago has been run innumerable times. But more recent experiments to demonstrate the existence of new particles in massive accelerators carried out by huge teams or to show the genetic modifications in fruit flies over dozens of generations cannot be easily replicated.

In the present system of science in the United States, an individual scientist is commonly in the state of the doctor without an AMA code. Many scientific associations have, of course, adopted codes of behavior, but these are sometimes nominal codes not much advanced beyond the banal and nearly vacuous Hippocratic Oath (for the medical rules, see the appendix to this chapter; the full text is in Lloyd 1950/1983, 67). Yet scientists are very much like doctors and lawyers in that their working lives are highly institutional. Therefore, their conduct should be determined in large part by reference to their institutional settings, just as the 1980s revisions of the main legal and medical professional codes responded to institutional constraints.

We may now be in the stage of transition between the primitive conditions of full self-regulation and legalized regulation by public agencies. Doctors and lawyers are under legal as well as professional self-regulation, but they have managed to keep the latter dominant, even if malpractice suits in the United States increasingly push the regulation of medical conduct into the courts. Scientists have generally been slower to create capacities for professional self-regulation, and they may have waited too long to preempt direct public regulation. The public regulation of doctors has recently been dominated by concerns with the costs and distribution of health care. The public regulation of scientists may quickly assume many of the panoply of issues that might seem to matter from other regulatory regimes covering, for example, doctors, lawyers, and corporations.

In imagining how scientists should behave without a professional code, consider the analogous case of medicine *if there were no AMA code of behavior*. If there is no such code and you are a doctor, what principles should you follow? A first answer might be that it would be good to do more or less the same things specified in the actual code. But this answer is incoherent. It becomes right to do all of what the code prescribes only on the assumption that various others, also governed by the code, are doing their parts. Your actions alone cannot ensure any such thing. Moreover, you could not possibly justify spending the time to work out the principles of the code that creating the code has required from large numbers of people with varied experiences working over several years. Indeed, it would violate an obvious ethical consideration for you to take out all that time rather than to deliver health care to those in need, which is what you are actually educated and trained to do. In the best of all institutional settings, there would be specialists to determine the morality of various practices and to secure the trustworthiness of doctors.

So what should you the doctor do without a code of behavior? Obviously, you should behave in ways that you can reasonably expect to affect the health of others beneficially and not in ways that would harm their health. You should generally avoid conflicts of interest that might give you incentive to override your concern for patients' interests—for example, you probably should not own the hospital, laboratory, or drugstore to which you refer your patients (see Council on Ethical and Medical

Affairs 1992; Emanuel and Steiner 1995; Rodwin 1992). You might not be able fully to avoid the conflict of interest inherent in your recommending to a patient that she have an operation from you or in other contexts without getting in the way of your care for the patient. And it might not even occur to you that prescribing drugs to be sold by your office involves a conflict of interest. (Chiropractors, for example, may not see the conflict of interest in their very profitably supplying patients with the so-called supplements that they push very hard.) But if someone points out the conflict and explicates its logic, we may reasonably doubt your honesty if you insist there is no conflict. Many of the rules of the AMA code might not be mandated by clear reason (few of them are, even if we suppose a relatively simple theory of medical responsibility), and we ought not to conclude that you should deduce them on your own and act by them even though the AMA has not promulgated them.

Note that doctors without a formal code must combine an attitude of service with a concern for the truth of what serves. Scientists may generally have been able to act reasonably with no more than the natural confluence of individual interest with the truth. But in the age of institutionalized science, with career stakes outside the accumulation of scientific findings and with institutional interests often directly conflicting with truth, this formula is no longer so clearly adequate. The self-interest of scientists in not seeing their findings ridiculed or dismissed by other scientists may continue to be the chief regulator of their behavior, but now incentives must be reinforced from outside the scientist's personal research arena, or the scientist must be normatively governed by a desire for truth. In big science, it seems likely that institutionally it is easier to design and implement a formal regulatory system outside the scientist's research arena than to inculcate an attitude of service. The public cannot know which areas are adequately policed by incentives for truth-finding and which by institutional regulation to block harms committed by scientists and employers who have a conflict of interest. Of the four devices for aligning scientists' actions with truthful findings, therefore, the inculcation of norms is not likely to be the route to follow. We will want to use incentives to induce proper behavior when norms fail.

Business

For business firms, the principal problem of reliability is the apparent conflict between the organization's interests and the interests of those it serves and those who happen to be affected by its external effects. Some intraorganizational issues can generally be addressed in the way that such issues are addressed in all organizations, whether business firms or other formal institutions (see chapter 7). *Intraorganizational incentive systems commonly reduce the need for reliance on trust relationships just as they reduce the need for reliance on moral commitments* (Hardin 1996a). However, because the virtual definition of the purpose of a business organization is to increase or even maximize its profit, such an organization faces a massive problem of fitting its interests to behaving morally toward the larger world in various ways.

We do not address issues of competence, which are a major part of assessments of trustworthiness in general, but focus here only on motivational problems, which are the general focus of this book. The main issues for successful firms and their managers or owners that we address here are the conflicts between their profitability and their commitments to customers and to those subjected to their externalized costs.

Intraorganizational Conflict of Interest

There is one major intraorganizational issue in conflict of interest. Recall for a moment the four devices discussed earlier for matching organizational incentives to relevant behavior: simple self-interest, organizational incentive systems and role definitions, legal sanctions, and inculcation of norms. For business organizations, the most important of these seems likely to be designing a relevant incentive system for role holders in the organization. This can be uniquely tricky for certain roles. Consider the role of leadership of an organization whose product in a sense is profit. The incentive system for running such a company is to offer monetary rewards for producing money. At first, this might sound as easy as the incentive system for sales: simply giving the salesperson a fixed percentage of the income from sales. This device makes the salesperson relatively reliable in achieving the goal of the organization. But organizational leaders are not the sole producers of the profits that a company makes, and most of the profits commonly go to the owners, not the non-owning managers. Unfortunately, putting a company's resources in the control of a manager whose purpose is to bring in profits for the owner creates extensive opportunities—and incentive—for abuse of the powers of the manager to capture much of the profit (Berle and Means 1932, 354–55).

Intraorganizational reward can go badly wrong. Consider, for example, the recent scandals at Enron, Tyco, WorldCom, and many other corporations. Managers of these firms were offered stock options as bonuses. The scale of the bonus depended on the performance of the companies or the value of their stock in the stock market, which is often taken to be a good measure of corporate performance. Of course, the stock options themselves had value that was a direct function of the stock prices of the corporations. This latter fact gave the top managers of these corporations (and of many others) incentive to do what would raise the market price of stocks in their firms. One way to do this is through more profitable production and marketing. Another easier but sometimes criminal way is through accounting and other tricks to make the company look more prof-itable than it is to outsiders, who therefore rate the stocks as having greater value. The managers of many firms invented many forms of manipula-tion of the apparent profitability of their firms, driving their stock prices very high. At some point the hidden liabilities of these firms became evi-dent, and their stock prices fell drastically, in some cases virtually to zero.

An early figure in this con game was "Chainsaw" Al Dunlap, whose nickname referred to his cutting thousands of employees and even parts of the companies that he managed. He used phony devices to show false profits and claimed large bonuses as rewards. At Nitec Paper Corporation, he secured phony profits that "amazed the owners and led them to pay Dunlap $1.2 million." He went on to Scott paper, where ap-parently similar accounting tricks earned him a bonus of $100 million—hidden liabilities totaling $99 million were uncovered only later. The Securities and Exchange Commission (SEC) accused him of similar fraud at Sunbeam Corporation, from which he walked away with hun-dreds of millions of dollars while bankrupting the company (Floyd Norris, "How Chainsaw Al Avoided Enron-Style Publicity," *International Herald Tribune*, September 7, 2002, p. 11).

For a quick sense of the scale of the abuse of this incentive system, the *Financial Times* surveyed the twenty-five largest business failures dur-ing the three years 1999 through 2001. "Senior executives and directors of these doomed companies walked away with some $3.3 billion in salary, bonuses, and the proceeds from the sales of stock and stock options" (Cassidy 2002, 64). This was $132 million per company. The rest of the stockholders in these companies were wiped out as the stock values collapsed.

One might agree that managers should be rewarded for the gains for which they are responsible. The difficulty then is to determine what dif-ference they actually make. One proposed way to accomplish this would be to index the price of the options to the Dow Jones or Nasdaq indexes for all stocks or for stocks in the same industry (Rappoport 1999). That way, in an era in which stock prices are generally rising, corporate execu-tives are rewarded only for what marginal additional growth in value might be attributed to their personal leadership. During the 1990s, when almost all stocks shot upward in value, it is not credible that almost all ex-ecutives were suddenly more effective than their predecessors had been. Even with indexing to the general level of stock prices, however, man-agers can be massively rewarded for accidental reasons having nothing to do with their performance (Cassidy 2002, 77). Perversely, managers are enabled to make staggering profits on their stock options even when the stock price falls (72).

There is a trivial slip, however, in the logic of using stock options to give managers, as agents of owners, incentive to enhance the wealth of owners. They are given incentive to do *anything* that makes the public perceive their company's value to be greater, and that can include actions that reduce or even wreck that value in the longer run. Eventually, manipulated stock prices are apt to fall. In effect, the possibilities for enormous onetime gains introduce destructive endgame effects in which managers can reap huge rewards and leave others to clean up their mess as the managers go about their own lives after cheating vast numbers of others who might have supposed they were reliable. Many of the managers in the debacles of the 1990s stock bubble were probably honest enough under ordinary circumstances but succumbed to massive greed as their stock prices rose and later as the bubble threatened to pop, at which point they violated their agency roles and took what they could while bankrupting their principals. Some of them, however, such as Dennis Kozlowski of Tyco, Gary Winnick of Global Crossing, and Andrew Fastow of Enron, reputedly looted their companies in criminal ways. It is distressing that such criminal actions were often minor in comparison to the crudely legal but rapacious actions that most contributed to their wealth at the expense of countless stockholders. For example, Kozlowski was first accused of criminally avoiding payment of sales taxes in New York on art that he purchased with funds plundered from Tyco.

Already in the 1930s, Adolph Berle and Gardner Means (1932, 354–55) argued that the separation of control and ownership in the modern corporation might lead to grievous problems. This form of corporate governance creates "a new set of relationships, giving to the groups in control powers which are absolute and not limited by any implied obligation with respect to their use." Because the managers have absolute control of a corporation and "can operate it in their own interests, and can divert a portion of the [corporation's assets] to their own uses," the likelihood of "corporate plundering" arises. Berle and Means might have been astonished at the level such plundering reached several decades after they wrote. In the era of Smith's butcher, brewer, and baker, who were adequately regulated by their regard for their own interest, radical plundering of a firm owned mostly by others was not a possibility. Now it is easily possible, and we need devices other than simple self-interest, as enforced by the market, to regulate potential misbehavior in the corporate business world.

Extraorganizational Conflict

There are at least three quite different forms that external harms from corporations take. The most obvious is that some firms directly and deliberately dump pollutants into the air, onto the land, and into waterways. For example, many firms—especially but not only chemical firms—dump harmful wastes into rivers. General Electric deliberately dumped thousands of tons of polychlorinated biphenyls into the Hudson River, killing much of the river's aquatic life and harming people who lived downstream.[20]

A second form of external harm caused by corporations occurs when workers are put at risk of harm to reduce corporate costs. Many firms subject workers to gruesome harms rather than enclose their processes to protect workers. For example, the copper smelting industry long subjected workers to exposure to high levels of arsenic. Coal miners' black lung disease made pneumonia "the miner's friend" before pneumonia could be overcome with antibiotics to let the miner live on with painful, debilitating emphysema. The problems with this form of external harm are often made more acute because higher management structures the situation of risk to workers but only lower management is in a position to see how grave the risks are (see Wagenaar 1996, 319, passim).

The third form is the use of risky methods of hauling, mining, and manufacturing that sometimes, but not always, cause severe harms, more or less accidentally. Many of the most newsworthy environmental disasters have been the result of firms operating in ways that were risky but not necessarily harmful. For example, the *Exxon Valdez* ran aground and spilled thousands of tons of crude oil into Alaskan waters, onto pristine beaches, and onto helpless birds and other wildlife when the oil tanker was under the command of a known drunkard. Strangely enough, and contrary to the views of those inclined to think that the wreck of the *Valdez* was a major moral failing by Exxon, market incentives should have reduced the odds of such a wreck, which, after all, cost Exxon more than the company made in all of its oil transport on the seas (Wagenaar 1996).

The wreck of the *Valdez* was presumably as unexpected as the sinking of the *Titanic,* and certainly it was massively against Exxon's interests. Exxon's response was a very clear market response: it sold off its tanker fleet to eliminate the chance of any further such disastrous losses (Wagenaar 1996). We can sensibly suppose that the eventual result will be an even greater risk of such harms recurring than if Exxon had maintained its control over its tanker fleet and continued to internalize much of the costs of such risks. With its deep pockets, Exxon did compensate for some of its harms from the *Valdez* oil spill.[21] A future wreck might simply bankrupt any of the small firms that now handle Exxon's former share of oil shipping; because that company would then have little capacity to cover the losses it had caused, those costs would be almost entirely externalized.

Among the worst offenses in externalizing corporate harm, however, are those that, though much less dramatically newsworthy, are deliberately harmful for the sake of reducing the costs of manufacturing. In many cases, the corporation's cost savings are dwarfed by the scale of the harms. Although there have been many firms that increased their own costs in order to avoid such harms, it seems virtually necessary to bring government enforcement to bear to block such abuses in general. The other devices we have discussed—ordinary market incentives, inculcated norms, and organizationally induced self-interest—cannot work adequately to align corporate interests with the interests of the public, the customers, the workers, or even the general stockholders, all of whom are largely at the mercy of corporate officers and boards.

George Loewenstein (1996, 215) supposes that in the face of decisions on such issues of costs to the external actors and costs to the firm, managers would have to be altruistic to opt for reducing the costs of others: "Managerial behavior provides a virtually inexhaustible source of seemingly skewed trade-offs between personal well-being and that of others" (see also Hardin 1996b). Loewenstein then compellingly argues that behavioral decision theory "paints an extremely bleak picture of the possibilities for altruism in general, and managerial altruism in particular." In the end, therefore, these issues of corporate malfeasance contribute little to the understanding of trust and trustworthiness other than to compel us to recognize that greed can forcefully trump trustworthiness and that it must sometimes be constrained by powerful government regulation when market devices conspicuously fail. This may be the strongest case discussed in this book for the need to find devices other than reliance on trustworthiness to achieve mutually beneficial cooperative behavior.

Concluding Remarks

For reasons of increasing scale, individuals can no longer oversee the activities of most of the other people who affect them. All too often, ordinary people learn that some major institution is not working well only when it breaks down more or less catastrophically. Trust as encapsulated interest cannot fit our relationships with large institutions, nor can any other standard theory of trust. We do not trust large institutions for very good reasons. But we also want large institutions for very good reasons: they enable us to do things we could never otherwise do and they bring us prosperity beyond imagining in earlier eras.

In the era of individual entrepreneurs, such as shop owners, or of individual scientists who developed their own experiments and theory, the incentive structure was roughly that of Smith's butcher et al. They needed to do good work if they were to be rewarded well.[22] That incentive structure was a powerful regulator that made behavior relatively reliable. In the era of agency relations, agents remarkably often can find ways to benefit themselves while compromising the interests of their principals, as in the case of business managers. Or they can benefit themselves by compromising the public interest and arguing against what they might actually know to be the truth, as has been done by some scientists who work for industries, such as lead and tobacco, that have harmful external effects.

Institutional and technological changes in law have not been as dramatic as in medicine. But legal practice in the United States has been bifurcated into big-firm law and more nearly solo-practice law (Heinz and Laumann 1982), with the bulk of the ABA's "Model Rules" now concerned with big-firm law. Big law firms deal primarily with large corporations. Solo-practice and small-firm lawyers typically handle divorce and family law, smaller corporations, small suits, and contracts and incorporation.

In the contemporary settings of medical care and law, much of the concern is with the functional efficacy of various behaviors, where the function is service of some relevant kind as defined or constrained by institutional possibilities. For law and medicine, service continues to be focused on clients and patients, although increasingly there are intrusions of concern for the larger public, especially in medicine as it consumes ever more of the domestic product—about 13 percent annually in the United States for the past several years (National Center for Health Statistics 2002, table 113)—and an even larger fraction of national government expenditures. For science, there is hardly any reason for concern with service to particular clients, which, after all, are generally firms substantially capable of overseeing their own scientists' work. Indeed, we may even worry that scientists in a firm are at risk whenever their truths seem to run against the interests of the firm. *The principal concern in the trustworthiness of the scientists themselves is with service to the larger public, which may conflict with both their own interests and those of their firms.*

Despite strong claims made for the regulation of doctors and lawyers through their professional organizations, they appear to be hardly regulated at all. If corporate managers are to be regulated (on behalf of owners, employees, or the public), the devices most likely to work seem primarily to be devices that would remove much of the power that Berle and Means (1932) attribute to them. For example, accounting could be assigned to independent firms through some system that does not de facto give control to the managers through the rewards they can offer to the accountants.[23] Record-keeping more generally could be made far more public with easy access by external interests, such as stockholders and public agencies. Virtually every device that might be made to work would entail changing the incentives of the managers—in some cases merely changing the incentives that previously have led them to be duplicitous.

We have learned of the massively self-serving deals of some corporate managers through their trials for minor infractions and even, in the case of Jack Welch, the former head of General Electric, through a divorce proceeding.[24] The salaries and other emoluments of many people are legally on the public record. For example, faculty at some state universities have their salaries published. And the top executives of corporations in some states have their salaries published by law. Merely making the deals of future Kozlowskis and Winnicks public might change their behavior, perhaps less by embarrassing them than by embarrassing their corporate boards. In the end, however, conflicts between the interests of corporate agents and the interests of stockholders, employees, and the public are sure to continue. Competition between scientists might continue to be the chief regulator of scientific misbehavior in fields in which great financial gains are unlikely, such as cosmology or high-energy physics (as opposed to much of genetic science, in which breakthroughs may have enormous market value). Cases such as those of Schön and Ninov might seem to be more nearly pathological than self-interested just because their findings are on sufficiently important issues in their fields that others will almost certainly attempt to replicate them and thereby discover that the findings are false.

For scientists, self-regulation through a professional organization's code of conduct and public regulation through a formal, legally empowered agency might differ substantially, as suggested by the examples of the ABA and the AMA. It is commonly asserted that the ABA and the AMA and related professional organizations impose few serious sanctions and that they tend to view their members as part of the club to be protected against complaints from outsiders. For example, American criminal lawyers effectively cannot be held legally responsible for flagrant violation of their duty to represent their clients even when their irresponsibility brings such great harm as false conviction of their clients. Meredith Duncan (2003, 1255) says that "criminal malpractice actions are so difficult to win that, for the most part, criminal defense attorneys enjoy special protection from civil liability for substandard conduct." Of course, it is mostly former lawyers sitting as judges who make it difficult to win a suit against a lawyer. American doctors sometimes face threats of loss of professional membership if they serve as expert witnesses on behalf of plaintiffs suing for malpractice (Michelle Andrews, "Making Malpractice Harder to Prove," *New York Times*, December 21, 2003, p. 3-8).

The ABA and the AMA both arose to help establish a monopoly over determining who is qualified to be a professional, and their focus continues to be fairly heavily on protection of their members.[25] A public agency might be considerably more aggressive toward professionals. In addition, scientists might tend to enforce any ethics code more rigorously against less prestigious scientists. A public agency might have less respect for scientific prestige and might even find it especially newsworthy or career-enhancing to sanction major scientists. We are now in an era when high-profile regulation of scientists by public officials and agencies has become common. Unfortunately, such regulation may be disruptive, relatively inegalitarian, and highly distorted, as in Congressman John Dingell's attacks on particular scientists.

The market and the competitive self-regulation of scientists can be extremely powerful forces, but they have severe limits in the corporate era.

Professionals could be (but arguably are not) strongly regulated by their own organizations, which are more concerned with lobbying for and protecting their members than with constraining them. *Ordinary citizens outside any of these fields are generally unable to trust the relevant actors.* Citizens might often therefore think that external regulation by government agencies is more likely to produce reliable behavior from these specialized people and organizations. Certainly, citizens cannot individually develop relationships of trust with many of the people whose services they sometimes desperately need. They cannot expect their interests to be encapsulated in the interests of those whose services they need, but they want to be able to rely on these specialists.

The ABA and the AMA are too beholden to their own professional members to be entirely reliable in compelling their members to treat clients and patients well. Scientists faced with the prospect of benefiting themselves enormously through their actions while working, for example, with drug firms or in the development of genetic start-up firms cannot be expected to rein in their own behavior merely on behalf of the larger public. And business leaders, who are not all like Chainsaw Al Dunlap or Andrew Fastow and other rapacious executives of recent years, can too readily make their customers, employees, and stockholders the scapegoats for their own personally lucrative actions. Trust is not at issue in these relationships, and there is no way to raise it to a prominent place. We want alternatives to trusting because those we might have trusted are too often untrustworthy—*and we might be untrustworthy as well in their places.* Thus, most of us have no difficulty understanding their venality and their fundamental conflicts of interest with us.

Appendix: The Oath of Hippocrates

The oath (Lloyd 1950/1983, 67) is very brief, and more than half of it has nothing to do with medical care but only with loyalty to one's teacher, secrecy within the sect, and so forth. One provision is not to engage in sex with men or women. The specifically medical injunctions are these few:

> I will use my power to help the sick to the best of my ability and judgment; I will abstain from harming or wronging any man by it.

> I will not give a fatal draught to anyone if I am asked, nor will I suggest any such thing. Neither will I give a woman means to procure an abortion.

> I will not cut, even for the stone, but I will leave such procedures for the practitioners of that craft.

Chapter 7

Organizational Design for Reliability

W E NOW turn to situations in which it is clearly imprudent to rely on trust relations to secure desired goals. Midlevel organizational design provides alternatives to trust relations in promoting productivity and quality output in most workplaces, and especially bureaucracies and firms. These settings are the classical loci of principal-agent problems and often involve hierarchical relationships of unequal power. Typically, there is little basis for trust and some reason for distrust among principals and agents given the inherent conflict of interest in the relationship and the potential for exploitation. The primary means of aligning agents' interests with the principal's generally require organizationally induced self-interest, as discussed in the last chapter. Individuals are constrained to behave in ways that contribute to the goals of the organization through institutional arrangements and other devices for assessing and enforcing performance. Internal incentive systems and monitoring induce agents to be reliable even if they are not, by our definition, trustworthy.

Yet, ironically, in just these contexts so generally antithetical to trust relations, contexts in which hierarchical power relationships and conflicts of interest dominate, trust relations sometimes emerge as complements to monitoring and discipline. Trust relations can moderate the counterproductive consequences and negative externalities of hierarchical supervision with respect to workers' attitudes toward the job and their bosses. By supplementing formal institutions with informal relations of trust and reciprocity, employers may induce greater employee effort and loyalty. The whole subfield of management science, beginning with Frederick Taylor, seems dedicated to figuring out new and better arrangements for inducing agents to cooperate more enthusiastically with their principals and become more productive (Bassett 1993; Perrow 1972). A recurring theme in the organizational literature is that improvements in effort and output follow from organizational role holders treating each other as trustworthy. Institutions still play the role of punishing those who shirk, but monitoring is reduced and grants of discretion are increased.

In what follows we attempt to clarify when institutions and incentives supplant, complement, or are irrelevant to trust relations within organizational settings. In chapter 6, we laid out the four primary means for managing conflicts of interest. In this chapter, we argue that organizationally induced self-interest is the major determinant of employee reliability. Self-interest and legally backed enforcement, two of the possible alternatives, are unlikely to align principal and agent interests effectively, as explained in the last chapter and elaborated here. Institutional designs for organizationally induced self-interest, however, often promote opportunism or have other dysfunctional consequences. This has led many organizational theorists to consider individual commitments to trustworthiness or the introduction of trust relations as additional means for securing reliability. We argue that *trust relations and trustworthiness are, at best, complements to organizationally induced incentives.*

Institutions and Incentives

To the extent that it can be, reliability must be designed into organizations. Typically, institutional design takes the form of establishing incentives for proper behavior. Hence, in principle there need be little or no direct oversight or sanctioning. Instead, each agent of the organization simply faces a schedule of incentives that make the agent's self-interest and the organization's purpose congruent. Institutional design includes monitoring and penalties as well as, in some organizations or for some organizational actors, room for discretion. Few organizations of substantial complexity are likely to be so well designed, although some assembly lines come close.

Within firms and bureaucracies, although not always within politics, those who are meritorious receive bonuses, pay raises, and the like while those who are shirkers or ineffectual suffer demotions, loss of pay, and even loss of job. Regulations and laws that create the external environment of organizations make certain behaviors criminal or subject to civil penalties; to the extent that laws affect motivations and competence, they affect reliability and are an alternative to trust relations as a way of aligning interests. Those who run firms, bureaucracies, political parties, governments, and other complex organizations can have private goals that run counter to the official aims of the organization or to public interest; in such cases, managers often establish institutional incentives for reliability that are particular to their organization, as elaborated in the last chapter with respect to lawyers, scientists, doctors, and businessmen.

The major problem with dependence on external enforcement devices, however, is that it is nearly impossible to write a complete and perfectly enforceable contract. It is difficult to cover all eventualities. A formal contract between employer and employee is a good starting point—and often a legally required one—for defining mutual expectations, but in most work settings it is supplemented by additional rules specific to the organization. Nor are these rules always so clear-cut. They often depend on subjective judgments, good faith, and the other components of what have come to be called relational contracting, as discussed later.

In the last chapter, we considered the corporate management and organizational governance of various professions in which individuals do similar work and have relative status equality. Here we focus on situations of power asymmetry in which organizational governance requires devising a set of internal institutions that structure incentives in order to elicit optimal agent effort while reducing the transaction costs of establishing contractual terms with employees and monitoring their behavior. With the adoption of Ronald Coase's insights (1937) and Oliver Williamson's (1975, 1985, 1996) extensions of the Coasean approach, political economists joined more sociologically and psychologically minded theorists (Gulick 1937; Simon 1947) in searching for forms of organizational governance and institutional design that reduce the costs of monitoring and surveillance while ensuring efficiency and productivity.[1] Coase insists that economists cannot treat production as a black box into which inputs are placed and from which outputs emerge. Firms form in a market economy, he argues, when the costs of entrepreneurial coordination are less than the costs of coordination by means of the price mechanism. This is what Williamson labels as the choice between hierarchy and market and defines as a problem of governance. Governance issues include not only the determination of when vertical integration is more efficient than horizontal (Williamson 1975) but also arrangements that enable stockholders (principals) to elicit greater productivity from top management (agents) (for example, Holmstrom 1982; Jensen and Meckling 1976), and management (principals) greater productivity from workers (agents) (Holmstrom and Milgrom 1994; Williamson 1980).

The relationship between an organization's hierarchical superiors and its subordinates is the major focus of this chapter. The principal-agent approach clarifies how cooperation between principals and agents is possible, but only if coercion, credible commitments, incentives, and other alternatives to trust are in place to solve information problems and facilitate the creation of norms and standards comparable to those used by professionals and scientists. Institutions also provide a basis for cognitive shortcuts, reputation-building, and social networks and thus can solve problems of assessing the trustworthiness—or at least the type and behavior—of those who lie outside the circle of family and close friends.

Institutional Arrangements for Making Agents Reliable

Private firms and public bureaucracies share certain characteristics. Both involve principals—owners, a board of trustees, chief executive officers (CEOs)—who establish the purposes of the organization and have the ultimate power to hire and fire. Both depend on agents—those who carry out the work of the organization. Each type of institution can have a wide range of possible principals. In firms, some are owners and some are CEOs and thus agents of the owners. In government, some are appointed by elected officials and some are themselves elected officials. There can even be multiple principals, as is generally true for government (Gulick 1937). Is a bureaucracy accountable to Congress, the president, or both? To which of its publics is a service agency responsible? Relationships between supervisors (or foremen or managers) and employees also share features of principal-agent relationships. In each case institutions regulate the relationships, but the institutions themselves vary according to the nature of the organization and the connections being regulated.

Agents vary a great deal in terms of skill, pay, and discretion. All are employees of the organization and in some important sense subordinates. They are subject to contractual obligations and to some form of oversight. Even professionals, who tend to have significant control over their work, some power vis-à-vis their principals, and significant latitude in discretion, may have interests and loyalties divergent from management's. The film *The Insider* illuminates just such a case. A chemical scientist whose professional norms dictate that he work in the service of promoting health comes to question the goals of the tobacco company for which he works. In being a good professional and citizen, he proves unreliable as an agent of the company.[2]

Despite wide variation in the types of principals and agents, virtually all institutional regulation aims to encourage high-quality effort, manage the risks associated with undependable job performance, and establish a causal account of culpability when there is a failure in performance. Over time three categories of institutional devices have emerged to generate incentive compatibility between principals and agents within complex, hierarchical organizations: procedures for selecting agents; the rewards and penalties, including the threat of dismissal, that structure incentives; devices for monitoring and enforcement. The use and effects of these devices vary with the nature of the work and the agent, but some version of each applies in virtually all organizations. While these devices are conceptually distinct, they are often empirically intertwined.

Employers would prefer to select reliable employees at the outset. They seldom know for certain, however, who will prove reliable, let alone trustworthy, over the long run, and they must instead develop devices for making judgments about potential agents. Inherent in most hiring situations is an asymmetry of information in the form of problems of adverse selection: the applicants know more about their qualifications, character, and commitments than does the employer. The quality of the candidate is neither easily observable nor easily verifiable—that is, it cannot be "(costlessly) described ex ante in a contract and ascertained ex post by a court" (Laffont and Tirole 1993, 211). Recruiters must therefore devise means to elicit or work around hidden information about what kind of person the job applicant is.

The institutional solutions for problems of adverse selection often reduce risk but fail to allocate personnel efficiently or motivate employees to achieve at their highest level. When the marginal costs of checking the applicants' accreditation or references are too high, employers often respond by treating all applicants as if they represent fairly high risks (Akerlof 1984, 31–33). Given the high costs of applicant assessment, employers may give everyone a low job classification, a short-term contract, and low pay, no matter what their actual skill or motivation. This emulates the insurance model: those who do not experience fires pay the same rates as those who will. Other information-revealing devices include the wage that potential employees are willing to take and reliance on ascriptive characteristics that in principle reveal the quality of the applicant. According to standard economic theory, low-productivity or noncompetitive workers will accept an offer of pay below what the work justifies, thus presumably revealing their low quality.[3] Barbara Ehrenreich's (2000) experiences as a low-wage worker in the service economy are illustrative. She worked as a waitress, as a hospital aide, for a cleaning service team, and for a large, low-end, Wal-Mart–type retail outlet. There were only two requirements for these jobs: a survey that checked on her honesty and willingness to obey rules (and was easily manipulable), and a drug test (also, as it turned out, manipulable).

When background checks are too costly, employers do not rely on the selection procedures to weed out unsuitable workers or discover particularly promising employees. Rather, they rely on their own supervisors to make these determinations on the job. These low-level supervisors may use their power in arbitrary ways or to secure personal advantage. Some may even demand sexual favors or side payments. One consequence is the erosion of potential cooperative relations, let alone trust relations, between the supervisor and workers. Another possible effect is the perpetuation of either a pool of low-skill, low-wage workers or high unemployment (Gibbons and Katz 1991; Montgomery 1999). Adverse selection and the delegation of key decisions about promoting and firing allow individual employers to solve problems of reliability and manage risk, but in ways that are not necessarily optimal for the organization.

Structured into the principal-agent relation are incentives meant to motivate the employee while simultaneously attempting to guard against moral hazard (incentives for behavior that would harm the organization). This means that the incentive structure should induce effort to do a good job without also inducing shirking, theft, or other opportunistic behaviors. The wage and employment contract initially structures the incentives of the agents. The contract primarily focuses on the bases for compensation and dismissal. In principle, it lays out rewards for high effort as well as penalties for failure to perform. Contracts can be implicit rather than formal, and they are often difficult for the employee to enforce and the employer to monitor. Contracts are seldom complete; they are often replete with loopholes and perverse incentives. Unions long ago discovered that they could wage a legal slowdown by encouraging their members to work-to-rule, that is, meet only the legal obligations of their contract.

Such problems lead many organizations and supervisors to devise additional rules and devices to encourage reliable behavior within a given setting. For example, a principal may institute rules that reward high productivity with recognition: the employee of the month. Or a supervisor may design the workplace so that workers compete with each other to provide information and innovations to improve the work product or outcome. This last was the strategy of President Franklin Delano Roosevelt when he would ask two of his staff or even two cabinet members to research and make recommendations on the same issue (Neustadt 1980/1990).

The Limits of Organizationally Induced Incentives

If we assume that institutional arrangements work sufficiently well that they generally reward the meritorious and punish the opportunistic, we can relax our search for alternative devices for ensuring reliability. Unfortunately, we cannot always assume that the institutional arrangements work well. It is extremely difficult to design proper incentives, particularly when management is balancing multiple goals. The institutional design and its structure of incentives all too often produce unintended consequences in the form of moral hazard, displacement of goals, and other perverse incentives. Surveillance and monitoring may produce insubordination rather than compliance.

Max Weber's (1968) ideal bureaucracy presumed certain preconditions before it could operate effectively, including a monetized economy, an extensive educational system, and some level of democracy. There are still many polities throughout the world that lack these preconditions, and the organizational design problems they face are often daunting (see chapter 9). However, even where the preconditions clearly exist, bureaucracies face immense difficulties in getting the incentives right. *It may be as hard to design an ideal organization as to write a complete contract.*

Perverse Incentives

Max Weber (1968, 956–1005) long ago observed the tension between the rules ensuring that bureaucrats will treat clients objectively and the flexibility required to serve clients well. Many scholars (notably, Blau 1955, 232–41; Merton 1957/1968, 195–206; Perrow 1972) have subsequently elaborated the dysfunctions of bureaucracy, emphasizing the difficulty of establishing appropriate criteria for job performance. They have documented the phenomenon of the displacement of goals in which employees adhere to bureaucratic rules rather than determine how best to serve the intended purpose of the agency. In an effort to make workers more reliable, bureaucratic rules and incentive structures may in fact promote moral hazard, resistance to supervisors, and other behaviors that make employees less likely to become trustworthy.

When contracts compensate only certain aspects of the work, there are likely to be "dysfunctional behavioral responses" (Prendergast 1999, 8, 25–28). A classic example comes from Peter Blau (1955, 36–56). The reliance by an employment agency on statistical records of agent performance undermined information-sharing among workers and encouraged them to take on only the easy placements they could chalk up as completed cases. Another common dysfunctional organizational practice is to reward conformists and dissuade innovators. These institutions are effectively privileging one form of reliability over another. A nice illustration—with a twist—is Koichi Tanaka, who works for Shimadzu of Japan. He conceived a mass spectrometry method that will substantially aid the development of cancer-fighting drugs. The method was patented by the company and won him a slight bonus. Tanaka remained "a lowly corporate employee whose talents were largely unrecognized by the conservative, hierarchical domestic authorities" of Shimadzu—until he won the Nobel Prize! (Watts 2002).

Ambiguities in the organization's goals in terms of who the clients are and how best to serve their interests are common in public-service bureaucracies (see, for example, Brehm and Gates 1997; Feldman 1989; Lipsky 1980; Weick 1969), but ambiguities can also characterize businesses, law firms, and financial organizations. Often the tasks are complex and the consequences of actions not fully foreseeable (Simon 1947). Assessing competence can then become quite difficult. Employees may be loyal, they may try hard, and they may be highly trained, skilled, and educated. All of these factors enhance their competence but do not ensure it. Moreover, when an institutional design compensates for individual shortcomings by some form of team production, a causal account of individual responsibility becomes nearly impossible.

The Paradox of Control

Because of the conflict of interest inherent in principal-agent relations, organizations tend to rely on hierarchical authority, formal contracts, and a high degree of surveillance to elicit employee reliability. However, heavy dependence on rules and procedures can create the "control paradox" (Miller 2004) or the "paradox of trust" (Murnighan, Malhotra, and Weber 2004). The formal features of the governance system may be more likely to produce agent resentment of principals than enhanced performance.

There are many examples. Distrust was prevalent within the highly bureaucratized work environment of a 1950s gypsum plant (Gouldner 1954). A series of studies of "Kay Electronics" (Sewell 1998; Sewell and Wilkinson 1992), the fictional name of a Japanese-owned manufacturer of consumer electronics, found that publication of task completion tends to increase obedience but not improvements in the work process. Blau (1955) describes the negative effects on the quality of the output of public bureaucrats when surveillance and evaluative techniques become more depersonalized and intrusive. As the power of supervisors increased, the employees felt less enabled to exercise discretion and more likely to be punished for doing so—to the detriment of their clients.

The changes that Blau (1955) details were intended to be reforms that would improve productivity. Such reforms, it seems, can often backfire. When a total quality management (TQM) program was applied to a research lab in a major U.S. technology corporation, the research scientists responded with resistance and nonconformity. TQM had been applied successfully to other parts of the corporation, where more routine tasks were carried out, but the scientists felt they should not be subject to the same kind of scrutiny as nonprofessional workers (Sitkin and Stickel 1996).

The principal-agent and most traditional management models rest on some form of command and control in which incentives are largely material and there is considerable surveillance and the threat of severe penalties. But monitoring is a two-edged sword. Observations of performance are essential for evaluations for promotions and raises, but they also signal lack of trust or even imply distrust. The effect can be confirmation of the impression that agents already have that their managers are enemies rather than partners in a common enterprise, especially for those already suffering from perceptions of low status, low power, and low discretion (Fox 1974; Kramer 1996). A superior's attitude may be revealed in how he designs subordinates' "task rules and the supervisory, inspection, and other control systems which govern him" (Fox 1974, 26). The effect is a reinforcing and vicious cycle (27), such as the one Alvin Gouldner (1954, 160) observes: "The supervisor perceived the worker as unmotivated; he then carefully watched and directed him; this aroused the worker's ire and accentuated his apathy, and now the supervisor was back where he began."

The mechanisms that connect more monitoring to reduced output seem to be largely psychological. Surveillance and job uncertainty can generate paranoid social cognition even among otherwise normal individuals. Those under observation become hypervigilant, suspicious, and susceptible to the sinister attribution error, judging others as more distrustful than they probably are (Kramer 1994; 1998, 262–63). Increases in resentment and even sabotage are one consequence (Brehm and Gates 1997; Cialdini 1996; Kramer 1999, 590–93). Reductions in effective information-sharing and in the problem-solving capacity of the organization are others (Zand 1972).

A long history of workplace experiments and innovations in management philosophy reveals that it is not easy to design effective incentive structures for regulating the relations between supervisors and subordinates and ensuring work effort and loyalty by employees (Perrow 1972). When organizational design works well, its devices constrain employees or offer them information and incentives that make them more reliable from the perspective of the firm. On the other hand, when institutional arrangements signal distrust by management of employees, they may provoke resistance rather than cooperation among employees and make it more difficult to secure the reliability, even trustworthiness, of the workers.

Building Trust Relations

The unintended and dysfunctional consequences of incentive structures are not simple design flaws. If they were easily corrected or better understood, we would see more models of sustained good practice and less debate about the best governance systems for organizations (for a research program that pursues this line of argument, see, for example, Gibbons 2003; Baker, Gibbons, and Murphy 1994). Trust relations between principals and agents may be a supplement to price and authority as a means to encourage productivity, discourage opportunism, and promote loyalty to the firm (Barnard 1938; Bradach and Eccles 1989, 104; Brehm and Gates 2004; Breton and Wintrobe 1982, 4–6; Fox 1974; Miller 1992). In this view, the more the workplace fosters trust relations among subordinates and with their superiors, the more likely it is that subordinates will become trustworthy, or at least reliable, in exercising competence and effort to serve the ends of the organization.

We consider evidence for the claims that "trust and/or trustworthiness beget trustworthiness" in each of the three primary workplace relationships. In the process, we contrast these claims with the somewhat different argument from the encapsulated interest account of trust: networks and relations of trust among those in a particular workplace can complement the formal organizational design to the advantage of the organization only when the relationships are personal and ongoing, and they are oriented toward information-sharing and negotiation meant to improve the efficiency and effectiveness of the work process over time. Networks and relations of trust are detrimental to the organization when they promote the protection of worker or supervisory prerogatives or power that inhibits the efficient and effective achievement of organizational goals. Although this last point should go without saying, it is often neglected by those who romanticize the role of trust within organizations.

Trust Among Workers

Horizontal trust often emerges among employees in a workplace, but not always, and these relations are not always sustained when they do appear. Nor do trust relations always work to the advantage of the organizational leadership.

Even selection devices can facilitate employee trust relations by evoking a presumption of similarity among those chosen and therefore an initial basis for bonding and perhaps trust. The cohort effect is notable and well documented among those from elite educational institutions who take their place in high-status businesses (Whiteley, Thomas, and Marceau 1981) and among workers in industrial settings (for example, Goldthorpe et al. 1968). It is even apparent in low-wage workplaces. Barbara Ehrenreich (2000) soon discovered that other workers, before developing any real knowledge of her, offered help and advice and assumed reciprocity as well as trustworthiness in relationship to the boss and their own personal confidences.

Trust relations that contribute to coordination across occupational divisions can be to the advantage of the firm or bureaucracy. For example, a field study of 194 managers and professionals confirmed the importance of affect-based trust in improving work performance (McAllister 1995). Social bonding may make workers more willing to share information and to help and instruct each other. Productive information-sharing also occurred in the more socially cohesive section of the state employment agency that Blau studied (1955, 71–72).

But trust among coworkers can also be disadvantageous to the organization. A cohesive group may control information and then use it to exert autonomous control or to give themselves negotiating power with management. This was what happened with the maintenance workers in the French factory that Michel Crozier studied (1964, 153–54). They prevented others from touching their machines, used rules of thumb rather than publicly available explanations or manuals, and exerted strong internal discipline and control among their members. As Crozier notes, "These practices are necessary for preserving the group's absolute control over machine stoppages" (153). Police officers present a quite different example of a subgroup that defends its prerogatives by controlling information, in this case by cooperating to conceal corruption, brutality, and other illegal and inappropriate actions from managers and the public (Brehm and Gates 1997; Lipsky 1980; Meier and Close 1994; Reiss 1971). In both these examples, workers built trust relations among themselves, but these relations were based on distrust of others. As we saw in chapter 4, the creation of in-group/out-group boundaries heightens distrust and inhibits cross-group cooperation.

Labor unions often build on networks and relations of trust established through family, ethnic, and work interactions and, simultaneously, on relations of distrust with the ability to produce material selective incentives and coercive devices. In this case, networks and relations of trust can be the linchpins for the institutions that help them maintain their solidarity with each other and in opposition to management. The history of the International Longshore and Warehouse Union (ILWU) is a case in point (Levi and Olson 2000; Nelson 1988). The work required teams that became dependent on each other over numerous repeat interactions, but worker solidarity across the teams emerged out of conflict with management, particularly the strike of 1934. Victory in that strike gained the union recognition and substituted the union-run hiring hall for the boss-run shape-up in allocating workers to jobs. Work became regular, but access to it depended on union membership, which was restricted. Embeddedness in a social network provided the information the union required about the trustworthiness of a potential member. The union-run hiring hall furthered the construction of trust relations: workers gathered daily to get their work assignments and, in the process, share information and build friendships.

Whether the ILWU hinders or facilitates management goals has turned out to be highly situational. Dependence on union cooperation ensures that workers have power relative to management, but strikes, slowdowns, and resistance to managerial innovations clearly are disadvantageous to the employers. On the other hand, negotiation sometimes allows Pareto optimal improvements. This was certainly the case in the 1950s when management introduced containerization on the West Coast. Management had to compensate workers but, in return, was able to introduce a major technological change at lower costs than were faced by most of its counterparts around the world, whose workers refused to bargain.

Although horizontal trust relations among employees sometimes seem easy to build, they are also often likely to be fragile. This is particularly true when they are used to equalize power asymmetries at the workplace and defend against management incursions. Management then has an interest in inhibiting horizontal trust through institutional changes and divide-and-conquer strategies that create competition and distrust among workers and undermine effective collective action. For example, management can introduce a contrived basis of promotion to stimulate individual competition (Breton and Wintrobe 1982).

In those instances where workers sustain horizontal trust, it is often the by-product of informal workplace institutions and norms that help build and sustain collective action. Such trust relations among employees are likely to facilitate overall organizational efficiency, however, only when there are also complementary cooperative relationships with supervisors and top management. Employee relationships with hierarchical unequals are thus the next subject of inquiry.

Supervisors and Subordinates

When organizational scholars discuss the importance of trust relations as a complement to incentives and monitoring, they are generally referring to relationships among hierarchical unequals. In chapter 3, we explored some of the determinants of trust relations in contexts of power asymmetry. An inherent conflict of interest and power disparity does not necessarily negate the possibility of mutual gain, but it remains a question whether actual trust relations are the basis for cooperation in these settings.

There are two plausible claims here. First, if subordinates believe superiors are trustworthy, the subordinates are more likely to reciprocate with loyalty and productivity. They are also more likely to engage in "gift exchanges"—that is, work effort and loyalty beyond the minimum standard (Akerlof 1982; 1984, 145–74). This is both an institutional and psychological process. The second plausible claim is that when supervisors treat workers as if they are reliable, workers are more likely to become reliable. This is what some scholars (Ayres and Braithwaite 1992; Braithwaite and Makkai 1994; Braithwaite 1995; Miller 1992; Pettit 1995) seem to mean when they talk about trust begetting trustworthiness. According to this line of reasoning, organizations are likely to get workers to exert more work effort and exhibit greater loyalty to the organization if management grants workers discretion, reduces surveillance, and in other ways treats employees as if they are honest and well motivated. Both of these claims could fit with the encapsulated model of trustworthiness, to the extent that they are grounded in ongoing personal relationships that provide information about the partners in the exchange and future-based reputations. But do either of these claims have empirical support? It is to this question that we now turn.

Recent research on the first claim confirms a positive link between workers' reliability and their perceptions of management trustworthiness (Brehm and Gates 2004; Dirks and Skarlicki 2004). Supervisory behavior can reveal the extent to which supervisors encapsulate and will defend the interests of their subordinates. Such behaviors include the development of personal relationships, indicators of benevolence, and credible assurances that management will protect employees against layoffs, speedups, and other threats. Many superordinates do seem to expend considerable effort to construct, manage, and maintain images of interpersonal trustworthiness (Elsbach 2004), but of course these signals can be spurious. More reliable are behaviors that reveal supervisory concern about the well-being of subordinates. This is the finding of an important ongoing research program on supervisor-subordinate relationships (Brehm and Gates 1997, 2004; personal communication from John Brehm, November 8, 2004). Once supervisors establish the boundaries of appropriate subordinate behavior within the organization through training, they gain greater latitude in the assignment of tasks by protecting subordinate discretion. Protection can even require that a supervisor take responsibility for the actions of those she supervises, giving them political "cover" (Brehm and Gates 2004, 43).

The relationships just described are the basis for what economists have called relational contracting (Gibbons 2001, 339–43; Macaulay 1963; Macneil 1980; Williamson 1975) and other social scientists have long described as the informal organization of the workplace (Barnard 1938; Blau 1955; Gouldner 1954; Simon 1947, 1951), or sometimes implicit contracting (for example, Shanteau and Harrison 1987). Relational contracts are the self-enforcing rules and norms that develop within a specific workplace; they depend on both local knowledge and ongoing relationships among the contracting parties. Relational contracts arise in situations of uncertainty and vulnerability, and they are enforced by reputational concerns that encourage each party to take the interest of the other into account. Relational contracts create reputational bases for confidence among the contracting parties engaged in ongoing personal interactions and thus are consistent with the encapsulated interest account of trust.

Within organizations, these informal and relation-based contracts complement formal contracts. They include provisions for terminating the relationship when there is evidence of low effort and for providing rewards with evidence of high effort, but they "incorporate a much broader range of subjective information" for evaluating performance than do formal contracts (Levin 2003, 835). Recent experimental evidence confirms the intuition that long-term relational contracts not only are more efficient than the alternatives but depend on cooperative relations to be productive. By signaling fairness with high wages at the outset, the employer is more likely to induce high effort from the employee, and the "establishment of a long-term relationship is further supported by a gradual increase of mutual trust" (Brown, Falk, and Fehr 2004, 27). By our logic, relational contracting offers an encapsulated interest account of trust because it depends on an orientation toward maintaining the relationship over time.

There is also some preliminary evidence for the second claim: a positive effect from supervisors treating employees as if they are reliable even when there is relatively little information about their actual character or competence. Reducing surveillance, using the carrot before the stick, and providing employees with discretion on the job are indicators that supervisors respect and grant discretion to workers; the result is likely to be a significantly higher rate of work effort and lower rate of shirking and sabotage (Ayres and Braithwaite 1992; Braithwaite 1985; Brehm and Gates 2004; Scholz 1984). For example, a detailed statistical and interview-based study of Australian nursing homes (Braithwaite and Makkai 1994) found that regulators' subjective trust of those whom they were regulating evoked trustworthy (in the authors' terminology) behavior, goodwill, and compliance. A detailed case study of a relatively poor white South Australia neighborhood also illustrates that government officials who treat clients and claimants as if they are reliable tend to elicit more honesty, openness, and compliance with government demands than when officials assume clients to be cheaters (Peel 1995, 1998).

Even in these accounts, "trust" is not enough. Coercive institutions provide credible commitments that supervisors will enforce the rules if need be and assurances that others will cooperate, an increasingly common claim in the organizational literature (see, for example, Braithwaite 1985; Levi 1997, 22–23). The nursing home supervisors and the neighborhood residents were aware that regulators and social workers could resort to coercion if need be. Even so, for those advocating this perspective, and in contrast to the encapsulated interest account of trust, the hierarchical superior does not have to know much about her claimants, clients, and subordinates; she need only treat them as if they are reliable to achieve the desired compliance much of the time.

The effect of trustworthy supervisors and supervisory expressions of confidence in subordinates is likely to vary considerably with the kind of work involved as well as with the education, training, and personal characteristics of the employees. Unfortunately, there are few systematic comparisons of contexts. This is an important issue for a serious research program on trust and trustworthiness in organizations. Although we do seem to know that the more vertical the hierarchy the less supervisory trustworthiness, on the one hand, and respect for workers, on the other (Argyris 1957, 1964; Crozier 1964; Gouldner 1954), we know far too little about why greater power asymmetries are introduced into some work settings and not others. Historically, distinct systems of rules and regulations tend to be associated with different managerial beliefs about the trustworthiness of employees in different categories and roles (Barber 1983, 14–17; Creed and Miles 1996, especially tables 2.2 and 2.3; Fox 1974; Kramer 1999, 577–78). There are also important cross-national differences in organizational design, particularly in relationship to the latitude provided workers by supervisors (Gordon 1996; Hall and Soskice 2001; Maurice, Sellier, and Silvestre 1986). Yet these findings are still inadequate for assessing whether there are systematic sources of power asymmetries in work settings.

The establishment of trust relations between subordinates and the supervisors with whom they work closely is possible under the right circumstances. Ongoing relationships in a context where interests are often interdependent, reputations matter, and individuals actually get to know each other personally can produce networks of trust as we understand them. Relational contracts and other informal devices for establishing trust relations can emerge as complements to formal organizational design in ways that contribute to organizational productivity. But what do we make of the claims that supervisory trustworthiness or trust begets trust by employees and therefore their reliability in the absence of relational contracts? Although the evidence does suggest that trust relations can emerge among particular supervisors and subordinates as they test each other and take greater risks with each other, it does not confirm the stronger claims. Rather, the evidence better supports an account of a positive employee response to supervisors who signal confidence in their employees and commit to treat them well. The mechanism by which the supervisors elicit better employee performance and loyalty is some form of reciprocity or, possibly, norm of cooperation, rather than by means of trust relations per se. Or at least there is not yet support for the argument that trust relations are a critical factor here.

Top Management

Even more problematic is the assertion that top management can win the trust of its employees. Agents often have reasons to distrust principals. Whether the boss is a canny bureaucrat ("Yes, Minister"), a brilliant entrepreneur, or simply a distant CEO, employees have good reason to be wary and to doubt that there is much congruence of interest between them; there are certainly no grounds for encapsulated interest. A focus by principals on short-term profit, the uncertainties associated with shifts in management, and employee job insecurity heighten bases for distrust and increase conflict and resentment at the workplace.

Even the highest ranking of agents must concern themselves with the trustworthiness of principals. These are among the problems addressed in the literature on team production and other devices for aligning the interests of stockholders and CEOs (Alchian and Demsetz 1972; Jensen and Meckling 1976; Miller 2000). Examples abound of breakdowns in this relationship. Daniel S. Goldin believed he had a job as president of Boston University, but just as he was to assume office the board of trustees expressed lack of confidence in his leadership and effectively fired him—albeit with a $1.8 million severance package (Bartlett 2003; Sara Rimer, "Turmoil at the Top at Boston University," *New York Times,* October 27, 2003, p. A-16). In several major financial companies, senior managers resigned when they did not receive the year-end bonuses they believed they had been promised (Levin 2003, 836).

More central to the concerns of this chapter are the relationships between top management and the organization's employees. Chester Barnard's (1938) argument about the importance of trustworthy leadership in eliciting work effort from employees is once again in vogue. Moreover, it is put in terms of organizational leadership that can be "trusted." One current version derives from the trust-honor game (with the term "trust" used vaguely), in which employees are only likely to exert effort if top management can credibly commit to "honor" the "trust" of employees by repaying performance and loyalty with reasonable wages, relative security, and generally fair treatment (Kreps 1990). The game has multiple equilibriums, but players can reach mutually beneficial outcomes in some circumstances. One means is the creation of a corporate culture in which top managers develop reputations for upholding principles that take the interests of workers into account. The result might be better performance by employees (see also Miller 1992). Such logic resonates with popular perceptions. For example, a recent newspaper article on downsizing argued that companies that "avoid cutting jobs reap huge benefits in loyalty and productivity" (Daniel Altman, "Downsizing Could Have a Downside," *New York Times,* December 26, 2002, p. C-1).

To convince employees of their dedication to the "corporate culture," managers must hold their reputations hostage to these principles and devise other forms of credible commitment. The devices are numerous and various. Tying their pay and promotions to those of their subordinates is one means of signaling reliability, and there are examples of this in both the business and association worlds. Aquila executives voluntarily reduced their compensation packages in November 2001, and the president of Delta Airlines forfeited his last quarter of pay in 2004 while in the process of negotiating with the pilots to forgo benefits. Social movement union presidents often helped write and then were tied by constitutional arrangements limiting their pay (Levi, forthcoming). Strong beliefs in the trustworthiness of owners may require their credible commitment to refrain from maximizing short-term profits, which they can do only by delegating control of key workplace decisions to hired management (Miller 2000, 319, passim; 2004). For example, rules that ensure that shareholders will be passive residual owners permit managers to make and fulfill implicit contracts with the workforce. This makes managers more likely to engage in a "gift exchange" in which they can promise to protect workers against layoffs, to give them higher pay than what the market would normally provide, and to reduce surveillance and monitoring in return for higher worker performance and loyalty (Akerlof 1982, 1984; Miller 2004).

There are other kinds of credible commitments that leadership can make to assure employees that they will uphold the principles of their corporate culture. By voluntarily limiting their discretion through the construction of constraints on their power, they may in fact increase their power. In some circumstances, the institutionalization of devices for dealing with labor-management conflict may reduce distrust and possibly even increase cooperation by making the commitments of both workers and managers credible. On the other hand, institutions that promise but fail to level the playing field may provoke further distrust (Levi, Moe, and Buckley 2004). The same logic applies to unsuccessful negotiations, as suggested by the case of Firestone tires, discussed in chapter 4.

Organizational leadership is generally too removed from workers for corporate culture to rely primarily on the devices that are implicated in an encapsulated interest account of trust. Top management cannot develop personal relationships, networks of trust, or relational contracts. Corporate culture does seem to involve a kind of reciprocity, in which the employee does more only as long as she believes top management is holding up its side of the bargain by living up to the principles inherent in the corporate culture. The evidence is more negative, however, than positive. When management defects, employees are likely to feel betrayed, with detrimental consequences for job performance and firm loyalty (Darley 2004; Frey 1993, 1994, 1997; Kramer 1999, 592–93). There is further support for this contention in a series of experiments using double auctions that help account for why employers do not reduce wages even when labor supply conditions would suggest they should: managers fear that such an act will be viewed as hostile by the workers and generate negative reciprocity (Fehr and Falk 1999).

On the positive side, above-market wages may elicit extra work effort (see, for example, Fehr et al. 1998), and so may other signals of the reliability of top management (Dirks and Ferrin 2002; Dirks and Skarlicki 2004; Miller 1992, 2000).[4] For most employees, however, their direct supervisors are far more likely to be the referents for trust relations, since they are the individuals with whom workers have ongoing and personal interactions (Dirks and Ferrin 2002).

Corporate cultures that promote reciprocity and cooperation are not always easy to create or preserve. Even when management seems to be trustworthy and responsive, employees are likely to be hypervigilant, given the great costs to them if they misperceive the intentions and credibility of bosses. Moreover, industrial, electoral, and other environmental changes easily undermine the reasons management might have to preserve a forward-looking reputation for upholding its corporate principles. For instance, the merging of McDonnell Douglas and Boeing undermined the cooperative corporate culture of Boeing. Management no longer came from the ranks of the Boeing engineers or shared their values. Boeing's shift of corporate headquarters from Seattle to Chicago was a further signal of the distance it was creating between leadership and even its highest-ranking professionals. The transformation in corporate culture was one of the reasons for the 2000 strike by Boeing engineers, the largest strike by private white-collar workers in U.S. history.

It is difficult to imagine trust as being at issue between employees and top management. Although reputation and credible commitments may enhance the reliability of top management in the eyes of employees and thus evoke a positive reciprocal response in the form of greater work effort and loyalty, there is probably no trust here. Employees have no grounds to form trust beliefs concerning a set of managers with whom they have no personal relationships and no basis for an expectation of encapsulated interest.

Concluding Remarks

At first glance, employment provides a good example of the principles discussed earlier in this book. A worker is entrusted with more responsibility as she demonstrates her competence and reveals her motivations. Employment relations often start over exchanges with relatively small stakes. As the agent proves trustworthy and as knowledge about her is accumulated, the stakes increase. But this is a very incomplete story. Institutional design within formal organizations is generally less about trust-building than about resolving conflicts caused by hierarchical power relationships and ensuring agent reliability in the absence of information on employee characteristics and motivations.

Trust relations and trustworthiness can emerge as a consequence of the informal organizations that are prevalent within many firms and bureaucracies. Sometimes these trust relations benefit clients or top management, but they are just as likely to make life easier for workers on the line and to create obstructions for those trying to supervise or gain from employee effort. Context and circumstance are important in determining who gains and who loses from these relationships, but despite the huge literature on organizations, relevant context remains inadequately specified. Moreover, trust between workers, trust relations between supervisors and subordinates, and the reliability of top management are all precarious, subject to shifts in incentive structures either from the top down or from exogenous changes.

Incentives for the alignment of principal and agent interests are at the heart of organizational design. Although networks of trust can be important complements to rules, incentives, and surveillance and may even inhibit some dysfunctional aspects of organizational design, they remain secondary and supplementary to the organizational design as means for eliciting reliability and cooperation.

Chapter 8

State Institutions

S TATE INSTITUTIONS affect cooperation in two principal ways. First, government acts as a third party, providing security for and external enforcement of various interactions and exchanges among its constituents. If there is sufficient confidence in the government's capacity to enforce the laws without extracting too high a rent in return, state institutions create a context in which cooperation becomes possible. Under some conditions, they may even facilitate the establishment of trustworthiness by allowing individuals to begin a relationship with small risks while they learn about each other. Second, government actors are in a relationship with those to whom they provide benefits and from whom they extract payments in money or service. To the extent that these government actors operate within rules and institutions that ensure transparency, integrity, and respectful behavior, they may be more successful in eliciting cooperation and compliance from citizens and subjects.

Government's third-party coercion is a major device for ensuring the reliability of interaction partners. Yet, despite significant experience with and scholarship on what makes for an effective state, state-building continues to confound policymakers and scholars (for a review of this literature, see Levi 2002). Organizations and institutions that promote cooperation without trust and support complex markets and governments are themselves the products of a long and contested historical process. Organizations and states, using third-party intervention, offer an alternative device for ensuring the reliability of a wide range of interaction partners. The problem, as history teaches us, is that organizations have a tendency toward oligarchy (Michels 1962), and states a tendency toward predatory behavior and banditry (Levi 1988; North 1981; Olson 1993). Such tendencies undermine the reliability of both the leadership and the institution itself. They may also undermine a state's ability to generate the context for the emergence of trust relations among those it governs. Even stable democracies with well-designed institutions for constraining government officials face problems of assuring citizens that they are well served by those institutions and the policies they produce.

Positive assessments of government reliability, or what some people might label government trustworthiness, are key to cooperative behaviors by constituents, both with each other and with government. However, different characteristics of the state are salient in these two settings. When government is a third party, at issue is its demonstrated competence and fairness in enforcement and monitoring. When government is a party to the relationship, evident respect for citizens and procedural justice are likely to be the key indicator of reliability. Competence matters, but the way government treats its clients and claimants seems to matter as much, if not more.

In both circumstances, however, government's power relative to that of the other actors is large. Its asymmetric power raises general issues about the reliability of its personnel in exercising self-restraint. Abuses of power in the form of exploitation, discrimination, or inordinate use of force are strong gauges of government unreliability, and they are likely to produce distrust of government and its agents.

In exploring how cooperation is facilitated by state institutions, we must first reflect on the nature of the requisite state institutions. We then take up how such state institutions promote (or fail to promote) constituent cooperation with each other and with the state. Simultaneously, we discuss major alternative claims about the relationship between government and trust. In the next chapter, we apply these arguments and those developed earlier in the book to domains where the state is either ineffective or attempting to establish its authority.

Credible Commitments, Competence, and Fairness

There are parallels between the features we look for in assessing personal trustworthiness and what we consider to be the determinants of government reliability. Competence and context are important for both, and questions of motivation clearly color our judgments of public officials, especially, perhaps, during elections. Yet most talk of "trust of government" is an oxymoron: citizens operate without the quality and depth of information provided by interpersonal relationships (Hardin 1998b, 2002b). The problems faced by citizens in assessing the reliability of government and its officials are multiple. The complexity of the modern state and the controversy over appropriate performance measures create huge information problems. Citizens may not be paying much attention (Hibbing and Theiss-Morse 2002), or they may make judgments (also tending to be information-poor) of individuals, such as presidents and prime ministers, rather than the government itself (Citrin 1974; Hetherington 1998; Levi and Stoker 2000, 480–81; Weatherford 1987). Widespread aversion to government intrusions and large bureaucracy leads to conflations of dislike with distrust. Strongly held religious convictions can lead to the dismissal of facts that contradict faith, as may have occurred in the 2004 U.S. election (Garry Wills, "The Day the Enlightenment Went Out," *New York Times,* November 4, 2004, p. A-25).

Well-ordered states do not rely only on citizen capacity to select officials who are honest, effective, and committed to acting in the public's interest. Well-ordered states embed even the most popular and honest government officials in institutions designed to weed out the incompetent and corrupt. Well-ordered states do not give public officials full discretion but require some form of procedural justice and rule under law. When we are assessing the reliability of governments and politicians, what we ultimately put our confidence in is the quality of the institutional arrangements within which they operate.

A sine qua non of a reliable state is the capacity to combat external enemies and to regulate the criminal elements of the domestic population. Thus, one of the trickiest questions of state-building is establishing sufficient coercive power while also satisfying citizens that it will not be wielded lightly. Before citizens and subjects of a state can rely on its institutions to provide safeguards or be willing to comply with government extractions, they must first have confidence that government will in fact protect them from the exploitations of others as well as from the predations of state agents. Since at least Hobbes, state design has required addressing the question of how to cede sufficient power to central states to provide social order without also ceding them excessive power to exploit and dominate (see, for example, Weingast 1997). This was one of the questions Madison and the Federalists squarely faced.

In chapter 2, we discussed how to establish trustworthiness with credible commitments and the individual strategies that make those commitments credible. Overcoming the huge power asymmetry between government personnel and most citizens requires more institutionally based credible commitments. These usually take the form of checks and balances within the government structure or automatic penalties for overstepping bounds. Credible commitments in government, as in personal relationships, derive from the dependence of one branch of government on another or government dependence on a group of constituents who control significant economic or political resources. Important historical instances abound. Acceptance of the constraints imposed by parliamentary elites on borrowing and budget-making was key to the maintenance of crown rule in seventeenth-century England (North and Weingast 1989) and ancien régime France (Root 1989). From the time of the Napoleonic Wars to the Second World War, various forms of delegation and taxation transformed the British government into a "chained Leviathan" (Daunton

1998, 2001). As we saw in chapter 4, the U.S. Constitution establishes institutions for delimiting the power of the state.

Reliable states must also have the capacity to detect offenders and free riders, a capacity that requires a costly infrastructure able to engage in extensive monitoring and information-gathering. This is not the place to rehearse the vast literature on the presuppositions for or variations in state capability to develop the necessary apparatus and resources; suffice it to say that monitoring, sanctioning, and information-gathering can be greater or lesser and can take a wide variety of forms (see, for example, Kiser and Schneider 1994). Moreover, if the monitoring is too intrusive or is seen as illegitimate, it may cause more problems than it solves. There is evidence that this is as true for states as for other formal organizations. Draft registration in nineteenth-century France and the United States (Aron, Dumont, and Ladurie 1972; Levi 1997, 44–51, 62–65, 85–102) illustrates the multiple difficulties. Registrars had to traverse the country and often search out young men at their homes, acquire birth dates and health information, and assess their suitability for the army. The work was time-consuming and dangerous, given the antagonisms of some communities to the state power the registrars represented. Between 1863 and 1865, thirty-eight employees of the U.S. Bureau of the Provost Marshal were killed and sixty wounded (Levi 1997, 64). Even during the very unpopular Vietnam War draft, there were no reports of casualties among draft board members or recruiters.

Gathering information to assist in service provision or to allocate voting representation can be problematic even for wealthy democratic governments with sophisticated modern techniques at their disposal. The recent debate over the U.S. census is a case in point. Staff must be able to locate those who are to be queried, conduct the questionnaire dispassionately, and protect anonymity. When there are questions about any of these dimensions or about the quality and uses of the survey instrument itself, it is hard for the personnel to assert competence.

By this account, the personal attributes and values of government personnel matter, but they are of less import in assessments of state reliability than are the institutional arrangements for managing coercion and enforcement and for upholding transparency, accountability, and fairness (for a different perspective, see Braithwaite 1998; Brennan 1998). This is not to say, however, that personal characteristics do not matter at all. Indeed, as argued in chapter 3 in the discussion of procedural justice, the key to viewing a process favorably may hinge more on the transparent integrity of the decisionmakers than on their competence per se.

This seems especially true in democracies, where in principle the official must answer to the voter. Yet the vote is a blunt instrument, one not particularly well suited to holding elected officials accountable. Voting can be understood as a game of incomplete information and considerable moral hazard (Fearon 1999). It is nigh impossible for citizens to become fully informed about what the incumbent has done in office or what either a challenger or incumbent will face or do in the future. Moreover, the nature of campaigns gives candidates incentives to conceal information that would harm their chances for victory, including at times their true policy aims. The empirical evidence confirms this logic. Politicians often switch from the mandates and platforms on which they ran (Stokes 2001a, 2001b). They do this because they learn something new once in office or, what seems more often the case, because they knew they could not win if they had revealed their ideas in the campaign. Other empirical evidence confirms how difficult it is for citizens—or perhaps how unwilling they are—to punish incumbents even when they fail to deliver important economic benefits; this is the finding of a detailed statistical analysis of 135 democracies since 1950 (Cheibub and Przeworski 1999).

Given the informational deficits of voters and the limits of the vote as an instrument of accountability, it should not be surprising that judgments of character sometimes trump assessments of competence. Perhaps that is why there is so much loose talk about which candidates for office we can "trust." At least some of the volatility of electoral politics derives from the fact that perceptions differ so sharply over the values and character of politicians we do not and cannot really know.

Constituents face multiple problems in determining whether government is serving their interests well, acting within the rule of law, and abiding by standards of procedural justice. One consequence can be intense political conflict over policies and politicians. Moreover, even when by any possible objective standards government is reliable, its constituents may not perceive it as so—and vice versa. This is most definitely the stuff of politics but not, we suggest, an issue of trust or trustworthiness. Rather, the institutional arrangements of government offer an alternative to trustworthiness as a basis for cooperation among citizens and with government.

The Role of the State in Interpersonal Cooperation

The backdrop of state-enforced law creates a context in which individuals feel safe to begin to take risks—or at least small risks with each other—without having to rely on trust. As argued in chapter 2, certain contexts provide sufficient security to enable those who have something to gain from mutual cooperation to find means of assessing each other's potential trustworthiness. A well-functioning state can offer such a context. It enhances the sense of security, promotes cooperation, and evokes a willingness to take risks even among strangers or relative strangers. With a reliable state in place, the advantages of "good" over "bad" government can become as evident as they are in the contrasting frescoes on the walls of Siena's City Hall. Ambrogio Lorenzetti's *Allegory of the Good Government* (1338–40) depicts a beautiful city with its walls open, its guards relaxed, and its people moving freely in and out of the gates as they engage in trade, toil in their fields, meet together, and play. In *Allegory of the Bad Government*, the city is in disrepair, the fields are desolate, and there are threats to order both inside and outside the walls.

The eighteenth-century Spanish conquest of Naples exemplifies the role of the state in promoting—or, in this case, undermining—cooperative behavior (Pagden 1988). Spanish governors consciously destroyed mutual trust and public-spiritedness and fostered suspicion and self-regard among the conquered citizens. They did this by a variety of divisive actions and mystifications that made it more difficult for people to cooperate, on the one hand, and to acquire accurate information about each other and their rulers, on the other. Ironically, "the degeneration of the necessary guarantors of the well-ordered community led inevitably to the collapse of the economy" (Pagden 1988, 137). Bad government drove out the positive effects of good government.

There is little debate that a reliable state, operating through property rights and their enforcement, supports social order and markets. There is evidence that it stimulates economic growth. There is also good reason to believe that the state can have a positive effect on the reliability of corporate actors. Once people have confidence that the laws delimit obligations among trading partners and that the state possesses sufficient capacity and will to punish the noncompliant, they are more willing to risk trading or otherwise cooperating with a wide range of partners, including those who are strangers. This is largely because such a state reduces the risks inherent in cooperation and exchange.

The importance of efficient and effective governmental institutions for improving the economic and political performance of countries with poor economic and democratic records is an increasingly standard claim by many economists and political economists (see, for example, Leblang 1996; North 1981, 1990; Olson 1982; Widner 2001). Even important quasi-governmental bodies, such as the World Bank and the International Monetary Fund, are now recognizing that they were misguided in their earlier indifference to the quality of governmental institutions. Francis Fukuyama (1995, pt. 2) labels countries whose business is largely based in families and networks "low-trust societies" because there is little trust of anyone outside the networked community. Such countries, he argues, can develop large-scale industry only with a highly interventionist state. With state enforcement of contracts, sellers and buyers no longer have to worry about certain kinds of betrayal and are thus better able to enter into cooperative relations. Norms and shared beliefs that support cooperation and exchange may also be important (Bowles 1998; Greif 1995; North

1990), but rules and formal institutions seem to be the necessary condition for economic and democratic development.

Recent cross-national empirical evidence supports the claim of a positive relationship between the reliability of states (those with effective rule of law) and economic growth. These studies use indicators of rule of law, probability of expropriation, corruption, bureaucratic quality, and infrastructural quality, derived from the surveys of experts, to produce measures of contract enforceability, governmental credibility, and government efficiency. They find a significant correlation between these measures and economic growth in a large sample of countries (Kaufmann, Kraay, and Zoido-Lobaton 1999, 2002; Knack and Keefer 1995).[1]

Using the World Values Survey (WVS), scholars have also investigated the causal direction of the common finding of a positive relationship between the same dubious "trust" questions in the General Social Survey and economic growth. "Trust" here refers to "generalized trust" or "social trust," denoting general attitudes toward others in society, a definition distinct from ours. Some find that trust is highest in countries where there is relative equality, higher standards of education, ethnic homogeneity, and effective government institutions "that restrain predatory actions of chief executives" (Knack and Keefer 1997, 1251; see also Knack and Zak 2002; Zak and Knack 2001). Others (for example, Whiteley 2000) read the data as supporting Robert Putnam's (1993a, 1993b, 2000) thesis that social capital is the causal engine from which economic growth flows and that institutions, including government, play a subordinate role. Yet others (most notably, Uslaner 2002) argue that neither the state nor social capital accounts for the strong positive correlation between trust and economic prosperity and that the level and perception of economic inequality is far more important.[2]

The dispute over the direction of causality reveals the limits of relying only on surveys. The inadequacies are fourfold. First, the concepts are underspecified, as becomes clearer in the next section. Second, the samples tend to be large and aggregated. Third, the samples, especially in some major cross-national surveys of government or business practice, tend to have serious selection biases. Fourth, without supplementary and detailed knowledge of the cases, it is difficult to sort out what makes government institutions reliable and effective.

Fortunately for the debate over the role of state institutional arrangements in enhancing economic growth by promoting the cooperativeness of actors, there is considerable complementary evidence. Some studies look at how policies intended to improve worker skills and training in advanced capitalist countries also offer information that enables employers to assess each other as reliable and therefore engage in decentralized cooperation (for example, Culpepper 2003; Hall and Soskice 2001; Mares 2003; Swenson 2002; Thelen 2004). This finding is consistent with the game theory literature on coordinating expectations and locating focal points in situations of private order with multiple equilibriums (for example, Gibbons and Rutten 2004). Or take the case of Chinese local governments, confronted for the first time since the 1950s with private industry and private investment. Variation in the institutions of local government shapes the officials' interests and incentives, which in turn explain most of the regional variation in private investment (Whiting 1998, 2000). A similar argument seems to apply to post-Soviet central Asia and Russia (Luong Jones and Weinthal 2004).

There are huge variations among polities in the extent to which people lock their doors or buy alarm systems and are willing to offer assistance to strangers or to cooperate without assurances that their effort will be repaid (Coleman 1990, ch. 5). Culture may account for some of the difference, but it is more likely that government institutions are the key. Just as there are good reasons to believe that governmental institutions provide the backdrop for assessing the reliability of potential partners in an economic exchange, they also may provide the backdrop for a sense of general security that facilitates social cooperation (Fukuyama 1995; Levi 1996, 1998; Yamagishi and Yamagishi 1994).

Sometimes the government directly produces the conditions and organizations that generate networks of engagement that make trust relations possible (Herreros 2004). In the United States the development of the post office in the nineteenth century supported the communication and diffusion of organizations that in turn produced the world that Tocqueville described (Carpenter 2001; Skocpol 1997). Government's electoral incentives can influence the level of police protection that makes riots against a detested minority more or less likely (Wilkinson 2004). Government can be an important initiator of the business, political, and other associations that enable Muslims and Hindus to regularly interact in civic associations and that make their cities less vulnerable to religious riots. In the "Bhiwandi experiment," for example, the police chief systematically established a neighborhood committee structure that ensured regular and organized interactions between the two groups (Varshney 2002, 293–95). The apparent result was peace in a locale that had frequently been wracked by violence.

Other evidence suggests that reliable government has an important effect on promoting trust among citizens. Negatively, we know that poor governmental performance, particularly well-publicized corruption, may reduce both confidence in government and, to some extent, beliefs about the trustworthiness of others (Della Porta 2000; Hart 1978; Pharr 2000). More positive substantiation comes from John Brehm and Wendy Rahn (1997). Using the American NES (National Election Studies) and GSS (General Social Survey) data, they analyze the relationships between civic participation, "generalized trust," and confidence in government. The strongest effect is that of confidence in government on trust (or what we would call perceptions of trustworthiness), as Margaret Levi (1996, 50–51) argues. Brehm and Rahn conclude that government behavior and policies can increase or decrease social capital (see also Herreros 2004).[3]

But what are the causal mechanisms that enable reliable government to generate cooperation and possibly even the potential for trustworthiness among citizens? Perhaps fair treatment of constituents by government officials leads those constituents to believe others in the polity will also be fair and trustworthy, as though there were a simple spillover (Rothstein and Stolle 2003). This is not a compelling or substantiated logic. A more promising line of argument is that *the backdrop of reliable government encourages citizens to take the small risks with others that facilitate their learning who is reliable, even trustworthy, and how to distinguish the reliable from those who are not.* This argument is, of course, consistent with our view about how trust relations are built. We return to these issues in chapter 9.

Interaction with Government

Robert Putnam (1993a, 1993b, 2000) makes the strong claim that social capital, particularly the trust among the population produced by interpersonal networks and civic associations, has a causal effect on the formation of an effective government. He takes the surveys as evidence for a decline in both social capital (as he defines the term, but see chapter 5) and responsive government. Alternatively, Sidney Tarrow (1996, 2000) argues that political mobilization may be the key to better government; it brings people together and develops civic competence through involvement in the parties vying for power or groups agitating for change. Finally, Margaret Levi (1988, 1996, 1997, 1998) maintains that government itself may also have an important role to play in eliciting citizen behaviors that in turn promote reliable and responsive government.

Building on Tocqueville (1835/1990, 1840/1990), for whom group association is the forum for learning democracy, but going further, Putnam argues that involvement in such groups as soccer clubs, bird-watching associations, and choral societies provides individuals with trusting relations and networks that make them more likely to cooperate generally. Membership in voluntary associations produces engaged and vigilant citizens who will demand responsive, well-functioning, and democratic government. Thus, Putnam worries about what he perceives as the decline in the quality of America's associational life (see also Skocpol 2003).

Putnam's is a problematic claim. The process by which specific reciprocity transforms into a more generalized reciprocity is far from clear theoretically and seriously in doubt empirically (Levi 1996). There is no good reason why those who cooperate with each other in a small group should believe that those outside the group are also trustworthy, and even less reason to believe that others are trustworthy if the cooperation is limited to a narrow situation such as bird-watching or bowling together. To the extent that voluntary associations produce social capital, they are more likely to produce bonding than bridging capital, that is, they are more likely to enforce intragroup than intergroup cooperation, as a recent and exhaustive study of American voluntary associations confirms (Kaufman 2002).[4]

Perhaps it is not associational life, however, but political mobilization that produces better and more trustworthy government, as Tarrow (2000) supposes and as he illustrates with the popular demand for better health care following the "Mad Cow" outbreak. An analysis of the 1996 U.S. national elections indicates that elections can be a context for increasing social capital by increasing citizens' sense of efficacy and "trust in government" and "by engaging people in a rite that allows them to renew their attachments to national society" (Rahn, Brehm, and Carlson 1999, 140). There is also a group of scholars who share with Putnam a concern about what they perceive as a decline in civic engagement, but they argue that the cause is less a decline in the number or membership of organizations than in the mobilization of those who belong (Clemens 1999; Skocpol 1997, 2003; Skocpol et al. 1999).

The consequences of political mobilization for confidence in government, however, are not always positive (Fiorina 1999; Newton and Norris 2000, 72–73); they seem to vary with time, government, and group involved. For example, the recent American tax revolts, exemplified by referenda in California and Washington, appear to have contributed to the belief that government has too much money and does not spend well what it has. These campaigns reduce rather than enhance citizen confidence in government.

Our position is distinct from that of both Putnam and Tarrow. In our perspective, state institutions tend to shape the way citizens respond to them, and sometimes these responses help produce better government. The more citizens perceive government as reliable in terms of both its competence and its goodwill, the more likely they are to comply with or even consent to its demands and regulations (Ayres and Braithwaite 1992; Levi 1988, 1997; Tyler 1990a, 1990b, 1998). Competence here is not generalized but domain-specific. For example, in tax collection the payers must have good reason to believe that the extractions are going toward the purposes for which they were intended and not into the pockets of corrupt officials (Brewer 1988; Levi 1988; Lieberman 2003). In the provision of health care, the training and quality of the health professionals and the cleanliness of the hospital are among the indicators of competence. But even in these contexts, how constituents are treated by government employees may be more important than what they pay or what they get.

What accounts for variation in citizen compliance and consent is less the perceived competence of the government—although that matters—than the perceived goodwill and fairness of the governors. Confidence in the benevolent motivations as well as the competence of state agents makes citizens more cooperative with government and enables its agents to be more effective. This line of argument and the evidence supporting it are consistent with the findings reported in the previous chapter on hierarchical relationships in firms and bureaucracies. For example, government regulation may be most effective if it keeps punishment in the background and uses persuasion and collegiality to induce compliance (see also Braithwaite 1985, 1998). When government actors fail to display confidence in citizens, or when they demonstrate active distrust, citizens are more likely to become wary of government interventions and less likely to consent willingly to the government's bureaucratic requirements (Lipsky 1980; Peel 1995, 1998). *Treating clients with respect appears to beget reciprocity. Distrust tends to evoke resistance, evasion, and dishonesty.*

Some of the most detailed work testing various propositions about the relationship between official behavior, citizen attitudes, and citizen responses comes from investigations of tax compliance (see, for example, Frey and Feld 2002; Lieberman 2003; Slemrod 2003). In the most developed research program to date, John Scholz (1998, 161) and various collaborators have investigated how "trust heuristics make compliance conditional on the action of governing elites and of other citizens." When government bureaucrats and politicians are perceived as fair, benevolent, and capable of controlling free-riding, citizens are more likely to comply with their demands (Pinney and Scholz 1995; Scholz and Lubell 1998). These findings on tax compliance are consistent with the findings of research on the role of due process and fairness in explaining why people obey the law (Tyler 1990a, 1990b; Tyler and Huo 2002) or contingently consent to extractions of taxes and military service (Levi 1988; 1997; Tilly 2005).

Illustrative of our logic is noncompliance with Australian tax laws in 1981 in the aftermath of a variety of scandals around Supreme Court interpretation of tax rules to the particular advantage of the well-off (Levi 1988, 158–72). The Court's actions elicited protests from unions and increases in tax evasion by those who felt the tax agencies and laws were discriminatory and unjust—and generally unreliable as a democratic and purportedly welfare-enhancing institution. This is a case, however, where government action was able to reestablish confidence. Tax inequity was one reason Bob Hawke and the Labor Party were elected in 1983 after nearly a decade of Conservative rule. In 1985 Hawke called a National Tax Summit to initiate revision of the tax laws. To establish the legitimacy of the process and its resulting regulations, the summit involved a wide range of groups and actors. Although the effort quickly deteriorated, it helped reestablish the reputation of the government as a dispassionate tax collector.

The history of francophone Canadians offers an example of a group who believe their interests are ill served by the central government, both by its institutions and by its leaders. They have learned that they almost always lose in the federal parliament on issues about which they feel strongly as a group but on which the anglophone majority has the opposite position. It is thus not surprising that they were far less willing than anglophone Canadians to volunteer for military service in World Wars I and II and far more likely to engage in draft resistance (Levi 1997, ch. 6). Their long-term solution has been to demand provincial autonomy, especially for Quebec, and to threaten secession as a block to discriminatory legislation. Although the particulars are different, within the United Kingdom Scotland uses a similar strategy in its relationship to England.

To the extent that government actors are both competent in relation to and beneficent toward a particular group, they are reliable. *Government reliability is established, reinforced, and conveyed through institutional arrangements that reward positive and effective interactions with constituents and guarantee due process without discrimination.*

The Effects of Distrust of Government on Democracy

The findings reported in the previous section tend to contradict Putnam. It is not interpersonal trust among citizens that makes government effective. Rather, reliable state personnel promote citizen confidence in, compliance with, and support of the state—or at least those state institutions with which citizens have had positive experiences. On the other hand, citizen distrust of government, or at least skepticism about its competence and goodwill, can have very negative effects on cooperation with government, and possibly among citizens.

There are three very different kinds of claims concerning citizen distrust of government: the perception that the state and its officials are unreliable; the necessity of designing distrust into government institutions; and rising popular distrust of government. The first claim mirrors our arguments in the previous section: the state and its officials may prove unreliable or be unable to convince citizens of their reliability. In some instances, distrust is a response to acts of government that demonstrate its inequitable treatment and even ill will toward a given group. African Americans, francophone Canadians, and the Basque are among the many examples of groups who have had negative experiences with well-entrenched democratic governments. Their judgments about the unreliability of government tend to be based on assessments of government fairness in the making and implementation of policies in addition to assessments of competence and accountability. Any institution, and especially any state institution, has major distributional consequences. Although standards for evaluating those distributions shift over time and vary among groups within the polity (Ensminger and Knight 1997; Knight 1992; Levi 1990, 1997), those to whom the standards are not being applied are rational and right to lack confidence in government.

Failures in due process and abrogations of civil rights and liberties undermine the credibility of the state and perhaps its effectiveness. This is not a contradiction of the first of our claims, but the other side of it. If an effective and reliable state helps build the confidence of citizens in each other, an ineffective, malevolent, or otherwise unreliable state offers no foundation for the flourishing of trust relations and confidence within the polity. We address these kinds of situations in the next chapter.

The second claim, the stuff of liberal theory, has to do with government accountability. Processes of accountability positively affect how people perceive and respond to governments and political parties (Hibbing and Theiss-Morse 2002), and "institutionalizing distrust" (Braithwaite 1998) may enhance accountability. As argued here and extensively in chapter 4, the reliability of the state hinges on an institutional design that builds in distrust. Perverse as it may sound, scrutiny and heightened attention to the actions of government agents may enhance general citizen confidence in government. Certain forms of deep distrust, however, lead to political mobilization intended to discredit the state, and some such mobilizations succeed in doing so.

The third claim is the popular view that there is increasing distrust of government and its officials, with negative consequences for political participation and good government. There is often a bit of whimsy in public assessments of when public officials have been successful and when lucky in achieving the ends they sought. How much of the economic upturn of the 1990s in advanced capitalist countries can be attributed to state policies or laws, let alone Alan Greenspan or Margaret Thatcher? Regular, periodic and fair elections combine with mechanisms of monitoring to offer some assurance that democratically chosen officials are fulfilling the public trust. However, as literatures on mandates (Stokes 2001a, 2001b), representation (Bianco 1994; Przeworski, Stokes, and Manin 1999), and voter ignorance (Popkin 1991) make clear, it is difficult for the public to fully comprehend the circumstances or assess the private information that elected officials must consider in making their policy decisions. It is hardly unusual for a candidate to make a promise during the campaign that she fails to keep once in office. The problem for the public is in determining the reason for her promise-breaking. Was she purposely deceiving the public beforehand? Or did she gain new information after the election? Or did she choose policies that would better serve a public that would object to these policies ex ante?

Whether the perception of a decline in citizen confidence in government is well or ill founded, it may nonetheless affect the level of support for government (Mishler and Rose 1997; Misztal 1996; Sztompka 1999). Recent research, for example, finds that a reduction of confidence in the U.S. government leads to a reduction in support for welfare, race-targeted, and other redistributive programs (see, for example, Hetherington 2004).

Most of what we know, or think we know, about citizen perceptions of the reliability of government comes from surveys, but as we have demonstrated, inferences from these surveys are problematic. There is conceptual confusion, leading to a conflation of two distinct, if related, phenomena: confidence in political actors, institutions, and processes and judgments about their trustworthiness. There is an issue of the extent to which the same questions capture comparable attitudes in different segments of the population or across time. In addition, there is an issue of domain-specificity (Levi and Stoker 2000, 499): trust varies with the task, context, and people involved, as in our three-part model of trust. That is, we typically trust any actor with respect to a specific domain, but not over all domains. The survey questions on trust in government and politicians were developed with a set of assumptions that are now highly contested, even by those most closely associated with the National Election Studies. For example, Nancy Burns and Donald Kinder (2000, 4) note in their report on the design and evaluation of new "generalized trust" questions for the NES: "We suspect that trust is domain-specific, but the measures of trust that dominate the empirical literature are based upon an entirely different assumption: namely, that people have in mind stable views about the trustworthiness of human nature in general."[5]

Concluding Remarks

A stable and effective state not only allows citizens to feel secure on the streets and in the shops but provides a context for individuals to begin to take risks with each other, learn about each other, and eventually cooperate and exchange even where the costs of defection are high. The quality and behavior of state institutions, agencies, and law play an important role in providing the background conditions for individuals to treat each other as reliable and discover who is trustworthy. Enhancements in civic engagement, economic growth, compliance with government policies, and even corporate responsibility are among the possible effects.

Our major effort here has been to offer an account of how and why state institutions have such positive consequences. In the process, we have contradicted the Tocqueville thesis, as revised by Putnam, that civic association promotes democracy and better government generally. There is some evidence of a correlation between dense civic associational life and effective government, but not the clear causal link suggested by Tocqueville or in Putnam's social capital argument. Our claim is that a responsive, fair, competent, and benevolent state is a reliable, even trustworthy, state and thus is likely to succeed in eliciting compliance and consent from citizens. It is in this sense that state effectiveness depends on the acquiescence and confidence of citizens. Government is a key player in bringing this result about, not just a beneficiary of preexisting trust within the polity.

At the same time, we have argued for the liberal view advocating institutionalized distrust of government. "Healthy skepticism" keeps constituents alert, and therefore public officials responsive, but only if transparency is designed into state institutions so that wary citizens may be constructively vigilant. It is likely that widespread, deep distrust of government, going well beyond liberals' "healthy skepticism," can undermine the state's institutional arrangements and provoke a breakdown in general cooperativeness, as elaborated in chapter 9. Survey evidence within the advanced democracies hardly indicates such a level of distrust; nor is there the kind of deep-seated distrust of the state that post-Soviet countries sometimes evidence. It is now generally accepted that the best-known and most widely cited surveys are problematic for evaluating trust in government. Instruments should reveal the domain-specificity of both "trust" and "distrust," as befits the paradigm that A trusts B with respect to x and not with respect to everything.

Institutionalized distrust is consistent with the existence of a state that enhances cooperation and is itself the beneficiary of the citizen cooperation it helps to create. State institutions that make their agents accountable and credible, ensure their competence, and encourage "healthy skepticism" provide the conditions under which citizens can risk cooperating with each other and with their government.

Chapter 9

Trust in Transition

W E HAVE noted that cooperation built on trust relations and established within one context or for one particular purpose does not necessarily translate into cooperation in other contexts or for other purposes. Networks of trust can easily become networks of distrust; those within the network are trusted and those without distrusted. In this chapter, we synthesize these claims and attempt some general statements about the processes that take place when individuals cannot, with confidence, turn to the state or well-defined organizations to protect them. We illustrate the limits of building or relying on trust relations as the basis for creating well-ordered societies. We observe, once again, that the recognition of the pervasiveness of distrust may be a better assumption than the importance of trust for constructing the organizations and institutions that enable us to cooperate.

The problem of cooperation is particularly acute in large-scale transitions in the polity, economy, and society that destroy or transform institutions, organizations, social networks, and even personal relationships. The high instability that accompanies transitions undermines many of the bases for reliable expectations about the behavior of others. There is reduced certainty about who is likely to be trustworthy or with whom one can cooperate productively. Trust relations themselves are in transition.

We do not systematically analyze every kind of transition. Nor do we provide a typology of transitions and their effects on trust relations, trustworthiness, reliability, and cooperation. Rather, our intention is to show how our conceptual apparatus can contribute to understanding the conditions under which interpersonal trust leads to or obstructs cooperation during and in the aftermath of transitions.[1] By doing so, we clarify the importance of alternatives to trust and trustworthiness, and we highlight the relatively small role that trust relations play in social, political, and economic life.

In this chapter, we focus on three of the devices that can produce trust relations, trustworthiness, and alternative bases for cooperation: embeddedness in ongoing and dense personal relations; social networks; and organizations and institutions with means to ensure the reliability of those with whom individuals would like to trade, collaborate, or safely interact. Transitions revise expectations about the likely behavior of others because they increase uncertainty and alter the settings in which people interact, hold each other accountable, and build reputations. Transitions typically transform the tasks and expertise that are required and therefore necessitate revisions in judgments of competence. When they discredit old values or bring new values into play, they also require revised judgments of motivations. Perhaps most importantly, transitions alter power relationships, which affect not only cognitive appraisals of who is trustworthy or reliable but also access to resources and information. Thus, *transitions significantly modify what people know or believe about each other, and therefore their perceptions of who is trustworthy or reliable.*

Transitions include a wide range of phenomena. Even the governmental shifts that occur regularly in parliamentary and presidential democracies or the ups and downs of the stock market might count as transitions, for they assuredly produce uncertainties. Our focus here, however, is on two kinds of transitions; both are characterized by the obliteration of many, if not most, past bases of stable expectations about the interests, motivations, and competence of those once trusted or considered reliable. The first is extensive migration experienced by an identifiable group within the larger society. The second is a regime shift that involves societywide change.

Migration is an important case because it allows us to consider the role played by trust relations or alternative devices when people move to a new economic and political context. Regime shifts, both economic and political, permit analysis of the breakdown and reconstruction of institutions and other arrangements for promoting cooperation. Both kinds of transition also raise issues about when trust is constructive and when it is detrimental to harmonious intergroup relations, widespread exchange, and productive cooperation. Migration and regime shifts exemplify a wide range of large-scale problems for which many policymakers and social analysts have advocated trust-building. We suggest that the role of trust relations is limited. Indeed, *trust relations are often a barrier to the integration of different groups into a society, the development of effective markets, state-building, and widespread and productive cooperation.*

Massive migrations tend to transform family and community structures and change power and status hierarchies. They nearly always require adaptation to new economic and governmental institutions. Given that the nature and guarantees of trustworthiness change, individuals must create new grounds for conveying their own trustworthiness and assessing that of others. Some of these may have the effect of helping individuals become integrated into the larger society; some may create or confirm boundaries and identities that inhibit productive interactions with those outside the group.

Nearly all regime change, whatever its effects on preexisting networks and communities, entails the development of new organizations and institutions. This has consequences for the available kinds and sources of information about others and for the locations of interaction. Major regime shifts involve significant transformations of the government, the economy, or both. Examples include revolutions, military conquests, and swings from authoritarianism to democracy (or back again), colonial to autonomous states, traditional to market economies, and socialism to capitalism. Regime transformations that involve the violent destruction of villages, communities, and ethnic, racial, or religious groups may also destroy prior bases for interpersonal trust. However, some have the opposite effect: an external threat may create greater dependency within the network or community, and mobilization for change may create new trust relations and new bases of cooperation. Some regimes, most notably totalitarian ones, purposely generate distrust, encouraging individuals—even members of the same family—to spy on each other.

Two major questions arise in considering trust in transition. The first is how to rebuild bases for cooperation among individuals. An equally important concern is the extent to which the relations, networks, and organizations that emerge during transitions to solve problems of trust and cooperation inhibit the construction of efficacious institutions in the post-transition period.

The Problems of Large-Scale Transitions

When old relationships break down, so do expectations about others. The encapsulated interest account of trust depends on ongoing repeat interactions. Transitions can undermine the probability of repeat transactions, however, and the capacity to monitor and sanction others. Mass migration can take a migrant from a world of individuals with iterated, close-knit interactions to a world of strangers. It can become harder to locate those who prove untrustworthy and more costly to punish them if found. Regime change, by definition, destroys organizations, laws, and institutions that previously facilitated cooperation and exchange. It generates uncertainty about who is likely to be trustworthy.[2]

When past social networks, organizations, and institutions are eradicated, the social effects can be devastating. Economic exchange may be reduced to barter and bazaars, even in countries, such as postwar Germany, where more elaborated markets once prevailed. One effect can be a Hobbesian state of nature, as the economist Steve Cheung describes in World War II Hong Kong, or as the director Vittorio de Sica reveals in the Italy of *The Bicycle Thief* (1948).[3] The U.S. South exemplifies what happens when former bases for cooperation disappear. In the aftermath of the Civil War, slaves once entrusted with children and valued property became subjects of distrust and fear. Traditional patterns of reciprocity were destroyed.

The sources of transitions can be exogenous, but the dynamics of the destruction and construction of trust relations and trustworthiness are usually endogenous and depend on the particularities of the situation in which individuals find themselves. Although we seem to know something about the conditions under which trust declines, we are only just beginning to systematize knowledge about how to build trust where it does not exist and how to reconstruct it when it dissolves—or, what is more likely, how to look to alternative bases for cooperation. The asymmetry of trust and distrust (see chapters 1 and 4) appears to find confirmation in the dearth of research on the process of rebuilding trust. Yet trust and trustworthiness can survive or be established even in circumstances of extreme risk and vulnerability. The extant literature, as discussed later, offers examples of trust relations arising among some but not all groups in the aftermath of a transition and offers some guidelines about the kinds of trust that are likely to emerge. Of even greater relevance for our argument is the growing body of research on institutions designed to ensure credible commitments. By reconsidering these studies in light of the factors that affect trust, trustworthiness, and reliability, we can elaborate a more analytic and potentially generalizable account of how cooperation arises in situations where trust relations are limited or nonexistent.

Trust and trustworthiness are important in the context of transition to the extent that they promote cooperation. The real object of concern is what contributes to the creation or reconstruction of effective societies, economies, and polities in which people can cooperate and exchange to mutual benefit. Cooperation and exchange may not always, however, be socially productive. We need to be sensitive to the conditions under which cooperation serves a few at high cost to the many.

Transitions that shatter extended networks, organizations, and institutions leave few, if any, alternatives to trust relations based on family and close personal connections. Individuals are likely to become reliant on their intimates to rely on them in a wider array of ways than they do when organizations are dense and institutions are vigorous. When instability, organizational weakness, and institutional fragility characterize the transition, trust relations are likely to become the primary bases for cooperation and exchange, assuming that intimate social networks are still sufficiently intact.

Exclusive reliance on trust relations can prove inadequate in the long run. This is the case when it severely restricts the scope and range of contracting and cooperation. Moreover, betrayal, distrust, and enmity within families and neighbors are as plausible as trusting relationships. Witness the history of tribal and feudal warfare on virtually every continent. Over time and under some circumstances, individuals create devices that enable them to assess a wider circle of individuals as relatively trustworthy, or at least reliable. This circle can come to include casual acquaintances and even some strangers. Such devices can encompass, at the one extreme, the simple identification of partners with whom to establish repeat transactions and, at the outer boundary, the elaboration of governments and markets. The need to survive and to thrive might lead to a search for increased opportunities. Extended trade and cooperation become more likely to the extent that potential interaction partners are embedded in a network that offers information about who is trustworthy and provides punishments for those who demonstrate they are not. The most common and immediate source of such relationships is a shared tribal or ethnic background, language, race, or religion—in other words, reliance on stereotypes, as elaborated in chapter 2. However, there are other equally common and effective forms of private order, as we shall see. When there are incentives to search for a wider range of interaction partners and allies, there are incentives to create a more encompassing social network that contains mechanisms for ensuring trustworthiness and reliability among the participants.

Although the trustworthiness embedded in social networks enhances trade and cooperation, it can also be restrictive (Cook, Rice, and Gerbasi 2004). Bases for membership can simultaneously constitute bases for exclusion that limit economic opportunities and create significant political problems, especially if the networks support intergroup hostility or political dominance by a particular faction.

We have so far focused on the production of trust, trustworthiness, and reliability. We must also consider how trust, trustworthiness, and reliability contribute to the development of social networks, organizations, and institutions. They sometimes complement the development of productive organizations and good government, as argued in chapters 7 and 8. *Trust relations and social networks can also block the development of effective alternative devices,* as we clarify in this chapter. There is no inevitable evolutionary path from trust relations to the networks of trust to the trustworthiness and reliability embedded in organizations and institutions. Trust relations may inhibit the development of welfare-enhancing political and economic institutions. Social networks may provide bases for enhancing trade and cooperation within the network, but at the price of economic and political exclusivity that can reduce even wider opportunities for trade and cooperation. States, organizations, and institutions can become predatory or inefficient. When no one risks the construction of other devices, or when those devices fail, trust relations may become the primary basis of cooperation. When certain groups develop social networks that inhibit or permeate further efforts at institution creation and change, then good government and effective markets are less likely.

Mass Migration

Personal relationships—and therefore trust—tend to become more generally significant in a world where most others are strangers and where supportive institutions are few or nonexistent. Families often migrate together, and individuals often migrate to join other family members. Reliance on family members for housing, welfare, and work is common among immigrants. Bitter enmity and betrayals certainly can exist among family members, but trust is also more likely to be embedded within familial and friendship relationships than among strangers. Particularly in the absence of organizations and institutions to ensure trustworthiness, trust relationships can become the major foundation for cooperation and exchange.

Migration creates different problems from those faced by a stationary community. Immigrants reach cities or new countries in search of jobs and capital, and they often lack the language, legal status, or know-how to find employment without assistance. Owing to the high costs of search, they generally turn to those whom they know or who possess a stereotypical attribute, such as shared nationality or religious sect, which may signal presumed trustworthiness. Most often, family or ethnicity is the basis of social networks for migrants who face otherwise uncertain environments.[4] High risks, such as those associated with illegal immigration, further increase migrants' reliance on networks. Moreover, many immigrant entrepreneurs have incentives to hire those within their family or network (Waldinger 1986, 271–74). Employers want an efficient means to recruit a reliable labor force. They may turn first to their family and intimates, but as the business grows they cast a wider net for reliable workers. Third-party endorsement and the dependence of the worker on membership in the network reinforce the reliability produced by the limited alternative opportunities for the immigrant employee. In addition, employers may find that hiring those with a shared background reduces workplace conflict by enabling them to rely on cultural norms and bases of authority rather than more costly dispute resolution devices (273–74).

Similar considerations may apply to those in need of capital. In chapter 5, we discussed the use of ethnic networks to obtain credit. Borrowers are subject to what Alejandro Portes and Julia Sensenbrenner (1993, 1325) label "enforceable trust," based largely on the possibility of ostracism from the enclave of ethnic entrepreneurs in a situation where the alternative sources of capital and jobs are nearly nonexistent. The loans are conceivable because of mutual dependence and lock-in.

Even family can sometimes fail to prove effective in new environments. For example, the migration of the Frafra from the Ghanaian countryside to the city of Accra weakened the hierarchy and gender segregation of the traditional family and undermined their former trust relationships (Hart 1988; see also Kerri 1976; Little 1965). Exchange and cooperation can emerge in these new circumstances, but kinship is no longer the primary ordering principle. New networks are established among virtual strangers, permitting credit and debt. The purveyors of goods develop beliefs and expectations about their potential clients, but they ensure their relative trustworthiness by establishing the expectation of repeat interactions. Keith Hart (1988, 190) notes that "the pretension of familiarity is the normal rhetoric of economic life in a place like Accra." By labeling these relationships as friendship, traders justify and make effective the use of shaming techniques against defaulters. Although the process of figuring out who will be trustworthy is one of trial and error and has a high failure rate (Hart 1988, 191), it does permit the creation of markets in which credit can play a role.

Emigrants promise and often do send back large remittances to wives, children, and parents (Massey 1986; Philpott 1968; Stahl and Arnold 1986). Some ultimately return to their village with sufficient capital to buy land or businesses, and others have their families join them where they now work and increase their ties to their new country. Some simply disappear. Fiction and the sociological literature are replete with tales of family desertions as well as of personal disasters that prevented return or remittance.

Many of the catastrophes that befall migrants involve calculated risks, and in others misplaced trust plays a role. There is continuing loss of life by those who are put on unsafe boats, hidden in containers on ships, or loaded onto trucks and then left by their guides in the desert of the U.S.-Mexican border. The risk did not pay off. Trustworthiness beliefs or relations are seldom at issue. Examples of misplaced trustworthiness beliefs include instances of virtual enslavement by people who are trusted because of their links to the home community of the victim or their common heritage: "just as ethnic ties constitute the bases of trust in immigrant communities, so they are a source of apprehensions. . . . Those who appear trustworthy may entrap you in a suboptimal outcome, which you may apprehend only when it is too late to escape" (Nee and Matthews 1996, 375).

There are far too many stories of workers, especially those without papers, recruited upon arrival in their new country or transported from their home countries on the basis of unrealized promises to feed the entrepreneurial requirement for cheap labor. Ethnic or family links with the employer or recruiter can make these promises credible. Nor do these work situations need to be exploitative to limit the workers' future opportunities. Those without much human or financial capital who secure jobs through ethnic networks are likely to find themselves restricted to low-skill, low-mobility employment, whether within the ethnic enclave economy or the wider economy. Those who already possess capital, human or financial, are likely to have a quite different experience: ethnic ties facilitate their transition into high-skill and high-mobility employment (Nee and Sanders 2000; Sanders 1994).

Such negative experiences are likely to confirm the distrust beliefs of low-skilled ethnic emigrants about those outside their network whom they already perceive as the source of discrimination, and these experiences are also likely to contribute to the development and reconfirmation of distrust of those who are powerful and exploitative within their own community (Nee and Sanders 2000). On the other hand, highly skilled ethnic immigrants find confirmation of the trustworthiness of those in their network who have aided them, and they learn to distinguish who might be trustworthy or reliable in the wider world. These claims are consistent with Russell Hardin's (1993) street-level epistemology of trust and Toshio Yamagishi's (2001) conception of social intelligence, which is the capacity to judge who is likely to be trustworthy or untrustworthy.

Despite the evident advantages for economic advancement, there are limits to social networks with strong ties. Reliance on family and cultural markers tends to narrow the opportunities to those available within the network, to exclude those who do not share the relevant attributes, and to have consequences for economic growth.

Networks that create dependencies and obligations that lock in the immigrant with a particular employer or patron are especially problematic. They often "activate boundaries" (Tilly 2004). Ethnic networks with blocked exit and entry not only limit economic opportunities but also increase the potential for ethnic conflict (Wintrobe 1995). Lock-in can lead to exploitation, a conclusion that follows from the theory of repeated games (Dasgupta 2002). Networks can also create externalities that bring about collective inefficiency, given that the creation and maintenance of trust networks require investments and forgone opportunities (Wintrobe 1995, 46; Hechter 1987, 45–49).

Economic restrictions may especially be a problem in hierarchical networks (Dasgupta 2002), such as ethnic groups with strong patriarchal authority or patron-client relationships. When a new economic opportunity arises, those in similar structural positions not only will want to take advantage of it but are likely to renegotiate their contract with each other. Those in a more hierarchical relationship may have more difficulty exercising that option if the subordinate seeks a renegotiation and the more powerful does not. The compatibility of interests facilitates trust in the first case, and the conflict of interests fosters distrust in the second.

Networks can also legitimize demands on successful members as a consequence of "the same normative structure that makes the existence of trust possible" (Portes and Sensenbrenner 1993, 1339). The norms might include tithing or other contributions to the economic support of the less well-off or threats of exclusion from the group should the successful person fail to fulfill group obligations. Such norms, which depend on sanctions and communal norms, are alternatives to trust. Religious shifts and name changes are among the strategies used by individuals from diverse cultures, places, and periods to free themselves from such demands (Portes and Sensenbrenner 1993, 1339–40). Some simply begin to use the alternatives available in the host society to make themselves seem more trustworthy to lenders, employers, and employees. For example, Korean immigrant entrepreneurs rely on their ethnic networks in the initial stage of developing their business but later rely more on their own human and physical capital, thus significantly reducing their dependence on the Korean community (Yoon 1991).

There are, of course, organizations that attempt to facilitate the economic and political incorporation of immigrants into the larger society. In the United States and elsewhere, religious, philanthropic, party, and labor organizations have played that role—as have public schools (Gerstle and Mollenkopf 2001; Michels 1962). For example, the ethnic political machine linked immigrants to the political system while also tying them into a tight and bounded web of reciprocity. It promoted cronyism and corruption rather than universalism and the provision of public goods. The aim of the settlement houses, started by religious groups, philanthropists, and social workers in the late nineteenth and early twentieth centuries, was to provide training in language, citizenship, work, and homemaking skills to enable the immigrants to better adapt to the American way of life. The hope was to make them good citizens and employees with contacts outside their immediate neighborhoods and communities. Success varied. The workers' centers started by unions to help immigrant sweatshop workers in the late twentieth and early twenty-first centuries (Ness 1998) are a contemporary alternative. The aim is to provide skills for organizing against employers and demanding protection from government. The unions that pay for the centers want the immigrants to rely on each other and the union leadership to facilitate collective action.

In these and other instances, organizations and associations attempt to build on personal, relational trust to create additional bases for trustworthiness in both the economic and political spheres. Ultimately, however, it is political institutions that provide the protections and opportunities immigrants need to move beyond the close-knit networks and associations that may bond them with each other but fail to give them the capacity to trade or cooperate with others in the larger society. It is depersonalized laws and regulations that ensure them access to wider labor markets, alternative sources of capital, and education. Consequently, they are no longer so dependent on family and no longer need to be bound by the restrictions of kin and tradition.

What distinguishes those cases in which trust relations are likely to be positive and to produce exchange and cooperation with members of the host society and those in which trust relations lead to exploitation and inhibit incorporation into the new country? Slaves and captives fit into the second category by definition, but many who feel forced to make the exodus may fit into either group. It appears that trust relations are useful and essential for both the process of immigration and the process of settlement where there is chain migration in which family and community members sequentially sponsor each other. There is still risk in migrating, but trust relations modify vulnerability. Where migrants have to rely on strangers, even if ethnically related, they are in the realm of high and relatively unmitigated risk, searching for signals of trustworthiness but with relatively little knowledge about or institutional protections against those in whom they must entrust their fate. Migrants, whether or not they are part of a chain, are likely to stay within narrowly bounded networks and associations unless government and other institutions make it safe to explore opportunities in the wider society and make it possible to develop capacities for assessing the reliability of those not intimately known. *The trust networks that facilitate migration may inhibit moving into the larger economy and society of the new home.*

Regime Shifts

Regime shifts take multiple forms, with varying effects on the destruction of trust and trustworthiness and on the potential paths to constructing new bases for cooperation. Revolutions and wars destroy social networks by literally annihilating participants in those networks. The razing of Native American or peasant Vietnamese villages, the shelling of Sarajevo, the massacres of Tutsis and Hutus by each other—these are but a few among countless examples of communities partially or wholly wiped out. In the destruction of such communities, the traditional bases for assessing trustworthiness were destroyed as well. Even those with only the most superficial knowledge of the pre- and postbellum American South, German history, or the recent events in the former Yugoslavia know that violent regime shifts in these communities made even those who once trusted each other as neighbors, friends, and relatives treat each other with suspicion if not downright hostility or worse. Even less violent shifts can have similar effects. Major economic transformations, such as the industrial revolution, the green revolution, or the reintroduction of capitalism into the former Soviet bloc also upset prior grounds for establishing and assessing trustworthiness. Even where strong networks of trust survive the transition, their capacity for securing valued resources may not.[5]

There are also regime shifts that may be said to derive from trust relations. Social revolutions and social movements often build on the close-knit ties developed in communities (Taylor 1988) or in the organizations and groups that mobilize for change (Eckstein 2001; Seidman 1994). Within the economy, trust relations and reciprocity often precede and buttress more complex market relations and credit systems. This certainly seems to have been the case in early modern England (Muldrew 1993). These bases for establishing trustworthiness do not always survive the transformation of the polity or economy, however, and sometimes evolve into exploitative relationships.

In the midst of major transitions and in their immediate aftermath, individuals may tend to rely on personal trust relations when and where possible. If they can, they develop social networks that enlarge the numbers of those with whom they can exchange and cooperate. However, some networks are short-lived, while others evolve into predatory organizations, such as roving bandits (Olson 1993) or the Mafia (Gambetta 1993; Varese 2001); some into governments that remain grounded in personal loyalties and patron-client relationships, such as caudillismo (Eisenstadt and Roniger 1984; Roniger 1990; Stinchcombe 1999, 69–70); and a few into networks with weak ties or even into impartial institutions. It is not inevitable that personal trust will evolve into networks or that networks will form the basis for more extensive trust or the institutions that might ensure widespread bases for cooperation.

Regime shifts, no matter the level of violence, change relations of power, alter norms, transform the organizational ecology, and transform institutions. However, the building of new bases for economic exchange has a logic somewhat distinct from that involved in creating political order and cooperation.

Economic Transitions

Even in the most advanced economies, cooperation among business people depends on some evaluation of each other's trustworthiness that is based, more often than not, on the assessment of the costs of defection from agreements. These costs may involve the loss of reputation, concrete punishment in the form of fines or incarceration, or exclusion from future trade. Networks, organizations, laws, courts, and political institutions provide information and enforcement. When these no longer exist, even long-term trading partners may be unwilling to transact with each other. The risks simply become too high. Personal relationships and reconstructed networks move in to fill the gap, but they easily become exclusive or predatory and can make further expansion of trade more difficult.[6]

We consider two very different kinds of situations that economic shifts produce. The first is a changing and widening of the terms of trade for a particular group but not necessarily for the society as a whole. In the second, the existing economy of an entire country is destroyed and sometimes replaced with a new kind of economic system—for example, when capitalism replaces state socialism. Other times, something closer to economic anarchy arises, as in post-Saddam Iraq.

The integration of a particular group into the larger economy often involves the transformation of intimate relationships into ones that are more market-dependent (see, for example, Ensminger 1992). However, the norms of traditional societies can inhibit efficient and wealth-enhancing investment by those who begin to succeed. Relational commitments facilitate truck, barter, and exchange but also enhance the possibilities of various forms of exploitation.

Aboriginal Australia provides an illustration of the negative externalities of a strong sharing norm. Family membership, which includes numerous connections and relationships, confers the right to demand a share in each other's earnings and possessions. One consequence of this norm is a high degree of egalitarianism, but another is the subjecting of anyone who succeeds to constant demands or "humbugging."[7] "The ethos of sharing on which so much Warlpiri exchange is based was difficult to reconcile with the competing demands the rare item generated" (Dussart 2000, 129). The strategies of successful Aboriginal artists are diverse. Some simply share what they have; one woman saved to buy a used car only to see it immediately driven off (and destroyed) by her grandchildren while she was left behind to walk home. Others share to improve their status or to have fun; one man played poker every night and lost what he had earned but did so as a self-conscious strategy. Others use their dealers to protect a significant proportion of their earnings in order to buy houses or pay for the education of their children. In the first two instances, the artists preferred the restrictions of the community even if it limited their economic advancement. In the third example, Aboriginal artists are exploring ways to evade the burdensome obligations of their communities.

Rotating credit associations, character loans, and other such devices support adaptation to the market and its extension by encouraging entrepreneurial behavior among small-business people, some of whom eventually earn enough and save enough to become creditworthy in the eyes of regular banks. The widely accepted view in the literature on rotating credit associations, however, is that they are intermediate and transitional, a means by which people learn what they need to know when "moving from a static economy to a dynamic one" (Geertz 1962, 242). Rotating credit associations may generally be a poor substitute for a credit market (Besley, Coate, and Loury 1994).

The Aboriginal artists as well as many participants in rotating credit associations have access to a relatively effective rule of law. This provides the artists with legal entitlement to their income should they choose to protect it from "humbuggers." It may provide additional penalties for rotating credit associations against credit defaulters (Hechter 1987, 109). There are many economic transitions, however, in which the state and legal apparatus are ineffective. Norms and relational commitments may still initially increase and ultimately limit the basis for judging who is likely to be a reliable interaction partner, but the penalties for default have to come from community relationships, extended networks, or nonstate institutions.

A different set of problems arises when a whole regime undergoes change. In the first set of cases, we have a community that must adapt to change. The existence of extant trust relations creates both opportunities and problems. In the second set of cases, extended networks are destroyed, and new bases of trustworthiness and reliability must be established. The first impulse is to rely on those with whom one has trust relations, but the reconstruction of the larger economy requires more than that. In a Moroccan bazaar, the costs of search and information encourage repeat interactions, which in turn help traders make judgments about strangers (Geertz 1978). To get beyond a variant of spot markets requires new forms of contracts, but also new forms of relational commitments. Effective trade, even within "primitive societies," depends on the transformation of "an arm's-length contract relationship into an intimate status relationship" (Posner 1980, 26).

As in the migration experience, personal relationships represent the first and usually most accessible way to attain dependable bilateral trading partners, especially where the state is ineffective. In immediate post-Soviet Russia, business dealings were disproportionately among personal acquaintances (42 percent), friends and friends' relatives (17 percent), and relatives (17 percent) (Radaev 2004a). Only 11 percent were with people previously unknown. This pattern reflects an attempt to deal with widespread opportunism and with uncertainty about the content and enforcement of both formal and informal rules. In such circumstances, business people choose to deal mainly with those with whom they have previous relationships that give them some reason to believe the other is trustworthy. Even then, they often take precautionary measures, such as insisting on prepayment or using other devices, such as lock-in, to ensure reliability.

Threats to cut off further trade become more credible, and the costs of defection higher, when lock-in is achieved by means of increased interdependence between the partners in bilateral relationships (McMillan and Woodruff 2000, 2426). A survey of Vietnamese firms during economic transition finds that "most deals among Vietnam's firms . . . rest on unorganized bilateral relational contracting" (2431–32). There is also a strong correlation between the level of credit offered to customers and the level of lock-in: the more competitors nearby, the less lock-in and the lower the credit. Presumably, fewer buyers would have a similar effect. The establishment of relational commitments helps resolve information problems in other markets as well, for example, where the buyer cannot assess the quality of the good (Kollock 1994) or the reliability of trading partners (Uzzi 1996).

Varied kinds of organized private order emerge among traders and among firms, suppliers, customers, and creditors in situations of "dysfunctional public order," that is, ineffective contract enforcement and rule of law by government (McMillan and Woodruff 2000, 2435–45). Examples range from the medieval law merchant to contemporary credit clearinghouses and industry associations, including both legal and criminal organizations. All of these organizations do one or both of two things in addition to expanding economic activity: they provide information about who has broken a contract, and they coordinate a response to breaches of contracts. At the root of these arrangements is the desire of trading partners to maintain their reputations in order to ensure continued business over time. The combination of information provision and investment in reputation makes it possible for individuals in these networks and relationships to assess the trustworthiness, or at least reliability, of others while also assuring others of their own trustworthiness. The fact that these trading arrangements derived from relatively closed networks makes the threat of ostracism especially effective against those who cheat; thus, negative reputation schemes are effective.

Multilateral trade relations depend on reliable middlemen, in the form of individuals, organizations, or businesses. Such middlemen generally have a monetary interest in creating a network of reliable trading partners, helping them locate each other as needed, and offering information about defections in ways that promote effective ostracism. Ethnically homogenous middlemen sometimes serve these purposes (Landa 1994, ch. 5), but there are a variety of possible arrangements. Tocqueville (1835/1990, 387–90) documents the establishment of business networks and organizations in the pre–Civil War United States as well as the importance of trust to business relations. Similar arrangements have emerged among contemporary Russian business people (Radaev 2004). The key seems to be in establishing means for punishing defectors through multilateral reputational mechanisms, such as those embodied in the cultural social networks of the Maghribi traders, the multicultural organization of the Hanseatic League, or the community responsibility system of medieval northern Europe (Greif 1989, 1995; see also Greif 1993; Greif, Milgrom, and Weingast 1994; Milgrom, North, and Weingast 1990). These are organized relationships, regulated by rules and norms, and they are closed networks in which forward-looking reputations matter.

The impetus behind the creation of private-order mechanisms is the desire to establish the reliability of unknown or barely known interaction partners. Not all resulting networks and organizations, however, are benevolent. Triads, cartels, mafias, and the like tend to emerge where opportunities exist for profit from illegal trade in alcohol, drugs, and prostitutes or from the establishment of private security or, more accurately, protection rackets. The so-called Russian Mafia is a case in point (Varese 2000, 2001). The original Sicilian Mafia developed during a period of economic, political, and demographic transition that produced and reproduced "endemic distrust" and led to a demand for private protection by resident landlords (Gambetta 1993, ch. 4 and passim). Ultimately, the Mafia became a full-fledged business, able to maintain itself even when public protection was feasible and even in the face of opposition from major government agencies (Gambetta 1993). It has been able to succeed in part because it created a market that produces and builds on distrust and in part because of the continued weakness of the central state. The Mafia provides productive alternative sources of investment for the capital accumulated by its leadership.

On the other hand, in Russia there may be a transition from protection rackets, extracting tribute, to private protection businesses, which are increasingly disciplined by market forces, eager to become respectable and legal, and willing to help in the fight against criminal elements (Volkov 2002). Such a transformation seems to depend on the growth of the market and of the state. Some observers (for example, Varese 2001) are skeptical that the Mafia is decriminalizing. But it does seem that there are significant variations in Mafia-like organizations across countries, owing to variations in unprotected markets (Varese 2004).

Organized private orders—both bilateral and multilateral, both benevolent and malevolent—are often trumped with the development of the rule of law and security arrangements that provide assurances about the reliability of actors outside these networks. For example, military conquest transformed long-distance trade in the Mediterranean, reducing the advantages of the Maghribi cultural marker. The Maghribi soon disappeared as a separate and distinct social group within the Jewish community (Greif 1989, 879; 1993). There are exceptions to this general rule, of course, as exemplified by failed governmental efforts to eradicate the Sicilian Mafia.

Often increased development of government and legal institutions brings with it specialization in the task of establishing reliability by verifying creditworthiness. For example, in France, the profession of notary, a fiscal intermediary, was both well established by the 1840s and regulated but not standardized by government (Hoffman, Postel-Vinay, and

Rosenthal 2000). There were regional differences in training, rules governing succession to the restricted positions, and other kinds of intermediaries, such as bankers. In the same period, credit agencies, which made their money from selling credit reports, were developing in the United States (Carruthers and Cohen 2001). They initially acquired the information on which the reports were based from local informants and correspondents. Brokers, banks, and other specialized intermediaries were also on the rise in this period, as were increased training and professionalization (Zucker 1986). The combination of organizational development and more competent intermediaries helped build confidence among lenders and borrowers and among suppliers and purchasers. These innovations facilitated networks with weak ties, more extensive markets, and larger businesses than were possible with reliance only on networks of individuals connected tightly through family or ethnicity.

These arrangements represent innovations in devising institutions that supplemented organizational and network bases for ensuring reliability. Well-designed rules, regulations, and monitoring arrangements facilitate the provision of information, the coordination of behavior, and the punishment of defectors. The most important institution for promoting trade is, of course, enforceable contract law. Its absence often gives rise to the variety of network and organizational institutions described earlier. However, its presence neither ensures the dissolution of networks that severely delimit exchange and cooperation nor necessarily drives out growth-enhancing networks and organizations. Effective legal and governmental institutions are not sufficient conditions for markets that are both wide and deep. They are nonetheless necessary conditions for both extensive economic exchange and well-run polities. Thus, it is to their transition that we now turn.

Political and Legal Transitions

Regime shifts often destroy extant institutions that supported reliability. The breakdown of legal institutions, most specifically effective police and court organizations able to enforce the law, tends to increase social anxiety about strangers on the street, taxi drivers, and shopkeepers—not to speak of partners in more complex exchanges and transactions. The breakdown of the regulatory apparatus more generally can produce a decrease in the reliability of various kinds of service providers who are no longer monitored or accountable.

In chapter 8, we discussed the issues involved in making government and its legal institutions reliable and the consequences for economic and political behavior. The focus here is on how the relations and networks of trust that are established and made useful during major political transformations affect the possibility of building confidence in government and law among those outside the foundational network of trust. Networks can play an important role in political transitions, just as they do in immigration and business. Networks may facilitate collective action and mobilization. Networks that enable elites to form trust relations with each other may support the establishment of governing coalitions. Networks that build trust relations between elites and non-elites—as in nineteenth-century Marxist societies of workers and intellectuals or the American abolitionist movement's coalitions of the wealthy and former slaves—may contribute to the formation of political parties and formal organizations. Such networks do not always or necessarily, however, form the building blocks of governments that promote economic growth or democracy. What these networks can accomplish and how they evolve are the subjects of the following discussion.

Tight social networks undoubtedly facilitate local solutions to common resource problems in the absence of the state, as revealed in the evidence of protection of forests and game in Africa (Barkan and Holmquist 1989; Barkan, McNulty, and Ayeni 1991; Bates 1991; Boone 2003; Gibson 1999), of water in Nepal and Turkey (Ostrom 1990, 1998), and of fish stock among the Pacific Northwest Native Americans (Singleton 1998), among other places and groups. In all these cases, trust relationships allowed individuals to have confidence that others would not free-ride in their joint protection of a common pool resource. Some of these cases have the structure of an assurance game, and others involve community norms rather than trust relations per se, but all depend on closed networks in which horizontal relations prevail. Networks can also be the basis for protection against military and criminal attack. Examples include the local militias formed by the American frontier colonists in response to their insecurity amid colonizers and Indians (Mahon 1983) and the night watches formed among citizens in the early days of capitalism. Both were prompted by the belief that it is essential to identify who is reliable in an unsafe environment, affiliate with them, and collectively fight those suspected of interests antagonistic to those within the organization.

The American and British militias evolved into national armies with territorial units. The night watches morphed into private security organizations, such as the Pinkertons, and into municipal police forces (Fogelson 1977). However, community-based and private protection services do not always transform themselves into public institutions. Gangs and protection rackets may be built on tight networks of trust, but they are predatory organizations that thrive as long as there is private gain and inadequate capacity to counter them. The Pinkertons and other private security companies in the United States eventually came under government regulation and were compelled to abide by the law to survive. Individuals who are involved with gangs and protection rackets usually intend to survive outside the law. When they achieve sufficient foothold and size, they make it difficult to establish effective law enforcement and impartial government—as in the case of the Sicilian Mafia or the gangs intertwined with Tammany Hall in nineteenth-century New York.

There are other kinds of illegal organizations that develop to protect customs and norms as well as property. The Luddites, the Ku Klux Klan, and a wide variety of nationalist terrorist groups are illustrative. These are not cases where government is lacking but where an economic or political transition has reinforced the belief that government is morally untrustworthy and must be defended against. The members of these networked groups usually trust each other but distrust government, and they are often very difficult to eradicate. They can threaten the rule of law and political stability until they are destroyed, die out, can be bought off, or emerge sufficiently victorious to consolidate order under their rule.

The persistence of oppositional organizations and voluntary associations creates one set of problems for the success of political transitions. Equally important is the persistence of legal networks within the government apparatus. The cohort that foments a successful revolution or military coup is often the group that governs. In the process, they learn which of the others are reliable, and they may distrust virtually everyone else. Usually their illegal and dangerous opposition to those in power requires concealing their identities as rebels until they have a good chance of victory. This is the principle of Leninism in theory (Lenin 1902/1963) and, in Lenin's case, initially in practice (Solzhenitsyn 1977). However, as is obvious from history—and Shakespeare—distrust often develops among the victors. This is especially the case when there is competition over important roles. The image that comes to mind is the scene from the stage musical *Evita* where the colonels plot together to take power, succeed, and then play musical chairs, as they always knew they would. All but Juan Peron are eliminated; in the musical, the others leave the stage, but in real life they may be assassinated, imprisoned, or simply given secondary roles in which they are closely monitored.

Patron-client relationships and other "precarious pyramids of personal political contracts" (Stinchcombe 1999, 69) often form the basis of governing factions as the state is built or rebuilt. In fact, some are far from precarious, lasting centuries (Gellner 1988; Searle 1988). Crony capitalism is a persistent problem today in Korea, the Philippines, and elsewhere (Kang 2002). Overthrowing particular heads of states, as was done with Ferdinand Marcos in 1986, does not necessarily get rid of the problem. Governing where there are murderous rivals often results in "a series of groups which are both cohesive and fragile, which perpetuate themselves by means of loyalty, and adjust to new realities by treason, whether formalized, pious or sudden" (Gellner 1988, 147).

New voluntary associations and political parties are also often grounded in networks, third-party intermediaries, and personalized relationships. The reemergence of old networks within the previously Soviet countries supports the reemergence of Communist successor parties (Grzymala-Busse 2002), which at the least raises questions about the nature of the change. Even new networks or networks based in resistance can become self-perpetuating elites under some conditions (Kitschelt et al. 1999). Thus, it is not surprising that survey evidence reveals that many citizens of Eastern Europe label their new political parties and governments as "untrustworthy" because they know how their members behaved in the past and thus they have rational doubts that these same individuals will live up to the promises of democracy and capitalism (Mishler and Rose 1997).

Past collaboration with a now-hated regime can taint current leaders in government and civil society (see, for example, Barahona de Brito, Gonzalez-Enriquez, and Aguilar 2001; Cohen 1995; Horne and Levi 2004). Consequently, several Central and Eastern European governments have now introduced lustration laws requiring that candidates for public office reveal their past and that their records be investigated thoroughly. The problem takes a different form in countries such as South Africa, where there is a desire to integrate past supporters of apartheid into the new regime. There the aim is to reintegrate people into the society through the truth and reconciliation process, which involves public confession and forgiveness.

Those who grew up within the new regime are more likely than their parents to come to their jobs with records untainted by past collaboration. Their socialization, education, and experience will also have been different. Hence, the new generations in Poland and, by implication, other Eastern European populations are liberated from the legacy of the "cultures of distrust" that marked their elders (Sztompka 1999, 190). From the perspective offered in this book, what is most likely to bring about generational shifts is an improved expectation about the responsiveness and reliability of government. Where that expectation is not met or is betrayed, distrust of the state is more likely, as is intergroup distrust. Perceptions of the reliability (or what the survey research labels "trust") of governments, parties, and leaders are said to be important in providing support for fragile democratic institutions in Eastern Europe and South Africa (Gibson 2001; Offe 1999; Rose 1994; Rose, Mishler, and Haerpfer 1998; Sztompka 1996, 1998, 1999), but so is healthy skepticism (Mishler and Rose 1997).

People once distrusted may be judged reliable in a transformed environment. Witness the universal plaudits for Mayor Rudolph Giuliani in the wake of the September 11 bombings! Even many of the severest critics of Giuliani's mayoralty credited him as an extraordinary manager of the city in the aftermath of the disaster. In transitions, shifts in perception of reliability may have as much to do with who is making the judgment as with the situation itself. For the British, Jawaharlal Nehru was a criminal, as was Nelson Mandela for the apartheid government of South Africa. Both spent time in prison, despised and distrusted by those who had a right to vote and govern in their countries. Upon the transformation of their governments and the power base upon which they rested, both of these men became popularly elected and respected heads of state, internationally acclaimed as world-class leaders. Within their countries, however, they were seen as representing the interests of particular networks and coteries and not necessarily the entire populace. Fears of post-independence violence in India were fulfilled after Nehru took power; fears of intertribal warfare continue to haunt post-Mandela South Africa.

The attribution of trustworthiness to one who was superb in a crisis or as a revolutionary leader or general can often be a chimera. Qualities that are effective for one purpose are not necessarily the best characteristics for another, and charisma often leads people to make choices on poor grounds. Nor are these leaders always as impartial and above the temptation of cronyism as it may once have appeared. These are cases where assessments of trustworthiness and reliability are mistaken owing to cognitive bias, misinformation, or a misperception of the salient qualities of leadership for the situation.

This discussion has reviewed the problems created by the networks of trust that emerge during the uncertainties of transition and that cling to special power and privilege after the transition is complete. We have shown that it is not trust relations or networks of trust but certain kinds of institutionalized reliability that are essential for stable, economically productive, and potentially democratic government.

Concluding Remarks

By undermining preexisting institutions, organizations, and networks, transitions alter the relationships among individuals and therefore the bases for trustworthiness and reliability. Positive reputations are lost and gained. Often the reliability of information is reduced during a transition, but nearly always the changes in the kind and quality of information lead to changes in the assessment of who is trustworthy or reliable. Individuals seem to turn to familiar trust relations in times of transition, at least initially. Ongoing relationships and close-knit networks provide information about motivations and interests through intimate knowledge of the others in the network, and they also provide incentives for reliability. However, trust relations are a limited basis for societywide cooperation and exchange, and they can be fragile or nonexistent even among family members. There are incentives to create networks based on weak ties, which offer access to a wider range of people. Such networks open up greater opportunities but also new risks. Reliance moves to friends of friends, and the incentives to maintain relationships are less direct.

The incentives and information provided through networks of weak ties may be incomplete and imperfect, and these networks definitely restrict the range of partners for cooperation and exchange. This is why societies increasingly rely on contract law and courts to regulate markets and on elaborated arrangements for monitoring, enforcing, and making accountable those who govern. Without reliable police, judges, governors, and citizens, the market and the state would be far more costly to manage. They would also be more unstable and unpleasant.

But how do reliable institutions and individuals emerge? We know more about what prevents than facilitates them. The relationships, networks, and organizations that provided the bases for cognitive assessments of reliability during the transition often inhibit further change. People may be fearful of others, not only those they do not know but also those they once knew well but in a different context. The activation of ethnic and other identities can make enemies of those who were once intimates. Some individuals may value the benefits and power they have under the current arrangement. To interact enough with others to begin to cooperate with them may require risks and losses too high to undertake.

This discussion has revealed that social scientists possess only a rudimentary understanding of the process by which trustworthiness established in one context gives people the means to develop confidence in each other and in institutions outside that context. We know it is hard to move from one coordination equilibrium to another, especially when there are many benefits to be gained from staying within the network and many risks involved in leaving it.

We have argued throughout this book that trust relations are less important in complex societies than the establishment of devices for ensuring trustworthiness and reliability. We also find that distrust and lack of trust are more likely than trust to drive the search for arrangements that reduce our risks and to motivate us to create the institutions and organizations that allow us to cooperate with each other and treat each other as trustworthy. The establishment of trust relations may indeed lubricate cooperation and exchange, as Kenneth Arrow and many others have argued. However, it seems to do so only if cooperation is among a small set of people or where the risks are low or institutional design removes the potential for serious exploitation. For most of us most of the time, when we cooperate, it is without trust.

Chapter 10

The Role of Trust in Society

IF WE reflect on the wide range of interactions in which we have to rely on others whom we would not be able to trust on the model of encapsulated interests, we must realize that it dwarfs the range of those interactions that are actually grounded in trust relationships. The latter might be our richest relationships, but they are not our most numerous. Hence, there is a great need for powerful and often sophisticated devices to secure cooperative interactions. Although there are many empirical studies of such devices, there has been little or no systematic effort to bring them together as we have done in this book. We have attempted to describe some especially important or interesting institutions and social practices, both historical and contemporary, for structuring interactions in ways that make cooperation work and social order possible. Because these institutions and practices, which work reasonably well without trust, might often eventually lead to trust through the ongoing relationships they help to constitute, *they often are genuine alternatives to trust.* And some of these practices might even exacerbate distrust, as must be true of the feud and the duel, both of which may have helped to secure social order in some ways even while threatening that order in specific moments.

At least since the time of Hobbes's *Leviathan* (1651/1968), the state has been seen as the primary instrument for facilitating peaceful and productive cooperation and social order. However, there are many institutions nearly as powerful as government in regulating individual behavior, and we have given some attention to these as well. Indeed, many institutions are more powerful with respect to certain behaviors than government could be. The family, the village community, the firm, and professional associations are among them. These institutions commonly have access to information on behavior that it would be difficult and expensive for government to collect, and they also have devices for delivering sanctions that are typically unavailable to government with its universalistic and rule-bound procedures. Government is especially capable of collecting aggregate information and applying very general, standardized rules. Although street-level bureaucrats, such as police officers and welfare workers, can sometimes craft responses to individual cases, such flexibility is most often *not* available to government officials.

The growth of such institutions, even to the point of tending toward being agencies of government, can substantially affect how they deal with individuals such as clients or patients. For example, the increasingly complex structure of medical delivery has radically affected the understanding of medical responsibility, which no longer resembles the quaint principles of the Hippocratic Oath.[1] That oath simply assumed that doctors would deal with *anyone* in need. Modern institutional medical agencies first must decide whom to serve and whom to exclude, and health service organizations and insurers, as more powerful actors than the patients they supposedly serve, frequently erect obstacles to getting medical care. Once such choices get in the way, it is hard to see the principles of medical care as being strictly concerned with what a universal doctor should do for a universal patient.

More generally, when great power differences exist between parties, it is rare that trust relations provide proper protection for the interests of the less powerful (such as patients or clients) or adequate safeguards against exploitation; this is true in business and law as well as medicine, not to mention in other contexts in which power relations are common. If trust relations emerge at all in such settings, they typically arise in the context of ongoing relations of mutual dependence in which *both* parties have at least something at stake, and often against the backdrop of institutional or organizational incentives that mitigate the potential for harm. In addition to the widely cited claim that trust is required for society to function well, it is often observed that social capital (sometimes defined as including trust) is in decline, with potentially negative consequences for social order.[2]

Social Capital in Decline?

One might say that sociology got its early life from the identification and analysis of informal social organization, which is to say that, although the label was not yet available, early sociology was substantially the analysis of social capital: how it worked and for whom it worked. Long before the observations of Stewart Macauley (1963) and Ian Macneil (1980) on the extralegal, informal aspects of contracts, Émile Durkheim (1893/1933, 162) analyzed the noncontractual elements of contracts, which he viewed as of social origin. Similarly, long before Mark Granovetter (1985) popularized discussions of the "embeddedness" of our lives and choices in broader social arrangements and its effects, Georg Simmel (1902/1964, 1908/1955) focused on "the web of group affiliations."

In recent debates, social capital has become a centerpiece in the analysis of democratic political participation. Perhaps the arena in which social capital would be democratically most important is the electoral arena, in which participation by citizens is neither extremely high nor dramatically in decline. Indeed, citizen participation in determining who will be the candidates for various political offices in the United States may well be increasing not through their voting so much as through their participation in many other ways. In the 2004 presidential election, young citizens with great skill at using the Internet had a substantial impact on every aspect of the campaign from the selection of the Democratic challenger to the re-election of the Republican president George Bush. The Internet represents a form of networking that far surpasses anything anyone could have done at such low cost two or more decades ago, and it is a form of social capital that has also grown enormously in that time (Lin 2001; Wellman 1998; see *Analyse und Kritik* 2004). Indeed, it is a standard quip that the movement against globalization has required the globalizing power of the Internet even to mobilize its supporters. Moveon.org may represent to date the most extensive use of the Internet to support political activism in history.

In Robert Putnam's (1995a, 1995b, 2000) argument for *declining* social capital, the evidence is a fairly systematic set of correlations of declines in various things, such as memberships in many and varied kinds of organized face-to-face groups. Everett Ladd (1996, 1999) presents contrary data and claims that certain major organizations (including parent-teacher associations and the Boy Scouts of America) face stiff competition from new organizations that are much harder to track because many are local and have no national headquarters. What is at stake in this debate seems to be not *individual access to social capital* but *groups' having social capital*, as discussed in chapters 5 and 9. Much of the argument turns on simple correlations: declining group memberships correlate with declining electoral turnout or declining confidence in government. Until we are given a causal mechanism for these correlations, we cannot even be sure what the problem is. Is it declines in individual access to social capital, or declines in groups' having social capital, or both?

Even if we grant that there are serious declines in general participation in Putnam's civic groups, it is virtually impossible to demonstrate empirically that the result of such declines is a government that is less competent or less responsive, especially given that "competence" and "responsiveness" are exceedingly hard enough to define, let alone measure. Many people think American national government is less competent and less responsive than in earlier times, but many do not, and this difference in perceptions might correlate better with political views than with causal understandings of government effectiveness. Some of us think any Republican or Tory regime is less responsive; others think any Democratic or Labour regime is less responsive. Declines in social capital may not be the issue, and more generally social capital defined as individual and group access to networks that provide resources or other forms of support may be put to good use or ill. Nothing in the definition of social capital requires that it be put to good uses only. Furthermore, social capital may constrain as well as enable.

The Social Evolution of Trust Relations

In chapter 6, we noted that science is evolving away from trust relationships toward externally regulated behavior. We noted there that the change toward big science done by huge teams of scientists with different, complementary specialties is necessarily detrimental to trust within science. The many scientists involved in a big particle physics project or in mapping the genome cannot oversee each other's work, and they cannot be involved enough in close dyadic or small-number interactions with each other to establish trust as encapsulated interest. (They also cannot have trust for each other grounded in moral commitments to trustworthiness or dispositions of character because they generally cannot know all the others in a huge team well enough to be able to assess their moral commitments or character dispositions.) These scientists depend on networks of control. Those networks might work well enough, but the knowledge they give is socially produced and not objectively assessable by the individual scientists.

This development in big science is interesting not because it is unusual but because it is so clearly similar to other arenas of public life (if a bit later in developing) in which *trust cannot play a large role because the relationships between all the relevant parties cannot be rich enough to ground trust.* The changes in scientific practice over the past five or six decades mirror the changes in professional practice in medicine and law. In medicine, practice has changed in large part because biological science has become radically more complex and richer than it was when the AMA was created. In any case, all three of these arenas point up how dramatically overwrought are all claims that social organization and cooperation require trust and how much they ultimately miss the mark.

A related but equally problematic claim is that the best means of overcoming the serious consequences of intergroup distrust is to develop trust. Consider one particularly commonplace claim: that we need to build trust between two—usually ethnic—groups to get them to live together in peace and end the murderous conflict between them. This pervasive supposition that we need mainly to lead people into trusting relationships to get them to be civilized is false. As Madison remarks in *Federalist* number 55, "Had every Athenian been a Socrates, every Athenian assembly would still have been a mob" (quoted in Hamilton, Jay, and Madison 1787/2001, 288). The road to peace in the Middle East or Bosnia or to harmony in the Sudan or Rwanda is not sensibly paved through developing trust. It is paved through constructing institutions that can operate successfully in such societies *despite the lack of trust, even despite pervasive and active distrust.* This is not a claim that somehow these societies are fundamentally different from societies that seem to be civilized today.[3] Highly civilized Great Britain went through a vicious and destructive civil war that wracked the society for more than a generation in the seventeenth century; that war was fought over religious differences that can only seem ludicrous to most Britons today. It was this vicious, brutal era that stimulated Hobbes to write his *Leviathan* and led him to believe that the creation of a powerful draconian monarch was the only hope for social order and civilization.[4]

As eventually happened in Great Britain, economic success commonly displaces religious conflicts (Hirschman 1977). More generally, when personal success in the economy trumps the individual's share of group success in politics, politics changes and ceases to be organized around exclusionary—even murderously exclusionary—groups. This is not the whole story, of course, because, for example, religious atavism can intrude even in an economically prosperous society, as it has done in the United States in recent years, so that people vote for so-called religious values that are extremely exclusionary and against their own economic interests. Furthermore, building bridges of trust between such exclusive groups is often difficult in the face of close-knit within-group trust relations that often breed distrust of outsiders.[5]

The evolution of social relations in complex societies away from communal groups and normative control to networks of informal association occasionally based on trust may have diminished the general role of trust in society, if only because so many of our activities are now based on arm's-length relations with those we barely know and yet cooperate with on a daily basis. But, as we argue, cooperation without trust can happen generally only against the backdrop of reliable political institutions and organizations that provide insurance against harm or failure.

The Roads Not Taken

Throughout this book, we have relied on a particular theory or conception of trust—a relational conception—and we have used it to explain many phenomena, from individual behaviors to institutional structures. We have discussed two other conceptions of trust that are often proposed in the literature: trust based on belief in another individual's trustworthiness because he or she is apparently morally committed or has a strong psychological disposition (perhaps of character) to be trustworthy. But we have not put these other conceptions to use here. Why?

Belief in another's moral commitment is possibly the most frequently cited definition of trust. But it has been put to use in almost no explanations beyond descriptive claims that *A trusts B because A believes that B is morally committed to being trustworthy.* Often the descriptive claims are far more elliptical than this in that they do not even acknowledge that the necessary element here is *trustworthiness*, not trust, which is merely the assessment of trustworthiness. It seems unlikely that such a conception can fit any substantial part of the findings we discuss in this book, especially any substantial part of the explanation of general social order. Both the moral and dispositional theories of trustworthiness are psychological conceptions and thus, ironically, must be very nearly irrelevant to sociological claims for the trustworthiness of institutions.

The claim that trustworthiness is a disposition of character is perhaps less often asserted, although it is implicit in the early work of Julian Rotter (1967, 1971, 1980) and explicit in the work of Toshio Yamagishi (2001). Sometimes the claim that trust is a matter of character or disposition is related to recognition of the importance of your reputation in motivating people to cooperate with you. It seems at least as likely that attention to reputation plays into the encapsulated interest view because the greater importance of reputation is forward-looking: because you have a good reputation, it is typically in your interest to live up to it in order to make yourself seem reliable for future dealings and to encourage others to develop cooperative relationships with you. The tendency to think of reputation as merely about someone's past actions severely downplays its significance. That view of reputation would be of central importance, however, to a dispositional theory of trustworthiness, because past reputation could be taken as evidence of your disposition.

The moral and dispositional accounts of trustworthiness are generally not a good way to go in explaining social choices and outcomes. A useful account should make trust and distrust analogous but contrary conceptions. But there is a strong asymmetry between trust and distrust in these two other accounts of trust. *There is no aura of morality or of deep psychological commitments in distrust, which is almost necessarily grounded in a reading of the intentions (or competence) of the object of distrust.* Someone distrusts you because of things you do or conflicting interests you have with that person. One might read backwards from distrust to say that any useful conception of trust should mirror it. But accounts that make trust part of either the morality or the psychology of the potential trusted party *do not mirror natural accounts of distrust.* All of us sometimes distrust specific others for reasons we can typically articulate and that have to do with the nature or past actions of those individuals. Of course, we must also ground our assessment of a particular person's dispositions or moral commitments in his or her nature or past actions. But you might rightly conclude that A is to be distrusted, while I think A is eminently trustworthy. What does such a conclusion imply about these more psychological approaches to trust?

If A's trustworthiness is grounded in a fixed moral commitment or psychological disposition, why should A rightly be trusted by some and distrusted by others? We can make easy sense of such differences only if we assume that *trust is relational: trust turns on specific interactions within specific relationships.* A is trustworthy to us because she has an ongoing relationship with us that grounds her trustworthiness toward us. She is untrustworthy to you because she does not have such a relationship with you, or because she has other interests that trump her maintenance of a cooperative relationship with you.

Such instances of highly specific, personalized distrust in the midst of many trusting relationships cannot be part of our standard, almost fixed stance toward those around us, whether moral, psychological, or rationally self-interested. If we want to analyze distrust in terms of these more psychological conceptions of trust, we must therefore either leave it untheorized (a common move when the discussion is at the vernacular level) or see it as something like the negative side of the encapsulated interest theory of trust because it is a more sociological, relational conception. The dispositional and moral theories of trust cannot logically handle distrust as a negative analogue of trust. Several years ago Robert Merton (in conversation with one of the authors in 1994) argued that we cannot finally expect to understand trust if we do not also come to understand distrust. The evidence of many examples analyzed in this book suggests the power of Merton's observation.

We can fully accept that someone distrusts A, whom we trust, without for a moment supposing that one or the other of us must therefore be mistaken in our judgment of A's character or morality. In such a case, we de facto reject any theory that says trust and distrust are inherently based in assessments of the character or the morality of the potentially trusted or distrusted person or agent. A moral theory of distrust can make sense only of certain relatively circumscribed cases and not of the general run of cases in our experience. The only compelling account of distrust in many cases—perhaps most cases that we can imagine or that we experience—is the analogue of the encapsulated interest theory of trust. *We distrust particular others because we are sure that their interests conflict substantially with our own on relevant matters or that they have no concern with our interests.* They do not encapsulate our interests in their own—perhaps not at all, but in any case not enough to override their own conflicting interests. We therefore expect them to go with their own interests against ours. Because they do not encapsulate our interests in their own, they do not substantially value maintaining a relationship with us. Hence, they are likely to prefer to act in favor of their own interests and against ours even at the cost of wrecking any chance of an ongoing relationship with us.

It would be quite difficult to suppose that another person's interests conflict with ours *only* if he is not morally committed to being trustworthy. To what range of possible actions would his trustworthiness apply—any and every action? Conflicts of interest are often embedded in social and institutional roles and thus cannot simply be about conflicting character dispositions or morals. In addition, it would be strange to suppose that an individual's character disposition requires actions against his own interests even on behalf of people whose relationship he would not especially care to maintain.

Finally, apart from the three conceptions of trust we discussed in chapter 1, there are other more idiosyncratic accounts of what trust is (for example, Becker 1996; Held 1968; Hertzberg 1988; Hollis 1998; Jones 1996; Mansbridge 1999; Seligman 1997; Williamson 1993). These perspectives on trust generally do not lead to coherent explanations of behavior or social structures, and they tend to remain idiosyncratic in the sense that few other scholars attempt to apply them. Many of these approaches unfortunately use the term "trust" in their definitions of trust as though taking for granted what it means or treating it as a primitive term. For example, Martin Hollis (1998, 10–11) says there are two forms of trust: trust in the predictability of others and trust of one another to do what is (morally) right (for a partial survey of the wide variety of such [often essentialist] accounts of trust, see Hardin 2002b). We have generally not dealt with these less systematic accounts here, and we suspect that most of them do not have wide application despite the fact that they often provide useful and clever insights.

Cross-Societal Differences

In the vast literature on trust, there has been relatively little focus on cultural differences in providing the conditions for building trust relations. On our view of trust as encapsulated interest, trust relations may vary from culture to culture as a result of differences in the social structures and institutions that exist to support cooperation and the norms that apply to social relations in general. Such differences and their implications for the analysis of cooperation without trust have yet to be investigated in any depth. In conclusion, we open this topic for brief discussion by noting that it is an important area for future investigation. What explains which devices are used under what conditions to secure cooperation, especially when trust relations are no longer viable as a prominent mode of achieving productive social exchange?

In this respect, we might ask whether the conditions for trust are better in some societies or cultures than in others. For example, people in one culture may be more inclined to take risks on cooperating with others (Buchan, Croson, and Dawes 2002). However, it is at least as likely that variation in trust relations has far more to do with the extent of their knowledge of others, consistent with the encapsulated interest view. Consider differences between long-settled and resettled villages in Zimbabwe (Barr 2004). Individuals are less willing to take risks in the resettled villages, but primarily because their kinship networks and information sources are less dense.[6]

There is even some doubt about the role of trust in some well-ordered societies. We earlier discussed the role of communal norms as an alternative to trust. Indeed, it seems that many traditional societies succeed in achieving mutual cooperation without trust, as the anthropologist Fredrik Barth (1985) has argued. For example, among the Swat, a tribe based in what is now Pakistan, men agreed to join the leader's army in exchange for the use of land, other material awards, and hospitality from landlords, who in turn owed fealty to the leader or Wali because of his role as a mediator in their disputes. According to Barth, no one in this society trusted anyone else or acted on the basis of morality. Instead, they used fear and respect to elicit obedience. Most importantly, they acted strategically to increase their power over others through the dependence of others on them. They distrusted those with whom they cooperated, but they cooperated as long as they perceived that they would individually benefit from the relationship.

Looking at contexts in which societies are undergoing massive change gives us some clues to what is necessary for trust (as opposed to what trust is necessary for). Trust as encapsulated interest depends on somewhat stable relationships so that the incentives of an ongoing interaction keep us trustworthy. When societies are radically destabilized, trust relations may collapse. Moreover, we might expect that trust relations would be more suitable in some earlier social states than they are today in the advanced industrial states or in the parts of the developing world that are in great flux. If we could graph the relative frequency of trust relations in regulating social cooperation over many generations, we might expect it to be curvilinear, with trust rising to displace control by social norms and then fading to be displaced by regulation by modern social institutions. Cooperation and coordination would be monotonically increasing throughout these developments. In many contexts, reliance on trust relations is not the most effective device for improving people's lives through social interactions.

With a clear conception of trust and how it works, we could use it not only to explain behaviors and social outcomes but also to explain differences in forms and degrees of cooperativeness in different soci-eties. This possibility leaves a large research agenda for the future.

Concluding Remarks

It is not surprising that trust has become a central issue in social science as well as in the popular press over the past several decades. As global-ization has taken hold and interconnectedness across continents has in-creased dramatically, citizens everywhere have become more wary of the stranger in their midst. In addition, the competition for resources world-wide has added to the worry of groups and nations about their future eco-nomic prospects. Locally, law, medicine, science, commerce, and many other aspects of our lives are increasingly a part of large systems in which the individual monitoring that is necessary for trust on any of the stan-dard explanatory accounts of trustworthiness is certainly beyond our ca-pacities (Luhmann 1980). *Societies are essentially evolving away from trust relationships toward externally regulated behavior.* Trust has force for us only in those contexts in which it is possible for us to judge others for their likely or actual trustworthiness in our dealings with them. Of necessity, this can include only a small fraction of the people on whose actions our lives depend. We interact directly and indirectly with millions of people, the overwhelming majority of whom we could not trust on *any* standard account of trust or trustworthiness.

One might claim that we have less trust in our lives than our forebears had in theirs. That claim is probably true if we are speaking of proportions of our interactions. *We do not have trust relations with most of the people we deal with.* In a small village a century or more ago, most people dealt only with other people who were well known to them as individuals who could be trusted or not trusted. In that era, however, trust might have been otiose much of the time because social norms carried sufficient force to induce people to be cooperative.

In the advanced industrial societies of today, we do not live enmeshed in such thick relationships, and we depend on trusting relationships with many people—especially those with whom we cooperate through net-works focused on particular matters—but we cannot establish such rela-tionships with vast numbers of others with whom we deal. Contrary to the claim that we have less trust in our lives in general, it seems likely that we have actual trusting relationships with a far broader and larger range of people than our forebears did. The proportion of trust in our relation-ships may have declined, but the incidence of trust has arguably increased substantially. Our lives are more complex, more productive, and more co-operative in more arenas than could have been true a few generations ago. Trust is surely increasing, not decreasing. But many other forms of coop-eration are also increasing. In particular, massive institutionalization of most of life makes modern society possible when mere trust could not have done so.

Still, we might be bothered by the declining overall proportion of trust relationships in our lives. The doomsayers who think that declining trust means declining social cooperativeness, however, may be wrong for the complexly varied reason that *we can motivate cooperativeness through manifold devices,* as discussed in earlier chapters of this book. Trust relations are certainly not the only route to cooperation, nor are they the most prevalent. Indeed, we have canvassed only a tiny fraction of the devices that societies use to secure cooperative social relations. Hollis (1998, 23) speculates that trust and economic progress have a perverse, perhaps circular, interaction. The more we trust each other, the better we are able to cooperate, and therefore the better are our prospects for economic progress. But with greater economic success we become more instrumentally rational, and therefore we trust less. However, he argues, we still need trust for economic progress. Our book presents many arguments for why we do not *need* trust in any such grand sense, even though at the personal level relational trust makes our day-to-day lives richer and more manageable. More often, however, and in many varied contexts, we cooperate without trust.

Notes

Chapter 1

1. Putnam (1993a, 1995b) initially made the claim much broader by including trust in what he refers to as social capital, a claim he revised in his later book (Putnam 2000). The ordinary language uses of trust are manifold and not well articulated, see Hardin (2002b, ch. 3) for a fuller discussion of alternative perspectives on trust.
2. The actor could be an agent for another individual or even a corporate actor, although that often complicates the assessment of trustworthiness (see chapters 2 and 6 on conflict of interests and chapter 7 on principal-agent relations).
3. Hertzberg (1988) is an exception to this claim, and Mansbridge (1999) is a partial exception in that she genuinely holds it to be morally required to trust.
4. Over the years, researchers have used other labels to describe what the NES questions measure, including "political cynicism," "disaffection," and "alienation" (see Citrin and Muste 1999).

Chapter 2

1. Recently several studies have probed the roots of different levels of cautiousness or risk-taking in various societies; see, for example, Weber, Hsee, and Sokolowska (1998) and Hsee and Weber (1999).
2. In addition, Stephen Standifird (2001) has studied the impact of reputation in one area of e-commerce: the importance of a trader's reputation on the final bidding price. While he finds positive reputational ratings to be only mildly influential in determining the final bid price, he finds negative reputational ratings to be highly influential and detrimental. In other words, Standifird finds "strong evidence for the importance of reputation . . . and equally strong evidence concerning the *exaggerated influence of negative reputation*" (279, emphasis added).
3. One example would be the well-known efforts on the part of Internet trading companies to develop reputation systems to facilitate transactions among unknown parties; see Kollock (1999) and McCabe, Rassenti, and Smith (1998).
4. In a vignette experiment, Vincent Buskens and Jeroen Weesie (2000) asked participants to reply to questions about a transaction between a buyer and a used-car dealer. The nature of the past relationship between the buyer and the dealer

and information about the likelihood of a future transaction were varied in the vignette. The study showed strong effects for past dealings as well as for reputational information from third parties about their past dealings on trust and on willingness to engage in the transaction. Surprisingly, a weaker effect was obtained for the shadow of the future (the implication that the buyer and dealer would transact again in the future), but this result may have been weak owing to the use of the vignette methodology.

5. Bacharach and Gambetta (2001) have developed a paradigm for studying the "second-order" problem of trust: determining whether one can trust the signals that are meant to convey trustworthiness.

6. There are more than three devices in the large literature on credible commitments, but some of these are devices to establish one's trustworthiness. A very important part of the literature is on devices to secure institutional commitments. For example, for monarchs to get taxes or loans under conditions that give them the power to renege on promised services or default as borrowers, they must find ways to tie their own hands (Levi 1988; North and Weingast 1989; Root 1989). They do this by ceding taxing and budgetary power to parliaments, whose members' interests are sufficiently different from the crown's and whose control of military and political resources is sufficiently great that they can punish rulers who break promises. Credible commitments were also at the heart of the institutional arrangements that made long-distance trade and economic growth possible in medieval Europe, as discussed in chapter 9.

7. Much of the literature is about the use of commitments in contexts in which trust is not an issue at all. For example, individuals find devices to commit themselves not to succumb to addiction or laziness (Elster 1979; Schelling 1978; see also Dixit and Nalebuff 1991; Nesse 2003).

Chapter 3

1. Continuing the analogy, Granovetter (2002, 38) identifies the behavioral differences that result from power and trust: "the behavioral consequences of power are domination and compliance; these are parallel to cooperation, the behavioral consequence of trust or solidarity." This theoretical view implies that there is little or no compliance as a result of trust and little or no cooperation that results from the exercise of power. It seems that trust, although perhaps limited in scope and depth, can emerge in the context of relations characterized by power inequality, and correspondingly that power can be exercised in the context of trust relations, even though, as Linda Molm (1997) suggests, it may be used quite sparingly in relations viewed as reciprocal, trusting relations.

2. Perhaps the most common definition of power in the political science literature is the definition introduced by Robert Dahl (1957): the ability of A to get B to do something that B would not have done otherwise. This is a version of what came to be known as the "power as social causation" perspective (see Clegg 2001). The debate in this literature, including the developments after the work of Dahl, contrast this view of power with the simple view of power as resources.

3. Power is defined by Emerson as inversely related to dependence. The greater the dependence, the lower the power. Dependence is a function of the value of what is being offered in exchange and the availability of that resource from alternative sources.

4. Even in the face of power inequality, however, Molm et al.'s (2000) findings suggest that trust can emerge if reciprocity is established in the exchange relation.

5. Power-balancing mechanisms include ways in which the power inequality is reduced. For Emerson (1964, 1972), these mechanisms involve coalition formation or collective action of the less powerful; efforts by the less powerful to find alternative sources of the resources they value to reduce their dependence; "status-giving" within a relationship to increase the perceived value of what one party receives from the other; and finally, withdrawal from the relationship.

6. In a study of thirteen vertical dyads, Roderick Kramer (1996) discusses empirical findings on what he calls "vertical trust" involving actors with different levels of power—in this case, employer-employee relations.

7. Molm (1997) investigates how risk and fear of loss constrain the use of coercive power in non-negotiated social exchange relations. An analysis of the use of strategic power helps explain why exchange partners in previous research have rarely used coercive power, even when their incentives and capacities to coerce were high. The findings suggest that using power is risky and that actors fear losses from the potential retaliation of their partners far more than they value the prospect of increased rewards. The risks of coercive power use are especially great in the context of relations of mutual exchange because of the high reward dependence of the actors who have the strongest incentive to use coercion.

8. I am indebted to Kathleen Morrison for raising these issues as the discussant of an earlier version of this chapter at a conference on trust at the University of California at Riverside, February 2004. See also chapter 5.

9. Tom Tyler and Peter Degoey (1996) argue, however, that the relational model of trust applies even to brief encounters with authorities. They argue that people are concerned primarily with benevolence and respect, so that encounters with authorities that violate these expectations (even if brief) reduce the general perceived trustworthiness of those authorities and thus the capacity for trust in them. We view this evidence as primarily related to a reduction in the perceived trustworthiness of those in authority. It is hard to argue that there could be a real trust relation in situations in which the encounters are brief or involve little or no expectation of future contact (see also Albrecht and Travaglione 2003; Boeckmann and Tyler 2002; De Cremer and van Knippenberg 2003; Shamir and Lapidot 2003).

10. It may well be the case that along with equality of power the continuity of the relationship is an important factor in such decisions. Such an argument would fit with our encapsulated interest model of trust, in which the shadow of the future is an important constraint on those who might exploit the vulnerability of a partner.

11. What Jeffrey Bradach and Robert Eccles (1989) refer to in their discussion of the significance of factors like flexibility and reliability seems to be trustworthiness

rather than trust. In many of their statements, "trustworthiness" should be substituted for the term "trust." For example, what the authors mean in the discussion here is that under uncertainty, *trustworthiness* is an important determinant of transactions.

12. In chapter 4, we discuss secrecy and lack of transparency as sources of distrust in their own right.

13. Procedural fairness generally refers to the use of procedures for evaluation and the determination of an allocation of rewards that are viewed as just. Procedural fairness depends on having clearly specified procedures that are transparent and applied systematically. Distributive fairness refers to an evaluation in justice terms of the actual distribution of outcomes based on distribution rules that are widely perceived as just (for example, based on need, equity, or equality under varying conditions).

14. In a comprehensive review of dependency theory and modernization theory, Brian Tamanaha (1995) makes the case that the rule of law is important in development but not necessarily to the degree to which some claim that it is required, since the law is a blunt instrument and one that must be developed in the context of a particular culture. "Much to the chagrin of those who wish to reshape society through law," he notes, "in most legal systems around the world lawyers are technicians who effectuate decisions made by others" (484). Tamanaha makes the argument that modern law is necessary but not sufficient for economic and political development.

Chapter 4

1. We are indebted to Robert K. Merton for this insight.

2. It is arguable that one cannot choose to trust and that one can only have trust happen to oneself, although one could choose to act as though one trusted.

3. One might hesitate on the latter claim, however, because the number that represents the degrees of separation between any two randomly selected people in the society might be very small. Stanley Milgrom (1967) thinks it is about six, although he drops from his count the majority of cases, in which people do not connect. If he is right, then anyone's networks include a fairly large fraction of the total population. A recent study (Kleinfeld 2002) finds that it is less than six when we succeed in connecting through the Internet with another person more or less randomly selected from the world, but that *in most cases by far there is no success in connecting*. That still leaves a huge fraction of the population who are not in any given person's trust networks, contrary to the implicit claim of only six degrees of separation (see also Watts 2003).

4. American religious demagogues, with the backing of President George W. Bush, and Spanish Catholics, with the backing of former Prime Minister José María Aznar (*New York Times,* December 21, 2003, p. 27), have pushed for a larger role of religion in political and public life. They would reverse the trends set by the U.S. Constitution and contemporary European developments. A proposed constitutional amendment to bar gay marriages would be the first U.S. amendment ever to reduce individual liberties rather than secure them against intrusions from government. Religious ascendancy seems likely to undercut civil liberties more generally.

5. In a note, Alan Krueger and Alexandre Mas (2003, 18) say that the fatality rate for the Decatur tires was about one death per 10 to 30 million tires. The fatality rate for parachute-jumping is reported as about one death per 13 million jumps.
6. Retailers' general success may have depended on timing. Before 1863, there was no national paper currency in the United States. Individual banks issued their own banknotes, which had the same face values but were not equally safe and therefore had different real values that, with bankruptcy, could suddenly fall to nothing. Hence, retailers were wary of advertising or marking prices before they knew which currency they would receive in payment.
7. Most of the discussion in the first three paragraphs of this section is a summary of Hardin (2002b, 98–100).

Chapter 5

1. Keith Hart (1988) portrays the very complex market arrangements that arise in almost ungovernable cities like Accra, Ghana.
2. Henry Farrell (2004) argues that the weakness of central state institutions in Italy fits with vigorous informal institutions at the local level in comparison to, for example, Germany, where the state is more rigidly in control and informal institutions are less important.
3. Dueling, for example, has been a crime in many times and places, but making it illegal generally did not stop it.
4. There are many forerunners, beginning apparently with Hanifan (1916) and including Jacobs (1961) and Loury (1977, 1987). A valuable compendium is Ostrom and Ahn (2003).
5. According to a thorough study of tort verdicts from 1985 to 1996, the win rates were low, the compensatory damages awarded were modest, and punitive damages were nonexistent. Moreover, both the win rates and the sizes of the awards declined over the twelve-year period (Merritt and Barry 1999).
6. Group or organizational capital would have the form of A (or some subset of A) getting A (or some subset of A) to do something to the benefit of the members of the group A; and the obstacle to be overcome is the logic of collective action that undercuts individuals' incentives to contribute to a collective as opposed to a merely individual benefit.
7. Shawn Hunt, an academically ambitious Brooklyn seventeen-year-old striving to get through high school and into university, says he talks to whites in "regular, straight up and down English." But that would not go over well with his black friends: "They'd be like—that's not what they're used to. They wouldn't take too good to that. They'd think I was funny" (Sara Rimer, "Shawn, 17: Running Past Many Obstacles," *New York Times,* April 25, 1993, p. 1, 2; see also Hardin 1995, ch. 4). If he spoke "straight up and down English" among his peers, they might soon have thought him worse than merely funny and been more comfortable with him out of their group. The life of such groups is commonly very much grounded in the pleasures of mutual activity; hence, the discomfort introduced by someone who violates the forms of that activity can motivate strong reactions and even sanctions.
8. For a substantial criticism of the politicized nature of Anderson's account, see anthropologist Laurie Kain Hart's letter to the editor, *New York Times Magazine,*

January 16, 2000, 7. Hart says that kunun bears no relation to the contemporary murderousness of Bosnia and Kosovo.

9. The text of this and many other dueling codes are available online. Wilson's name leads to many of these. Available at: http://onlinebooks.library.upenn.edu/webbin/gutbook/lookup?num=6085 (accessed February 15, 2005).

10. The duel may well have evened the life chances of aristocrats and lesser mortals somewhat, because the latter were exempt from dueling, although not from beatings. When Voltaire challenged the Chevalier de Rohan to a duel, the charming chevalier sent his servants to give the great man a beating for his effrontery (Gilmour 1992, 279).

11. Helen Ebraugh and Mary Curry (2000, 191–94) offer a succinct review of the range of practices captured by the term "fictive kinship." For a review of the American experience, see Chatters, Taylor, and Jayakody (1994).

12. An especially common and widespread form of fictive kin is the compadrazgo, the set of relations and obligations resulting from being a godparent that loosely form an "alliance for mutual protection and advancement." These relations, under different names, continue to exist throughout Latin America and the Mediterranean (Lomnitz and Sheinbaum 2002). The origin is in Catholic Church practices, and the relationship receives ritual formalization at baptism and confirmation. The compadrazgo ostensibly has its basis in a moral relationship, but it often serves economic and political as well as social and spiritual purposes (see Gudeman 1971 and responses in *Current Anthropology*).

13. There are numerous forms of rotating credit associations among immigrant groups in the United States. In New York, these include Jamaican partners, Trinidadian susus, Haitian mens, the Guyanan box, Dominican sams or sociedades, and Korean, Portuguese, and Jewish equivalents. Evidence of participation in such an association can be used to qualify for ordinary bank loans at several New York banks (Sasha Abramsky, "Newcomers Savings and Loan," *New York Times*, October 22, 2000, p. 14–4).

Chapter 6

1. The model is spelled out by H. L. A. Hart and Anthony Honoré (1959); a similar, far more accessible account is presented in McGill (1996).

2. For such views, see Veatch (1972) and Gewirth (1986, 283–87). Alan Goldman (1980) canvasses arguments for special principles of ethics for various professions.

3. See the survey of works in Barber (1983, 1–22) and much subsequent work. Two extensive readers are Windt and others (1989) and Appelbaum and Lawton (1990). On legal ethics, see Luban (1988). A symposium on academic ethics is in *The Monist* 79(4, October 1996). Much of the literature on professional and business responsibility focuses on whether it is right or wrong to perform an abortion or to pollute the environment. We do not address these issues of the ethics of behavior but focus instead on whether we can trust another actor to act in our interests.

4. Conflicts of interest are the focus of much of section 8 of the "Current Opinions of the Council on Ethical and Judicial Affairs," appended to the AMA's "Code of Medical Ethics" (in Gorlin 1999, 388–95).

5. In 1938 the AMA went even further to make the one-on-one practice of medicine virtually an ideology. It threatened to penalize any of its members who took part in group health practices, on the ground that such practice is unethical. The U.S. government blocked this perversion of "medical deontology" as a violation of the Sherman Antitrust Act (Chapman 1984, 118).

6. The medical code of the AMA is called the "Code of Medical Ethics." The ABA lawyers' code is now more aptly called "Model Rules of Professional Conduct." The "Ethics Manual" of the American College of Physicians is especially clear on the changing environment and shift of medical care away from one-on-one physician-patient relations to highly complex and organized medical care (see Gorlin 1999, 323–31).

7. There is a perhaps invented story among lawyers that some years ago a corporation reputedly gave up on trying to sue Exxon because all major law firms in the United States had Exxon as a client and they claimed they could not sue it without conflict of interest. One might suppose they could also not choose not to sue it without conflict of interest.

8. Consider a second case with the law firm Weil, Gotshal & Manges that illustrates how the issue of conflict of interest is made more crucial in our day of very large firms with huge numbers of clients. The case arose while Weil Gotshal was representing Fashion Boutique of Short Hills, New Jersey, against Fendi. In another case, it was also representing Prada, which then became part-owner of Fendi. Weil Gotshal did not advise the owners of the then-defunct Fashion Boutique of the conflict of interest. Fashion Boutique is, at this writing, in court suing Weil Gotshal for failed representation of its interests (Karen Donovan, "When Big Firms Trip over Their Own Clients," *New York Times*, October 3, 2004, p. 3-5.). This case shows just how subtle the problem of conflict of interest can be, because Weil Gotshal has in place various computerized devices for discovering whether it has a conflict of interest in any given case. In the case of the Fashion Boutique, the conflict arose after representation had already begun. But for gigantic firms such as Weil Gotshal, this problem must occur frequently enough to justify extra effort to find any such new conflict.

9. It is hard to see fraud rather than mere sloppiness in the data collection. Note the relative carelessness of earlier times in work of Nobel Prize quality, as discussed by Gerald Holton (1996, 69–71). So why is there such great concern with procedure? One credible answer is that others cannot genuinely replicate all experiments. Results must therefore be in a form that can be overseen and checked; otherwise, truth will not be an adequate check.

10. Gallo's case suggests to many that the longing for a Nobel Prize, which would seem to be a strong incentive for good scientific work, can also be a distorting incentive, because it massively rewards priority. Hence, I have incentive to keep my work secret from you while I attempt to find out about yours. I might even take unjustified shortcuts in order to get to a result sooner, perhaps at the risk of making my result less reliable.

11. Stephen Jay Gould (1993, 452) expresses a related view: "The factual correction of error may be the most sublime event in intellectual life, the ultimate sign of our necessary obedience to a larger reality and our inability to construct the world according to our desires. For science, in particular, factual correction

holds a specially revered place." One might suppose it is more revered to correct than to be corrected.

12. This view was expressed at the Wingspread conference "The Moral Role of Scientists," sponsored by the Midwest Consortium on International Security Studies, Racine, Wisconsin (October 1992).

13. "The Chemist's Code" can be found online at: http://www.chemistry.org/portal/a/c/s/1/acsdisplay.html?DOC=membership%5Ccode.html (accessed February 15, 2005).

14. Among Dingell's targets were David Baltimore and his coworker Thereza Imanishi-Kari, Robert Gallo, and Stanford University—all very high-profile targets.

15. For example, a major category of conflict of interest for doctors is the ownership of hospitals to which they refer patients; see AMA, "Code of Medical Ethics and Current Opinions, 8.032," in Gorlin (1999, 389–90).

16. For a general historical account of the problem of lead poisoning, see Warren (2000). Debates over children's exposure to lead continue, with the deliberate intrusion of conflict of interest on the federal Advisory Committee on Childhood Lead Poisoning Prevention with the George W. Bush administration's appointment of lead industry representatives to the committee (Ferber 2002; Michaels et al. 2002).

17. This case was complicated by errors in the contract between Dong and Boots.

18. Universities are somewhat craven in the face of large suits or even politicized actions. For example, the historian Michael Bellesisles (2000) has been attacked for falsifying data on gun ownership and gun use in the United States before the Civil War, which, he claims, started Americans on the path of their gun culture. The National Rifle Association (NRA) went after his book with a massive attack, and his employer, Emory University, forced his resignation from its faculty. Some press accounts (for example, Wiener 2002) make his claims sound eminently defensible against his attackers. Several major historians of the era stand behind Bellesisles's account, which won the Bancroft Prize. Along with many NRA members and many academics, Charlton Heston, former president of the NRA, attacked the book. An outsider might well wonder whether Bellesisles was forced out in the interest of his university rather than in the interests of truth in history. A peculiar novelty of this case is that Bellesisles's claims have been subjected to corroboration or "replication," as would be results in experimental physics when the stakes are very high. The perversity of the Bellesisles case is that the stakes seem not at all high for anyone involved. In particular, his historical account is exceedingly unlikely to influence policies on gun ownership. Of far greater concern than this anomalous politicized case are cases in the sciences, especially in the development of drugs whose value to a corporation can be staggering. But the pattern of university capitulation to outside pressures bodes ill for truth in science.

19. Donald Kennedy, editor-in-chief of *Science,* argues that all authors of a paper should be held fully responsible for the misdeeds of any of them, although he notes that this view puts him "in a quirky minority" (Kennedy 2003, 733; see also Davidoff et al. 2001).

20. This is merely one of countless such deliberate harms from lead, mercury, radioactive fallout, various fertilizers, poisons, and so on. For an eloquent

and accessible account of many of these harms, see Steingraber (1998); see also Warren (2000) on harms from lead.

21. The extent of those harms may be far from determined as yet (Peterson et al. 2003). At this writing, the full case of liability for harms has also not been settled. A lower court has assessed punitive damages of $4.5 billion (Adam Liptak, "$4.5 Billion Award Set for Spill of *Exxon Valdez*," *New York Times*, January 29, 2004, p. A-18).

22. One might wish to say the same for doctors, but an AMA study concluded that until about 1900 an ill person who went to a doctor in the United States was more likely to be harmed than benefited (Flexner 1910). The market was a failure for early medicine, which must often have killed those unfortunate enough to be able to afford the care of doctors.

23. Enron's main accounting firm was Arthur Andersen, which earned more from Enron as a consulting firm than as its auditor. One must wonder whether Arthur Andersen's accounting was distorted by its being a direct beneficiary and maybe even sometime designer of Enron's practices.

24. The press had a field day with this juicy story. Paul Krugman (2002, 64) says: "The messy divorce proceedings of Jack Welch, the legendary former CEO of General Electric, have had one unintended benefit: they have given us a peek at the perks of the corporate elite, which are normally hidden from public view." See also Leslie Wayne and Alex Kuczynski ("Tarnished Image Places Welch in Unlikely Company," *New York Times*, September 16, 2002, pp. C-1); N. R. Kleinfield ("Land of the Free, Home of the Perk; New Yorkers See Box Seats and Other Goodies as an Inalienable Right," *New York Times*, September 22, 2002, p. 1–41), and *New York Times* ("Courtside Tickets for Life," [editorial], September 15, 2002, p. 4–14). The last of these notes that "even the most jaded of executive compensation experts found Mr. Welch's richly accessorized retirement-to-grave security package grotesque."

25. Carleton Chapman (1984, 147), a cardiovascular specialist who was a national leader in medical education, argues that doctors have wrongfully supposed that what is good for doctors is good for their patients. He concludes that "two millennia of mistaken emphases with regard to the essential *raison d'etre* of the medical profession are surely enough."

Chapter 7

1. Thomas Hammond (1990) offers a useful assessment of the alternatives presented by Gulick (1937) and Simon (1947).

2. Nor can we always assume that institutions uphold the kinds of reliability we value. Interestingly, Americans have recently begun to lionize whistle-blowers. *Time* magazine anointed three whistle-blowing women as "The Person of the Year" for 2002.

3. The quality predictions of the theory tend to be highly inaccurate when the employer does not consider the supply and demand for labor, discrimination on the basis of race or sex, or other features of the context (Akerlof 1984, 14–15; Stiglitz 1987, 2–3, 16–17).

4. Similarly, there is reason to believe that an efficiency wage is a positive signal that builds trust relations and reciprocity (Wielers 1997). An efficiency wage

is a wage higher than supply and demand would produce (Weiss 1990). Although the statistical evidence for the existence of an efficiency wage is thin (Prendergast 1999, 44–45), there is some documentation of a trade-off between wages and supervision (Arai 1994; Rebitzer 1995). Efficiency wages also seem to work with a model in which monitoring for shirking serves as a screening device to weed out those who are opportunistic (Bar-Ilan 1991).

Chapter 8

1. A new survey instrument, the Business Environment and Enterprise Performance Survey (BEEPS), covers six thousand firms in twenty-six transitional economies. It is just beginning to be analyzed (see, for example, Raiser, Rousso, and Steves 2004). Although critics express concern about its generalizability, it may be the best instrument currently available.
2. Using the World Values Survey, some researchers argue that "generalized trust" is positively related to democracy and to economic development (Inglehart 1997; Norris 1999, 2002); others are less sure (Newton 1999; Newton and Norris 2000, 64). See also Dalton (1999).
3. Bo Rothstein (2001, 2004; Rothstein and Stolle 2003) disaggregates further and confirms the Brehm and Rahn (1997) finding, but also offers evidence that certain government agencies have a disproportionate effect on citizen confidence in each other.
4. Putnam (2000, 22–24) makes the intragroup-intergroup distinction. He argues that "bonding social capital is good for undergirding specific reciprocity and mobilizing solidarity. . . . Bridging networks, by contrast are better for linkages to internal assets and for information diffusion" (22). This distinction draws heavily on Granovetter (1973).
5. Until recently, there has been relatively little consideration of alternative survey indicators of political trust or of different notions of political trust. Some research using pilot items for the NES addresses this issue (Burns and Kinder 2000; Rahn and Rudolph 2000). However, as Wendy Rahn and Thomas Rudolph (2000) note, the items on faith in elections do not yet represent an improvement in the capacity of electoral surveys to measure factors that influence trust assessments.

Chapter 9

1. For alternative and more normative accounts, see Seligman (1997) and Misztal (1996). For an account that focuses on the United States, see Zucker (1986).
2. For an account of the social exchange literature on the development of trust relations under conditions of uncertainty, the limitations of social exchange networks, and the ways in which this literature might inform our understanding of transitions, see Cook, Rice, and Gerbasi (2004). Much of the discussion in this chapter parallels the findings cited there.
3. Cheung described the Hong Kong of his youth, the World War II years, in a seminar he taught on transaction cost theory in the mid-1970s at the University of Washington at Seattle.

4. This is what Charles Tilly (1998, 163–69) and others call chain migration. There is a huge literature on these questions; see, for example, Fukuyama (1995), Light (1972), Nee and Nee (1973), Nee and Sanders (2000), Portes and Sensenbrenner (1993), Sanders and Nee (1987), and Waldinger (1986).

5. Steve Pfaff pointed this out to us.

6. Samuel Bowles and Herbert Gintis (2000) offer an interesting model of this problem and attempt to determine whether the benefits of the network outweigh the costs of excluding other trading partners. See also the work of economic sociologists, especially Brian Uzzi (1996), who tries to assess when such embedded networks become counterproductive; Paul DiMaggio and Hugh Louch (1998), who analyze when consumer transactions are more likely to take place within personal networks; and Roberto Fernandez and his colleagues, who consider the personal contacts and references of employees in the hiring decision (Fernandez, Castilla, and Moore 2000; Fernandez and Weinberg 1997).

7. This account of Aboriginal Australia is based on Margaret Levi's personal experiences and researches. Clifford Geertz (1963) documents similar issues in Bali.

Chapter 10

1. The Hippocratic Oath primarily gives rules for behavior that might seem to apply to everyone, not merely to doctors, although it also proscribes surgery—as surely made good sense at the time. See the oath, which is very brief, in Lloyd (1950/1983, 67). The Babylonian Code of Hammurabi, set down during the eighteenth century B.C.E., gave extensive, detailed rules for the practice of medicine. But this was a legal, not an ethical, code, and some of its penalties for medical failures were harsh.

2. Putnam (1993a, 167) originally defined social capital as "features of social organization, such as trust, norms and networks that can improve the efficiency of society by facilitating coordinated actions."

3. Reputedly, when asked what he thought of Western civilization, Mahatma Gandhi said he thought it was a good idea. Indeed.

4. The relative success of the U.S. civil rights movement in the 1950s and 1960s did not signal the elimination of distrust between blacks and whites; distrust survives, and often for good reason. The struggle did result, however, in the universal enforcement of laws forbidding segregation and upholding integration and in punishment of those who broke those laws or engaged in violence against the advocates of civil rights.

5. This seems to have become increasingly the pattern of Islamist groups in French working-class suburbs. Even North African women whose home cultures did not demand the veil are succumbing to social pressure or revised religious beliefs and now wearing it. They are far less likely than before to mix with any men at all, or even with women who do not share their practice. Their trust relations have narrowed, and their distrust relations have increased in number and range.

6. The larger cross-cultural behavior experiments project (Henrich et al. 2004), of which this study is a part, compares ultimatum, dictator, and public goods games in fifteen small-scale societies. The authors find great variation in offers

and responses in these games across societies, and they conclude that the variation has little to do with individual differences and more to do with differences between groups. They conclude that "the higher the degree of market integration and the higher the payoffs to cooperation, the greater the degree of prosociality found in experimental games" (Henrich et al. 2004, 49). The experiments do not, for the most part, assess the variation in trust as encapsulated interest, but they do suggest that the search for indices of reliability and trustworthiness becomes more salient as individuals leave close-knit networks where social norms might suffice to regulate cooperativeness.

References

Aguilar, John L. 1984. "Trust and Exchange: Expressive and Instrumental Dimensions of Reciprocity in a Peasant Community." *Ethos* 12: 3–29.

Akerlof, George A. 1982. "Labor Contracts as Partial Gift Exchange." *Quarterly Journal of Economics* 97(4): 543–69.

———. 1984. *An Economic Theorist's Book of Tales.* New York: Cambridge University Press.

Albrecht, Simon, and Anthony Travaglione. 2003. "Trust in Public-Sector Senior Management." *International Journal of Human Resource Management* 14(1): 76–92.

Alchian, Armen, and Harold Demsetz. 1972. "Production, Information Costs, and Economic Organization." *American Economic Review* 62: 777–95.

Amato, Paul R. 1993. "Urban-Rural Differences in Helping Friends and Family Members." *Social Psychology Quarterly* 56: 249–62.

Analyse und Kritik. 2004. "Trust and Community on the Internet." *Analyse und Kritik* 26(1, December): entire issue.

Andersen, Susan M., Roberta L. Klatzky, and John Murray. 1990. "Traits and Social Stereotypes: Efficiency Differences in Social Information Processing." *Journal of Personality and Social Psychology* 59(2): 192–201.

Anderson, Scott. 1999. "The Curse of Blood and Vengeance." *New York Times Magazine* (December 26): 29–35, 44, 54–57.

Appelbaum, David, and Sarah Verone Lawton. 1990. *Ethics and the Professions.* Englewood Cliffs, N.J.: Prentice-Hall.

Arai, Mahmood. 1994. "Compensating Wage Differentials Versus Efficiency Wages: An Empirical Study of Job Autonomy and Wages." *Industrial Relations* 33(2): 249–62.

Ardener, Shirley. 1964. "The Comparative Study of Rotating Credit Associations." *Journal of the Royal Anthropological Institute of Great Britain and Ireland* 94(2): 201–29.

Argyris, Chris. 1957. *Personality and Organization: The Conflict Between System and Individual.* New York: Harper.

———. 1964. *Integrating the Individual and the Organization.* New York: Wiley.

Aron, Jean-Paul, Paul Dumont, and Emmanuel Le Roy Ladurie. 1972. *Anthropologie du conscrit français: d'après les comptes numériques et sommaires du recrutement de l'armée (1819–1826).* Paris: Mouton.

Arrow, Kenneth. 1974. *The Limits of Organization.* New York: Norton.

Ayres, Ian, and John Braithwaite. 1992. *Responsive Regulation*. Oxford: Oxford University Press.

Bacharach, Michael, and Diego Gambetta. 2001. "Trust in Signals." In *Trust in Society*, edited by Karen S. Cook. New York: Russell Sage Foundation.

Baier, Annette. 1986. "Trust and Antitrust." *Ethics* 96(2): 231–60.

Bailyn, Bernard. 1967. *The Ideological Origins of the American Revolution*. Cambridge, Mass.: Harvard University Press.

Baker, George, Robert Gibbons, and Kevin J. Murphy. 1994. "Subjective Performance Measures in Optimal Incentive Contracts." *Quarterly Journal of Economics* 109: 1125–56.

Baker, Laurence, Todd H. Wagner, Sara Singer, and M. K. Bundorf. 2003. "Use of the Internet and E-mail for Health Care Information: Results from a National Survey." *Journal of the American Medical Association* 289(18): 2400–2406.

Balkwell, James W. 1994. "Status." In *Group Processes: Sociological Analyses*, edited by Margaret Foschi and Edward J. Lawler. Chicago: Nelson-Hall.

Banfield, Edward C. 1958. *The Moral Basis of a Backward Society*. New York: Free Press.

Barahona de Brito, Alexandra, Carmen Gonzalez-Enriquez, and Paloma Aguilar, eds. 2001. *The Politics of Memory: Transitional Justice in Democratizing Societies*. Oxford: Oxford University Press.

Barber, Bernard. 1983. *The Logic and Limits of Trust*. New Brunswick, N.J.: Rutgers University Press.

Bardhan, Pranab, ed. 1999. Special issue on group lending. *Journal of Development Economics* 60(1).

Bar-Ilan, Avner. 1991. "Monitoring Workers as a Screening Device." *Canadian Journal of Economics* 24(2): 460–70.

Barkan, Joel D., and Frank Holmquist. 1989. "Peasant-State Relations and the Social Base of Self-help in Africa." *World Politics* 41(3): 359–80.

Barkan, Joel D., Michael I. McNulty, and M. A. O. Ayeni. 1991. " 'Hometown' Voluntary Associations, Local Development, and the Emergence of Civil Society in Western Nigeria." *Journal of Modern African Studies* 29(3): 457–80.

Barnard, Chester I. 1938. *The Functions of the Executive*. Cambridge, Mass.: Harvard University Press.

Barr, Abigail. 2004. "Kinship, Familiarity, and Trust: An Experimental Investigation." In *Foundations of Human Sociality*, edited by Joseph Henrich, Robert Boyd, Samuel Bowles, Colin Camerer, Ernst Fehr, and Herbert Gintis. New York: Oxford University Press.

Barron, John M., and Michael Staten. 2003. "The Value of Comprehensive Credit Reports: Lessons from the U.S. Experience." In *Credit Reporting Systems and the International Economy*, edited by Margaret J. Miller. Cambridge, Mass.: MIT Press.

Barth, Fredrik. 1985. *The Last Wali of Swat: An Autobiography*. New York: Columbia University Press.

Bartlett, Thomas. 2003. "How Not to Choose a President." *Chronicle of Higher Education* (November 14).

Bassett, Glenn. 1993. *The Evolution and Future of High-Performance Management Systems*. Westport, Conn.: Quorum Books.

Bates, Robert H. 1991. *Beyond the Miracle of the Market*. New York: Cambridge University Press.

Becker, Lawrence C. 1996. "Trust as Noncognitive Security About Motives." *Ethics* 107(1): 43–61.

Bella, David A. 1987. "Engineering and Erosion of Trust." *Journal of Professional Issues in Engineering* 113(April): 117–29.

Bellesisles, Michael. 2000. *Arming America: The Origins of National Gun Culture.* New York: Alfred A. Knopf.

Berger, Joseph, Bernard P. Cohen, and Morris Zelditch Jr. 1966. "Status Characteristics and Expectation States." In *Sociological Theories in Progress,* vol. 1, edited by Joseph Berger, Morris Zelditch Jr., and Bo Anderson. Boston: Houghton Mifflin.

———. 1972. "Status Characteristics and Social Interaction." *American Sociological Review* 37(3): 241–55.

Berlant, Jeffrey. 1975. *Profession and Monopoly.* Berkeley: University of California Press.

Berle, Adolph A., and Gardner C. Means. 1932. *The Modern Corporation and Private Property.* New York: Macmillan.

Besley, Timothy, Stephen Coate, and Glenn Loury. 1994. "Rotating Savings and Credit Associations, Credit Markets, and Efficiency." *Review of Economic Studies* 61(4): 701–19.

Bianco, William. 1994. *Trust: Representatives and Constituents.* Ann Arbor: University of Michigan Press.

Blau, Peter M. 1955. *The Dynamics of Bureaucracy.* Rev. ed. Chicago: University of Chicago Press.

———. 1964. *Exchange and Power in Social Life.* New York: Wiley.

———. 1994. *Structural Contexts of Opportunities.* Chicago: University of Chicago Press.

Blendon, Robert J., and John M. Benson. 2001. "Americans' Views on Health Policy: A Fifty-Year Historical Perspective." *Health Affairs* 20(2): 33–46.

Boeckmann, Robert J., and Tom R. Tyler. 2002. "Trust, Respect, and the Psychology of Political Engagement." *Journal of Applied Social Psychology* 32(10): 2067–88.

Boehm, Christopher. 1987. *Blood Revenge: the Enactment and Management of Conflict in Montenegro and Other Tribal Societies.* 2nd ed. Philadelphia: University of Pennsylvania Press.

Boone, Catherine. 2003. *Political Topographies of the African State: Territorial Authority and Institutional Choice.* New York: Cambridge University Press.

Bovens, Mark. 1998. *The Quest for Responsibility: Accountability and Citizenship in Complex Organizations.* Cambridge, U.K.: Cambridge University Press.

Bowles, Samuel. 1998. "Endogenous Preferences: The Cultural Consequences of Markets and Other Economic Institutions." *Journal of Economic Literature* 36(1): 75–111.

Bowles, Samuel, and Herbert Gintis. 2000. "Optimal Parochialism: The Dynamics of Trust and Exclusion in Networks." Unpublished paper. Department of Economics, University of Massachusetts, Amherst.

Bradach, Jeffrey L., and Robert G. Eccles. 1989. "Price, Authority, and Trust: From Ideal Types to Plural Forms." *Annual Review of Sociology* 15: 97–118.

Braithwaite, John. 1985. *To Punish or Persuade.* Albany: State University of New York Press.

———. 1998. "Institutionalizing Distrust, Enculturating Trust." In *Trust and Governance*, edited by Valerie Braithwaite and Margaret Levi. New York: Russell Sage Foundation.

Braithwaite, John, and Toni Makkai. 1994. "Trust and Compliance." *Policing and Society* 4(1): 1–12.

Braithwaite, Valerie. 1995. "Games of Engagement: Postures Within the Regulatory Community." *Law and Society Review* 17: 225–55.

Braithwaite, Valerie, and Margaret Levi, eds. 1998. *Trust and Governance*. New York: Russell Sage Foundation.

Brehm, John, and Scott Gates. 1997. *Working, Shirking, and Sabotage: Bureaucratic Response to a Democratic Public*. Ann Arbor: University of Michigan Press.

———. 2004. "Supervisors as Trust-Brokers in Social Work Bureaucracies." In *Trust and Distrust Within Organizations: Emerging Perspectives, Enduring Questions*, edited by Roderick M. Kramer and Karen S. Cook. New York: Russell Sage Foundation.

Brehm, John, and Wendy Rahn. 1997. "Individual-Level Evidence for the Causes and Consequences of Social Capital." *American Journal of Political Science* 41(3): 999–1023.

Brennan, Geoffrey. 1998. "Democratic Trust: A Rational Choice Theory View." In *Trust and Governance*, edited by Valerie Braithwaite and Margaret Levi. New York: Russell Sage Foundation.

Breton, Albert, and Ronald Wintrobe. 1982. *The Logic of Bureaucratic Conduct*. New York: Cambridge University Press.

Brewer, John. 1988. "The English State and Fiscal Appropriation: Taxes and Public Finance in England, 1688–1789." *Politics and Society* 16(2–3): 335–86.

Brewer, Marilynn B. 2000. "Superordinate Goals Versus Superordinate Identity as Bases of Intergroup Cooperation." In *Social Identity Processes: Trends in Theory and Research*, edited by Dora Capozza and Rupert Brown. Thousand Oaks, Calif.: Sage Publications.

Brockner, Joel, and Phyllis Siegel. 1996. "Understanding the Interaction Between Procedural and Distributive Justice: The Role of Trust." In *Trust in Organizations: Frontiers of Theory and Research*, edited by Roderick Kramer and Tom R. Tyler. Thousand Oaks, Calif.: Sage Publications.

Brown, Margaret L. 2004. "Compensating for Distrust Among Kin." In *Distrust*, edited by Russell Hardin. New York: Russell Sage Foundation.

Brown, Martin, Armin Falk, and Ernst Fehr. 2004. "Relational Contract and the Nature of Market Interactions." *Econometrica* 72(3): 747–80.

Buchan, Nancy R., Rachel T. Croson, and Robyn M. Dawes. 2002. "Swift Neighbors and Persistent Strangers: A Cross-cultural Investigation of Trust and Reciprocity in Social Exchange." *American Journal of Sociology* 108(1): 168–206.

Burns, Nancy, and Donald Kinder. 2000. *Social Trust and Democratic Politics*. Ann Arbor, Mich.: National Election Studies.

Buskens, Vincent, and Jeroen Weesie. 2000. "An Experiment on the Effects of Embeddedness in Trust Situations: Buying a Used Car." *Rationality and Society* 12(2): 227–53.

Carpenter, Daniel P. 2001. *The Forging of Bureaucratic Autonomy: Organizational Reputations and Policy Innovation in Executive Agencies, 1862–1928*. Princeton, N.J.: Princeton University Press.

Carruthers, Bruce, and Barry Cohen. 2001. *Predicting Failure but Failing to Predict: A Sociology of Knowledge of Credit Rating in Postbellum America.* Paper presented to Russell Sage Foundation trust workshop, California Institute of Technology, Pasadena (September 7).

Cassidy, John. 2002. "The Greed Cycle: How the Financial System Encouraged Corporations to Go Crazy." *The New Yorker* (September 23): 64–77.

Chapman, Carleton B. 1984. *Physicians, Law, and Ethics.* New York: New York University Press.

Chatters, Linda M., Robert Joseph Taylor, and Rukmalie Jayakody. 1994. "Fictive Kinship Relations in Black Extended Families." *Journal of Comparative Family Studies* 25(3): 297–304.

Cheibub, Jose Antonio, and Adam Przeworski. 1999. "Democracy, Elections, and Accountability for Economic Outcomes." In *Democracy, Accountability, and Representation,* edited by Adam Przeworski, Susan C. Stokes, and Bernard Manin. New York: Cambridge University Press.

Cialdini, Robert B. 1996. "The Triple Tumor Structure of Organizational Behavior." In *Codes of Conduct,* edited by David M. Messick and Ann E. Tenbrunsel. New York: Russell Sage Foundation.

Citrin, Jack. 1974. "Comment: The Political Relevance of Trust in Government." *American Political Science Review* 68: 973–88.

Citrin, Jack, and Christopher Muste. 1999. "Trust in Government and System Support." In *Measures of Political Attitudes,* edited by John P. Robinson, Lawrence S. Wrightsman, and Phillip R. Shaver. New York: Academic Press.

Clegg, Stuart R. 2001. "Power in Society." In *International Encyclopedia of the Social and Behavioral Sciences,* edited by Neil J. Smelser and Paul B. Baltes. Oxford: Elsevier.

Clemens, Elisabeth S. 1999. "Organizational Repertoires and Institutional Change: Women's Groups and the Transformation of American Politics, 1890–1920." In *Civic Engagement in American Democracy,* edited by Theda Skocpol and Morris P. Fiorina. Washington, D.C., and New York: Brookings Institution and Russell Sage Foundation.

Coase, Ronald. 1937. "The Nature of the Firm." *Economica* 4(3): 386–405.

Cohen, Don, and Laurence Prusak. 2001. *In Good Company: How Social Capital Makes Organizations Work.* Boston: Harvard Business School Press.

Cohen, Stanley. 1995. "State Crimes of Previous Regimes: Knowledge, Accountability, and the Policing of the Past." *Law and Social Inquiry* 20(1, Winter): 7–50.

Coleman, James S. 1988. "Social Capital in the Creation of Human Capital." *American Journal of Sociology* (supp.) 94: S95–120.

———. 1990. *Foundations of Social Theory.* Cambridge, Mass.: Harvard University Press.

Cook, Karen S. 2005. "Networks, Norms, and Trust: The Social Psychology of Social Capital." *Social Psychology Quarterly* 68(1): 4–14.

Cook, Karen S., and Robin M. Cooper. 2003. "Experimental Studies of Cooperation, Trust, and Social Exchange." In *Trust and Reciprocity: Interdisciplinary Lessons for Experimental Research,* edited by Elinor Ostrom and James Walker. New York: Russell Sage Foundation.

Cook, Karen S., and Richard M. Emerson. 1978. "Power, Equity, and Commitment in Exchange Networks." *American Sociological Review* 43(5): 721–39.

Cook, Karen S., and Russell Hardin. 2001. "Norms of Cooperativeness and Networks of Trust." In *Social Norms*, edited by Michael Hechter and Karl-Dieter Opp. New York: Russell Sage Foundation.

Cook, Karen S., Roderick Kramer, David Thom, Stephanie Bailey, Irena Stepanikova, and Robin Cooper. 2004. "Physician-Patient Trust Relations in an Era of Managed Care." In *Trust and Distrust in Organizations*, edited by Roderick M. Kramer and Karen S. Cook. New York: Russell Sage Foundation.

Cook, Karen S., and Eric R. W. Rice. 2001. "Exchange and Power: Issues of Structure and Agency." In *Handbook of Sociological Theory*, edited by Jonathan Turner. New York: Kluwer Academic/Plenum Publishers.

Cook, Karen S., Eric R. W. Rice, and Alexandra Gerbasi. 2004. "The Emergence of Trust Networks Under Uncertainty: The Case of Transitional Economies—Insights from Social Psychological Research." In *Building a Trustworthy State in Post-Socialist Transition*, edited by Janos Kornai and Susan Rose-Ackerman. New York: Palgrave Macmillan.

Cook, Karen S., Toshio Yamagishi, Coye Cheshire, Robin Cooper, Masafumi Matsuda, and Rie Mashima. Forthcoming. "Trust Building Via Risk-Taking: A Cross-societal Experiment." *Social Psychology Quarterly*.

Costigan, Robert D., Selim S. Ilter, and J. Jason Berman. 1998. "A Multidimensional Study of Trust in Organizations." *Journal of Managerial Issues* 10(3): 303–17.

Council on Ethical and Judicial Affairs, American Medical Association. 1992. "Conflicts of Interest: Physician Ownership of Medical Facilities." *Journal of the American Medical Association* 267(17): 2366–69.

Creed, W. E. Douglas, and Raymond E. Miles. 1996. "Trust in Organizations: A Conceptual Framework Linking Organization Forms, Managerial Philosophies, and the Opportunity Costs of Controls." In *Trust in Organizations: Frontiers of Theory and Research*, edited by Roderick M. Kramer and Tom R. Tyler. Thousand Oaks, Calif.: Sage Publications.

Crozier, Michel. 1964. *The Bureaucratic Phenomenon*. Translated by Michel Crozier. Chicago: University of Chicago Press.

Culpepper, Pepper D. 2003. *Creating Cooperation*. Ithaca, N.Y.: Cornell University Press.

Currall, Steven C., and Marc J. Epstein. 2003. "The Fragility of Organizational Trust: Lessons from the Rise and Fall of Enron." *Organizational Dynamics* 32(2): 193–206.

Dahl, Robert A. 1957. "The Concept of Power." *Behavioral Science* 2: 201–15.

Dalton, Russell J. 1999. "Political Support in Advanced Industrial Democracies." In *Critical Citizens: Global Support for Democratic Governance*, edited by Pippa Norris. New York: Oxford University Press.

Darley, John M. 2004. "Commitment, Trust, and Worker Effort Expenditure in Organizations." In *Trust and Distrust in Organizations: Frontiers of Theory and Research*, edited by Roderick M. Kramer and Karen S. Cook. New York: Russell Sage Foundation.

Dasgupta, Partha. 1988. "Trust as a Commodity." In *Trust: Making and Breaking Cooperative Relations*, edited by Diego Gambetta. New York: Blackwell.

———. 2002. "Social Capital and Economic Performance: Analytics." In *Social Capital: A Reader*, edited by Elinor Ostrom and T. K. Ahn. Colchester, Eng.: Edward Elgar.

Daunton, Martin. 1998. "Trusting Leviathan: British Fiscal Administration from the Napoleonic Wars to the Second World War." In *Trust and Governance*, edited by Valerie Braithwaite and Margaret Levi. New York: Russell Sage Foundation.

———. 2001. *Trusting Leviathan.* Cambridge, U.K.: Cambridge University Press.

Davidoff, Frank, Catherine D. DeAngelis, Jeffrey M. Drazen, John Hoey, et al. 2001. "Sponsorship, Authorship, and Accountability." *Journal of the American Medical Association* 286(10): 1232–34.

Davis, Michael. 1982. "Conflict of Interest." *Business and Professional Ethics Journal* 1(summer): 17–27.

———. 1998. "The Price of Rights: Constitutionalism and East Asian Economic Development." *Human Rights Quarterly* 20: 303–37.

De Cremer, David, and Daan van Knippenberg. 2003. "Cooperation with Leaders in Social Dilemmas: On the Effects of Procedural Fairness and Outcome Favorability in Structural Cooperation." *Organizational Behavior and Human Decision Processes* 91(1): 1–11.

Della Porta, Donatella. 2000. "Social Capital, Beliefs in Government, and Political Corruption." In *Disaffected Democracies*, edited by Susan J. Pharr and Robert D. Putnam. Princeton, N.J.: Princeton University Press.

Dijksterhuis, Ap, and Ad van Knippenberg. 1996. "Trait Implications as a Moderator of Recall of Stereotype-Consistent and Stereotype-Inconsistent Behaviors." *Personality and Social Psychology Bulletin* 22(4): 425–32.

DiMaggio, Paul, and Hugh Louch. 1998. "Transactions Between Friends and Between Strangers: Socially Embedded Consumer Transactions—For What Kinds of Purchases Do People Most Often Use Networks?" *American Sociological Review* 63(5): 619–37.

Dirks, Kurt T., and Donald L. Ferrin. 2002. "Trust in Leadership: Meta-analytic Findings and Implications for Research and Practice." *Journal of Applied Psychology* 87(4): 611–28.

Dirks, Kurt T., and Daniel Skarlicki. 2004. "Trust in Leaders: Existing Research and Emerging Issues." In *Trust and Distrust in Organizations*, edited by Roderick M. Kramer and Karen S. Cook. New York: Russell Sage Foundation.

Dixit, Avinash K., and Barry J. Nalebuff. 1991. *Thinking Strategically.* New York: Norton.

Draper, Elaine. 2003. *The Company Doctor: Risk, Responsibility, and Corporate Professionalism.* New York: Russell Sage Foundation.

Duncan, Meredith J. 1893/2003. "Criminal Malpractice: A Lawyer's Holiday." *Georgia Law Review* 37(4): 1251–1306.

Durkheim, Émile. 1933. *The Division of Labor in Society.* New York: Macmillan.

Dussart, Françoise. 2000. *The Politics of Ritual in an Aboriginal Setting.* Washington, D.C.: Smithsonian Institution Press.

Dwyer, Paula. 2003. "Breach of Trust." *Business Week* (December 15): 98–108.

Dyer, Jeffrey H., and Wujin Chu. 2003. "The Role of Trustworthiness in Reducing Transaction Costs and Improving Performance: Empirical Evidence from the United States, Japan, and Korea." *Organization Science* (special issue: "Trust in an Organizational Context") 14(1): 57–68.

Ebraugh, Helen Rose, and Mary Curry. 2000. "Fictive Kin as Social Capital in New Immigrant Communities." *Sociological Perspectives* 43(2): 189–209.

Eckstein, Susan, ed. 2001. *Power and Popular Protest: Latin American Social Movements.* 2nd ed. Berkeley: University of California Press.

Ehrenreich, Barbara. 2000. *Nickel and Dimed in America.* New York: Owl.

Eisenstadt, S. N., and Luis Roniger. 1984. *Patrons, Clients, and Friends.* Cambridge, U.K.: Cambridge University Press.

Ellickson, Robert C. 1991. *Order Without Law: How Neighbors Settle Disputes.* Cambridge, Mass.: Harvard University Press.

———. 1998. "Law and Economics Discovers Social Norms." *Journal of Legal Studies* 27(2, pt. 2, June): 537–52.

Elsbach, Kim. 2004. "Managing Images of Trustworthiness in Organizations." In *Trust and Distrust Within Organizations,* edited by Roderick M. Kramer and Karen S. Cook. New York: Russell Sage Foundation.

Elster, Jon. 1979. *Ulysses and the Sirens.* London: Cambridge University Press.

Ely, John Hart. 1980. *Democracy and Distrust: A Theory of Judicial Review.* Cambridge, Mass.: Harvard University Press.

Emanuel, Ezekiel J., and Nancy N. Dubler. 1995. "Preserving the Physician-Patient Relationship in the Era of Managed Care." *Journal of the American Medical Association* 273(4): 323–29.

Emanuel, Ezekiel J., and Daniel Steiner. 1995. "Institutional Conflict of Interest." *New England Journal of Medicine* 332(4): 262–67.

Emerson, Richard. 1962. "Power-Dependence Relations." *American Sociological Review* 27(1): 31–41.

———. 1964. "Power-Dependence Relations: Two Experiments." *Sociometry* 27(3): 282–98.

———. 1972. "Exchange Theory, Part II: Exchange Relations and Networks." In *Sociological Theories in Progress,* edited by Joseph Berger, Morris Zelditch Jr., and Bo Anderson. Boston: Houghton Mifflin.

Ensminger, Jean. 1992. *Making a Market: The Institutional Transformation of an African Society.* Cambridge, U.K.: Cambridge University Press.

———. 2001. "Reputations, Trust, and the Principal Agent Problem." In *Trust in Society,* edited by Karen S. Cook. New York: Russell Sage Foundation.

Ensminger, Jean, and Jack Knight. 1997. "Changing Social Norms: Common Property, Bridewealth, and Clan Exogamy." *Current Anthropology* 38: 1–24.

Farrell, Henry. 2004. "Trust, Distrust, and Power." In *Distrust,* edited by Russell Hardin. New York: Russell Sage Foundation.

———. Forthcoming. "Trust and Political Economy: Comparing the Effects of Institutions on Interfirm Cooperation." *Comparative Political Studies.*

Fearon, James D. 1999. "Electoral Accountability and the Control of Politicians: Selecting Good Types Versus Sanctioning Poor Performance." In *Democracy, Accountability, and Representation,* edited by Adam Przeworski, Susan C. Stokes, and Bernard Manin. New York: Cambridge University Press.

Fehr, Ernst, and Armin Falk. 1999. "Wage Rigidity in a Competitive Incomplete Contract Market." *Journal of Political Economy* 107(1): 106–34.

Fehr, Ernst, Erich Kirchler, Andreas Weichbold, and Simon Gachter. 1998. "When Social Norms Overpower Competition: Gift Exchange in Experimental Labor Markets." *Journal of Labor Economics* 16(2): 324–51.

Feldman, Martha S. 1989. *Order Without Design: Information Production and Policymaking.* Palo Alto, Calif.: Stanford University Press.

Ferber, Dan. 2002. "Overhaul of CDC Panel Revives Lead Safety Debate." *Science* 298(October 25): 732.

Fernandez, Roberto M., Emilio J. Castilla, and Paul Moore. 2000. "Social Capital at Work: Networks and Employment at a Phone Center." *American Journal of Sociology* 105(5): 1288–1356.

Fernandez, Roberto M., and Nancy Weinberg. 1997. "Labor Markets in Japan and the United States: Sifting and Sorting: Personal Contacts and Hiring in a Retail Bank." *American Sociological Review* 62(6): 883–902.

Ferrary, Michel. 2003. "Trust and Social Capital in the Regulation of Lending Activities." *Journal of Socioeconomics* 31(6): 673–99.

Fiorina, Morris P. 1999. "A Dark Side of Civic Engagement." In *Civic Engagement in American Democracy*, edited by Theda Skocpol and Morris P. Fiorina. Washington, D.C. and New York: Brookings Institution and Russell Sage Foundation.

Fischer, Claude S. 1982. *To Dwell Among Friends: Personal Networks in Town and City*. Chicago: University of Chicago Press.

Flanagan, Dennis. 1992. "Fraud in Science: A Media Event." Paper delivered at the conference, Knowledge and Responsibility: The Moral Role of Scientists. Wingspread, Wis. (October 9–10).

Flexner, Abraham. 1910. *Medical Education in the United States and Canada*. With an Introduction by Henry Pritchett. Report to the Carnegie Foundation for the Advancement of Teaching. Bulletin 4. New York: Carnegie Foundation for the Advancement of Teaching.

Fogelson, Robert M. 1977. *Big-City Police*. Cambridge, Mass.: Harvard University Press.

Fox, Alan. 1974. *Beyond Contract: Work, Power, and Trust Relations*. London: Faber and Faber.

Freidson, Eliot. 1986. *Professional Powers: A Study of the Institutionalization of Formal Power*. Chicago: University of Chicago Press.

Frey, Bruno S. 1993. "Does Monitoring Increase Work Effort? The Rivalry with Trust and Loyalty." *Economic Inquiry* 31(4): 663–70.

———. 1994. "How Intrinsic Motivation Is Crowded Out and In." *Rationality and Society* 6(3): 334–52.

———. 1997. "A Constitution for Knaves Crowds Out Civic Virtues." *Economic Journal* 107: 1043–53.

Frey, Bruno S., and Lars P. Feld. 2002. "Trust Breeds Trust." *Economics of Governance* 3(3): 87–99.

Fukuyama, Francis. 1995. *Trust: The Social Virtues and the Creation of Prosperity*. New York: Free Press.

Fuller, Lon L. 1981. "Human Interaction and the Law." In *The Principles of Social Order*, edited by Kenneth Winston. Durham, N.C.: Duke University Press.

Gambetta, Diego. 1993. *The Sicilian Mafia: The Business of Private Protection*. Cambridge, Mass.: Harvard University Press.

———, ed. 1988. *Trust: Making and Breaking Cooperative Relations*. Oxford: Blackwell.

Gambetta, Diego, and Heather Hamill. Forthcoming. *Streetwise: How Taxi Drivers Establish Customers' Trustworthiness*. New York: Russell Sage Foundation.

García, Jorge A., Debora A. Paterniti, P. S. Romano, and Richard L. Kravitz. 2003. "Patient Preferences for Physician Characteristics in University-Based Primary Care Clinics." *Ethnicity and Disease* 13(2): 259–67.

Garcia, Stephen M. 2002. "Power and the Illusion of Transparency in Negotiations." *Journal of Business and Psychology* 17(1): 133–44.

Geertz, Clifford. 1962. "The Rotating Credit Association: A 'Middle Rung' in Development." *Economic Development and Cultural Change* 10: 241–63.

———. 1963. *Peddlers and Princes.* Chicago: University of Chicago Press.

———. 1978. "The Bazaar Economy: Information and Search in Peasant Marketing." *American Economic Review* 68(2): 28–32.

Gellner, Ernest. 1988. "Trust, Cohesion, and the Social Order." In *Trust: Making and Breaking Cooperative Relations,* edited by Diego Gambetta. Oxford: Blackwell.

Gerstle, Gary, and John Mollenkopf, eds. 2001. *E Pluribus Unum? Contemporary and Historical Perspectives on Immigrant Political Incorporation.* New York: Russell Sage Foundation.

Gewirth, Alan. 1986. "Professional Ethics." *Ethics* 96(January): 282–300.

Ghatak, Maitreesh, and Timothy W. Guinnane. 1999. "The Economics of Lending with Joint Liability: Theory and Practice." *Journal of Development Economics* 60(1): 195–228.

Gibbons, Robert. 2001. "Trust in Social Structures." In *Trust in Society,* edited by Karen S. Cook. New York: Russell Sage Foundation.

———. 2003. "Team Theory, Garbage Cans, and Real Organizations: Some History and Prospects of Economic Research on Decisionmaking in Organizations." *Industrial and Corporate Change* 12(4): 753–87.

Gibbons, Robert, and Larry F. Katz. 1991. "Layoffs and Lemons." *Journal of Labor Economics* 9(4): 351–80.

Gibbons, Robert, and Andrew Rutten. 2004. "Institutional Interactions: An Equilibrium Approach to the State and Civil Society." Cambridge, Mass.: Sloane School, MIT.

Gibson, Clark C. 1999. *Politicians and Poachers: The Political Economy of Wildlife Policy in Africa.* New York: Cambridge University Press.

Gibson, James L. 2001. "Social Networks, Civil Society, and the Prospects for Consolidating Russia's Democratic Transition." *American Journal of Political Science* 45(1): 51–68.

Gilmour, Ian. 1992. *Riots, Risings, and Revolution: Governance and Violence in Eighteenth-Century England.* London: Hutchinson.

Ginsburg, Tom. 2000. "Does Law Matter for Economic Development? Evidence from East Asia." *Law and Society Review* 34(3): 829–54.

Gladwell, Malcolm. 1999. "Six Degrees of Lois Weisberg." *The New Yorker* (January 11): 52–63.

Gluckman, Max. 1956. *Custom and Conflict in Africa.* Oxford: Blackwell.

Goldman, Alan H. 1980. *Moral Foundations of Professionalism.* Totowa, N.J.: Rowman and Littlefield.

Goldthorpe, John H., David Lockwood, Frank Bechhofer, and Jennifer Platt. 1968. *The Affluent Worker: Industrial Attitudes and Behavior.* Cambridge: Cambridge University Press.

Good, David. 1988. "Individuals, Interpersonal Relations, and Trust." In *Trust: Making and Breaking Cooperative Relations,* edited by Diego Gambetta. New York: Blackwell.

Gordon, David M. 1996. *Fat and Mean.* New York: Free Press.

Gorlin, Rena A., ed. 1999. *Codes of Professional Responsibility: Ethics Standards in Business, Health, and Law.* 4th ed. Washington: Bureau of National Affairs.

Gould, Stephen Jay. 1993. *Eighty Little Piggies: Reflections in Natural History.* New York: Norton.

Gould, Susan D. 1998. "Money and Trust: Relationships Between Patients, Physicians, and Health Plans." *Journal of Health Politics, Policy, and Law* 23(4): 687–95.

Gouldner, Alvin W. 1954. *Patterns of Industrial Bureaucracy.* Glencoe, Ill.: Free Press.

Granovetter, Mark. 1973. "The Strength of Weak Ties." *American Journal of Sociology* 78(6): 1360–80.

———. 1985. "Economic Action and Social Structure: The Problem of Embeddedness." *American Journal of Sociology* 91(3): 481–510.

———. 2002. "A Theoretical Agenda for Economic Sociology." In *The New Economic Sociology: Developments in an Emerging Field,* edited by Mauro Guillén, Randall Collins, Paula England, and Marshall Meyer. New York: Russell Sage Foundation.

Green, Thomas Andrew. 1985. *Verdict According to Conscience: Perspectives on the English Criminal Trial Jury, 1200–1800.* Chicago: University of Chicago Press.

Greif, Avner. 1989. "Reputation and Coalitions in Medieval Trade: Evidence on the Maghribi Traders." *Journal of Economic History* 49(4): 857–82.

———. 1993. "Contract Enforceability and Economic Institutions in Early Trade: The Maghribi Traders' Coalition." *American Economic Review* 83(3): 525–48.

———. 1995. "Micro Theory and Recent Developments in the Study of Economic Institutions Through Economic History." In *Advances in Economics and Econometrics: Theory and Applications,* edited by David M. Kreps. New York: Cambridge University Press.

Greif, Avner, Paul Milgrom, and Barry R. Weingast. 1994. "Coordination, Commitment, and Enforcement: The Case of the Merchant Guild." *Journal of Political Economy* 102(4): 745–76.

Grzymala-Busse, Anna. 2002. *Redeeming the Past: The Regeneration of Communist Successor Parties in East Central Europe After 1989.* Studies in Comparative Politics Series. New York: Cambridge University Press.

Gudeman, Stephen. 1971. "The *Compadrazgo* as a Reflection of the Natural and Spiritual Person." *Proceedings of the Royal Anthropological Institute of Great Britain and Ireland* 1971: 45–71.

Gulati, Ranjay, and Harbir Singh. 1998. "The Architecture of Cooperation: Managing Coordination Costs and Appropriation Concerns in Strategic Alliances." *Administrative Science Quarterly* 43(4): 781–814.

Gulick, Luther. 1937. "Notes on the Theory of Organization." In *Papers on the Science of Administration,* edited by Luther Gulick and Lyndall Urwick. New York: Institute of Public Administration, Columbia University.

Gutmann, Amy, and Dennis Thompson. 1996. *Democracy and Disagreement.* Cambridge, Mass.: Harvard University Press.

Hall, Peter A., and David Soskice, eds. 2001. *Varieties of Capitalism*. New York: Oxford University Press.

Hamilton, Alexander, John Jay, and James Madison. 1787/2001. *The Federalist Papers*, edited by George W. Carey and James McClellan. Gideon ed. Indianapolis, Ind.: Liberty Fund.

Hamilton, Gary G., and Kao Cheng-Shu. 1990. "The Institutional Foundations of Chinese Business: The Family Firm in Taiwan." *Comparative Social Research* 12: 95–112.

Hammond, Thomas H. 1990. "In Defense of Luther Gulick's 'Notes on the Theory of Organization.'" *Public Administration* 68: 143–73.

Hanifan, Lyda J. 1916. "The Rural School Community Center." *Annals of the American Academy of Political and Social Science* 67: 130–38.

Hanlon, Gerard. 1998. "Professionalism as Enterprise: Service Class Politics and the Redefinition of Professionalism." *Sociology* 32(1): 43–63.

Hardin, Russell. 1982a. "Exchange Theory on Strategic Bases." *Social Science Information* 21(2): 251–72.

———. 1982b. *Collective Action*. Baltimore: Johns Hopkins University Press for Resources for the Future.

———. 1988. *Morality Within the Limits of Reason*. Chicago: University of Chicago Press.

———. 1989. "Ethics and Stochastic Processes." *Social Philosophy and Policy* 7(Fall): 69–80.

———. 1991a. "The Artificial Duties of Contemporary Professionals." *Social Service Review* 64(December): 528–41.

———. 1991b. "Trusting Persons, Trusting Institutions." In *The Strategy of Choice*, edited by Richard J. Zeckhauser. Cambridge, Mass.: MIT Press.

———. 1993. "The Street-Level Epistemology of Trust." *Politics and Society* 21(4): 505–29.

———. 1995. *One for All: The Logic of Group Conflict*. Princeton, N.J.: Princeton University Press.

———. 1996a. "Institutional Morality." In *The Theory of Institutional Design*, edited by Robert E. Goodin. Cambridge, U.K.: Cambridge University Press.

———. 1996b. "The Psychology of Business Ethics." In *Codes of Conduct: Behavioral Research into Business Ethics*, edited by David M. Messick and Ann E. Tenbrunsel. New York: Russell Sage Foundation.

———. 1998a. "Institutional Commitment: Values or Incentives?" In *Economics, Values, and Organization*, edited by Avner Ben Ner and Louis Putterman. Cambridge, U.K.: Cambridge University Press.

———. 1998b. "Trust in Government." In *Trust and Governance*, edited by Valerie Braithwaite and Margaret Levi. New York: Russell Sage Foundation.

———. 1999a. "Ethics in Big Science." In *The Proceedings of the Twentieth World Congress of Philosophy*, vol. 1, edited by Klaus Brinkmann. Bowling Green, Ohio: Philosophy Documentation Center.

———. 1999b. "From Bodo Ethics to Distributive Justice." *Ethical Theory and Moral Practice* 2(4): 337–63.

———. 1999c. *Liberalism, Constitutionalism, and Democracy*. Oxford: Oxford University Press.

———. 2000. "Democratic Epistemology and Accountability." *Social Philosophy and Policy* 17: 110–26.

———. 2002a. "Liberal Distrust." *European Review* 10(1): 73–89.

———. 2002b. *Trust and Trustworthiness.* New York: Russell Sage Foundation.

———. 2003. "If It Rained Knowledge." *Philosophy of Social Science* 33(1): 3–23.

———, ed. 2004a. *Distrust.* New York: Russell Sage Foundation.

———. 2004b. "Distrust: Manifestations and Management." In *Distrust,* edited by Russell Hardin. New York: Russell Sage Foundation.

———. 2004c. "Terrorism and Group-Generalized Distrust." In *Distrust,* edited by Russell Hardin. New York: Russell Sage Foundation.

Hart, H. L. A., and Anthony M. Honoré. 1959. *Causation in the Law.* Oxford: Oxford University Press.

Hart, Keith. 1988. "Kinship, Contract, and Trust: Economic Organization of Migrants in an African City Slum." In *Trust: Making and Breaking Cooperative Relations,* edited by Diego Gambetta. Oxford: Blackwell.

Hart, Vivien. 1978. *Distrust and Democracy: Political Trust in America and Britain.* New York: Cambridge University Press.

Hasluck, Margaret. 1954. *The Unwritten Law in Albania,* edited by J. H. Hutton. Cambridge, U.K.: Cambridge University Press.

Hayashi, Nahoko. 1995. "Emergence of Cooperation in One-Shot Prisoner's Dilemmas and the Role of Trust." *Japanese Journal of Psychology* 66(3): 184–90.

Hechter, Michael. 1987. *Principles of Group Solidarity.* Berkeley: University of California Press.

Heinz, John P., and Edward O. Laumann. 1982. *Chicago Lawyers: The Social Structure of the Bar.* New York: Russell Sage Foundation.

Held, Virginia. 1968. "On the Meaning of Trust." *Ethics* 78(2): 156–59.

Henrich, Joseph, Robert Boyd, Samuel Bowles, Colin Camerer, Ernst Fehr, Herbert Gintis, and Richard McElreath. 2004. "Overview and Synthesis." In *Foundations of Human Sociality,* edited by Joseph Henrich, Robert Boyd, Samuel Bowles, Colin Camerer, Ernst Fehr, and Herbert Gintis. New York: Oxford University Press.

Herreros, Francisco. 2004. *The Problem of Forming Social Capital.* New York: Palgrave Macmillan.

Hertzberg, Lars. 1988. "On the Attitude of Trust." *Inquiry* 31(3): 307–22.

Hessler, Peter. 2003. "Under Water: The World's Biggest Dam Floods the Past." *The New Yorker* (July 7): 28–33.

Hetcher, Steven A. 2004. *Norms in a Wired World.* Cambridge, U.K.: Cambridge University Press.

Hetherington, Marc J. 1998. "The Political Relevance of Political Trust." *American Political Science Review* 92(4): 791–808.

———. 2004. *Why Trust Matters: Declining Political Trust and the Demise of American Liberalism.* Princeton, N.J.: Princeton University Press.

Hewstone, Miles, Mark Rubin, and Hazel Willis. 2002. "Intergroup Bias." *Annual Review of Psychology* 53: 575–604.

Hibbing, John R., and Elizabeth Theiss-Morse. 2002. *Stealth Democracy.* New York: Cambridge University Press.

Hirschman, Albert O. 1977. *The Passions and the Interests: Political Arguments for Capitalism Before Its Triumph.* Princeton, N.J.: Princeton University Press.

Hobbes, Thomas. 1651/1968. *Leviathan,* edited by C. B. Macpherson. London: Penguin.

Hoffman, Philip T., Gilles Postel-Vinay, and Jean-Laurent Rosenthal. 2000. *Priceless Markets: The Political Economy of Credit in Paris, 1660–1870.* Chicago: University of Chicago Press.

Hollis, Martin. 1998. *Trust Within Reason.* Cambridge, U.K.: Cambridge University Press.

Holloway, Marguerite, and Paul Wallich. 1992. "A Risk Worth Taking." *Scientific American* (November): 126.

Holmes, John G., and John K. Rempel. 1985. "Trust in Close Relationships." In *Close Relationships: Review of Personality and Social Psychology,* edited by Clyde Hendrick. Newbury Park, Calif.: Sage Publications.

Holmstrom, Bengt. 1982. "Moral Hazard in Teams." *Bell Journal of Economics* 13(2): 324–40.

Holmstrom, Bengt, and Paul Milgrom. 1994. "The Firm as an Incentive System." *American Economic Review* 84(4): 972–91.

Holton, Gerald. 1995/1996. " 'Doing One's Damnedest': The Evolution of Trust in Scientific Findings." In *Einstein, History, and Other Passions: The Rebellion Against Science at the End of the Twentieth Century.* New York: Addison-Wesley. (Orig. pub. in 1995 by American Institute of Physics Press, Woodbury, N.Y.)

Horne, Cynthia, and Margaret Levi. 2004. "Does Lustration Promote Trustworthy Government? An Exploration of the Experience of Central and Eastern Europe." In *Building a Trustworthy State in Post-Socialist Transition,* edited by Janos Kornai and Susan Rose-Ackerman. New York: Palgrave Macmillan.

Horsburgh, H. J. N. 1960. "The Ethics of Trust." *Philosophical Quarterly* 10: 343–54.

Howard, Judith. 1995. "Social Cognition." In *Sociological Perspectives on Social Psychology,* edited by Karen S. Cook, Gary Alan Fine, and James S. House. Boston: Allyn and Bacon.

Hsee, Christopher K., and Elke U. Weber. 1999. "Cross-national Differences in Risk Preference and Lay Preferences." *Journal of Behavioral Decisionmaking* 12(2): 165–79.

Huici, Carmen, Maria Ros, Mercedes Carmon, Jose Ignacio Cano, and Jose Francisco Morales. 1996. "Stereotypic Trait Disconfirmation and the Positive-Negative Asymmetry." *Journal of Social Psychology* 136(3): 277–89.

Humboldt, Wilhelm von. 1854/1969. *The Limits of State Action,* edited by J. W. Burrow. Cambridge, U.K.: Cambridge University Press; 1993 rep., Indianapolis, Ind.: Liberty Fund.

Hume, David. 1739–40/1978. *A Treatise of Human Nature.* Oxford: Oxford University Press, 2nd ed., edited by L. A. Selby-Bigge and P. H. Nidditch.

———. 1752/1985. "Of the Independency of Parliament." In *David Hume, Essays Moral, Political, and Literary,* rev. ed., edited by Eugene F. Miller. Indianapolis, Ind.: Liberty Press.

Inglehart, Ronald. 1997. *Modernization and Postmodernization: Cultural, Political, and Economic Change in Forty-three Societies.* Princeton, N.J.: Princeton University Press.

Jacobs, Jane. 1961. *The Death and Life of Great American Cities.* New York: Random House.

Jensen, Michael, and William Meckling. 1976. "Theory of the Firm: Managerial Behavior, Agency Costs, and Ownership Structure." *Journal of Financial Economics* 3: 305–60.

Jones, Karen. 1996. "Trust as an Affective Attitude." *Ethics* 107(1): 4–25.

Kang, David C. 2002. *Crony Capitalism, Corruption, and Development in South Korea and the Philippines.* New York: Cambridge University Press.

Kao, Audiey, Diane Green, Alan M. Zaslavsky, Jeffrey P. Koplan, and Paul D. Cleary. 1998. "The Relationship Between Method of Physician Payment and Patient Trust." *Journal of the American Medical Association* 280: 1708–14.

Kaufman, Jason. 2002. *For the Common Good.* New York: Oxford University Press.

Kaufmann, Daniel, Aart Kraay, and Pablo Zoido-Lobaton. 1999. *Governance Matters.* Paper Policy Research Working Paper 2196. Washington, D.C.: World Bank.

———. 2002. *Governance Matters II: Updated Indicators for 2000–2001.* Paper Policy Research Working Paper 2772. Washington, D.C.: World Bank.

Kelley, Harold H., and John W. Thibaut. 1977. *Interpersonal Relations: A Theory of Interdependence.* New York: Wiley.

Kelman, Steven. 1990. "Congress and Public Spirit: A Commentary." In *Beyond Self-interest,* edited by Jane J. Mansbridge. Chicago: University of Chicago Press.

Kennedy, Donald. 2003. "Editorial: Multiple Authors, Multiple Problems." *Science* (August 8): 733.

Kerri, James Nwannukwu. 1976. "Studying Voluntary Associations as Adaptive Mechanisms: A Review of Anthropological Perspectives." *Current Anthropology* 17(1): 23–47.

Kiernan, Victor G. 1986. *The Duel in European History: Honor and the Reign of Aristocracy.* Oxford: Oxford University Press.

King, Anthony. 2000. "Distrust of Government: Explaining American Exceptionalism." In *Disaffected Democracies: What's Troubling the Trilateral Democracies,* edited by Susan J. Pharr and Robert D. Putnam. Princeton, N.J.: Princeton University Press.

King, Valarie. 2002. "Parental Divorce and Interpersonal Trust in Adult Offspring." *Journal of Marriage and Family* 64(3): 642–56.

Kiser, Edgar, and Joachim Schneider. 1994. "Bureaucracy and Efficiency: An Analysis of Taxation in Early-Modern Prussia." *American Sociological Review* 59(2): 187–204.

Kitschelt, Herbert, Zdenka Mansfeldova, Radoslaw Markowski, and Gabor Toka. 1999. *Post-Communist Party Systems: Competition, Representation, and Interparty Cooperation,* edited by Margaret Levi. Cambridge Studies in Comparative Politics Series. New York: Cambridge University Press.

Klein, Benjamin. 1985. "Self-enforcing Contracts." *Journal of Institutional and Theoretical Economics* 141: 594–600.

Kleinfeld, Judith. 2002. "Six Degrees of Separation: Urban Myth?" *Psychology Today* 35(2): 74.

Knack, Stephen, and Philip Keefer. 1995. "Institutions and Economic Performance: Cross-country Tests Using Alternative Institutional Measures." *Economics and Politics* 7: 207–27.

———. 1997. "Does Social Capital Have an Economic Payoff? A Cross-country Investigation." *Quarterly Journal of Economics* 112(4): 1251–88.

Knack, Stephen, and Paul Zak. 2002. "Building Trust: Public Policy, Interpersonal Trust, and Economic Development." *Supreme Court Economic Review* 10(fall): 91–107.

Knight, Jack. 1992. *Institutions and Social Conflict.* Cambridge, U.K.: Cambridge University Press.

Kollock, Peter. 1994. "The Emergence of Exchange Structures: An Experimental Study of Uncertainty, Commitment, and Trust." *American Journal of Sociology* 100(2): 313–45.

———. 1999. "The Production of Trust in Online Markets." In *Advances in Group Processes,* edited by Edward J. Lawler. Greenwich, Conn.: JAI Press.

Kramer, Roderick M. 1994. "The Sinister Attribution Error: Paranoid Cognition and Collective Distrust in Organizations." *Motivation and Emotion* 18(2): 199–230.

———. 1996. "Divergent Realities and Convergent Disappointments in the Hierarchic Relation: Trust and the Intuitive Auditor at Work." In *Trust in Organizations: Frontiers of Theory and Research,* edited by Roderick M. Kramer and Tom R. Tyler. Thousand Oaks, Calif.: Sage Publications.

———. 1998. "Paranoid Cognition in Social Systems: Thinking and Acting in the Shadow of Doubt." *Personality and Social Psychology Review* 2(4): 251–75.

———. 1999. "Trust and Distrust in Organizations: Emerging Perspectives, Enduring Questions." *Annual Review of Psychology* 50(1): 569–98.

Kramer, Roderick M. and Karen S. Cook, eds. 2004. *Trust and Distrust in Organizations.* New York: Russell Sage Foundation.

Kramer, Roderick M., and Dana A. Gavrieli. 2004. "Power, Uncertainty, and the Amplification of Doubt: An Archival Study of Suspicion Inside the Oval Office." In *Trust and Distrust in Organizations,* edited by Roderick M. Kramer and Karen S. Cook. New York: Russell Sage Foundation.

Kreps, David M. 1990. "Corporate Culture and Economic Theory." In *Perspectives in Positive Political Economy,* edited by James Alt and Kenneth Shepsle. New York: Cambridge University Press.

Krimsky, Sheldon. 2003. *Science in the Private Interest: Has the Lure of Profits Corrupted the Virtue of Biomedical Research?* Lanham, Md.: Rowman and Littlefield.

Krueger, Alan B., and Alexandre Mas. 2003. "Strikes, Scabs, and Tread Separations: Labor Strife and the Production of Defective Bridgestone/Firestone Tires." Working paper 9524. Cambridge, Mass.: National Bureau of Economic Research.

Krugman, Paul. 2002. "For Richer." *New York Times Magazine,* (October 20): 62–67, 76–77, 141–42.

Ladd, Everett C. 1996. "Civic Participation and American Democracy: The Data Just Don't Show Erosion of America's 'Social Capital.' " *The Public Perspective* 7(4, June–July): 1–22.

———. 1999. "Bowling with Tocqueville: Civic Engagements and Social Capital." *The Responsive Community* 9(2, Spring): 11–21.

Laffont, Jean-Jacques, and Jean Tirole. 1993. *A Theory of Incentives in Procurement and Regulation.* Cambridge, Mass.: MIT Press.

Landa, Janet Tai. 1994. *Trust, Ethnicity, and Identity: Beyond the New Institutional Economics of Ethnic Trading Networks, Contract Law, and Gift Exchange.* Ann Arbor: University of Michigan Press.

Lane, Christel, and Reinhard Bachmann. 1996. "The Social Constitution of Trust: Supplier Relations in Britain and Germany." *Organization Studies* 17(3): 365–95.

Larson, Magali Sarfatti. 1977. *The Rise of Professionalism: A Sociological Analysis.* Berkeley: University of California Press.

LaVeist, Thomas A., and Amani Nuru-Jeter. 2002. "Is Doctor-Patient Race Concordance Associated with Greater Satisfaction with Care?" *Journal of Health Social Behavior* 43(3): 296–306.

Lawler, Edward J., and Jeongkoo Yoon. 1998. "Network Structure and Emotion in Exchange Relations." *American Sociological Review* 63(6): 871–94.

Leblang, David A. 1996. "Property Rights, Democracy, and Economic Growth." *Political Research Quarterly* (49): 5–26.

Leider, Peter J., Ryan Solberg, and Thomas Nesbitt. 1997. "Family Physician Perception of Economic Incentives for the Provision of Office Procedures." *Family Medicine* 29(5): 318–20.

Leijonhufvud, Axel. 1995. "The Individual, the Market, and the Industrial Division of Labor." In *L'Individuo e il mercato*, edited by Carlo Mongardini. Rome: Bulzoi.

Leik, Robert K., and Sheila K. Leik. 1977. "Transition to Interpersonal Commitment." In *Behavioral Theory in Sociology*, edited by Robert L. Hamblin and John H. Kunkel. New Brunswick, N.J.: Transaction.

Leisen, Birgit, and Michael R. Hyman. 2001. "An Improved Scale for Assessing Patients' Trust in Their Physician." *Health Marketing Quarterly* 19(1): 23–24.

Lenin, Vladimir I. 1902/1963. *What Is to Be Done?* Translated by S. V. Utechin and Patricia Utechin. Oxford: Clarendon Press.

Levi, Margaret. 1988. *Of Rule and Revenue.* Berkeley: University of California Press.

———. 1990. "A Logic of Institutional Change." In *The Limits of Rationality*, edited by Karen Schweers Cook and Margaret Levi. Chicago: University of Chicago Press.

———. 1996. "Social and Unsocial Capital: A Review Essay of Robert Putnam's *Making Democracy Work.*" *Politics and Society* 24(1): 45–55.

———. 1997. *Consent, Dissent, and Patriotism.* Cambridge, U.K.: Cambridge University Press.

———. 1998. "A State of Trust." In *Trust and Governance*, edited by Valerie Braithwaite and Margaret Levi. New York: Russell Sage Foundation.

———. 2000. "When Good Defenses Make Good Neighbors." In *Institutions, Contracts, and Organizations: Perspectives from New Institutional Economics*, edited by Claude Menard. Colchester, Eng.: Edward Elgar.

———. 2002. "The State of the Study of the State." In *Political Science: State of the Discipline*, edited by Ira Katznelson and Helen Milner. New York: Norton, with the American Political Science Association.

———. Forthcoming. "Inducing Preferences Within Organizations." In *Preferences and Situations: Points of Intersection Between Historical and Rational Choice Institutionalism*, edited by Ira Katznelson and Barry Weingast. New York: Russell Sage Foundation.

Levi, Margaret, Matt Moe, and Theresa Buckley. 2004. "The Transaction Costs of Distrust: Labor and Management at the National Labor Relations Board." In *Distrust*, edited by Russell Hardin. New York: Russell Sage Foundation.

Levi, Margaret, and David Olson. 2000. "The Battles in Seattle." *Politics and Society* 28(3): 217–37.

Levi, Margaret, and Laura Stoker. 2000. "Political Trust and Trustworthiness." *Annual Review of Political Science* 3: 475–507.

Levin, Irwin P., Edward A. Wasserman, and Shu-fang Kao. 1993. "Multiple Methods for Examining Biased Information Use in Contingency Judgments." *Organizational Behavior and Human Decision Processes* 55: 228–50.

Levin, Jonathan. 2003. "Rational Incentive Contracts." *American Economic Review* 93(3): 835–57.

Lieberman, Evan S. 2003. *Race and Regionalism in the Politics of Taxation in Brazil and South Africa*. New York: Cambridge University Pres.

Light, Ivan. 1972. *Ethnic Enterprise in America*. Berkeley: University of California Press.

Lin, Nan. 2001. *Social Capital: A Theory of Social Structure and Action*. Cambridge, U.K.: Cambridge University Press.

Lipsky, Michael. 1980. *Street-Level Bureaucracy*. New York: Basic Books.

Little, Kenneth. 1965. *West African Urbanization: A Study of Voluntary Association in West African Urbanization*. Cambridge: Cambridge University Press.

Lloyd, G. E. R., ed. 1950/1983. *Hippocratic Writings*. Harmondsworth, Eng.: Penguin.

Locke, John. 1690/1988. *Two Treatises of Government*, student ed., edited by Peter Laslett. Cambridge, U.K.: Cambridge University Press.

Loewenstein, George. 1996. "Behavioral Decision Theory and Business Ethics: Skewed Trade-offs Between Self and Other." In *Codes of Conduct: Behavioral Research into Business Ethics*, edited by David M. Messick and Ann E. Tenbrunsel. New York: Russell Sage Foundation.

Lomnitz, Larissa Adler, and Diana Sheinbaum. 2002. "Trust, Social Networks, and the Informal Economy: A Comparative Analysis." Paper presented at Workshop 2, "Formal and Informal Cooperation," at the conference "Honesty and Trust: Theory and Experience in the Light of Post-Socialist Experience." Collegium Budapest (November 23).

Lorenz, Edward H. 1988. "Neither Friends nor Strangers: Informal Networks of Subcontracting in French Industry." In *Trust: Making and Breaking Cooperative Relations*, edited by Diego Gambetta. Oxford: Blackwell.

Loury, Glenn C. 1977. "A Dynamic Theory of Racial Income Differences." In *Women, Minorities, and Employment Discrimination*, edited by Phyllis A. Wallace and Annette LaMond. Lexington, Mass.: Lexington Books.

———. 1987. "Why Should We Care About Group Inequality?" *Social Philosophy and Policy* 5: 249–71.

Luban, David. 1988. *Lawyers and Justice: An Ethical Study*. Princeton, N.J.: Princeton University Press.

Luebke, Neil R. 1987. "Conflict of Interest as a Moral Category." *Business and Professional Ethics Journal* 6(Summer): 66–81.

Luhmann, Niklas. 1980. "Trust: A Mechanism for the Reduction of Social Complexity." In *Trust and Power*, by Niklas Luhmann. New York: Wiley.

Luong Jones, Pauline, and Erika Weinthal. 2004. "Contra Coercion: Russian Tax Reform, Exogenous Shocks, and Negotiated Institutional Change." *American Political Science Review* 98(1): 139–52.

Macauley, Stewart. 1963. "Noncontractual Relations in Business: A Preliminary Study." *American Sociological Review* 28(February): 55–67.

Mackie, Gerry. 2001. "Patterns of Social Trust in Western Europe and Their Genesis." In *Trust in Society*, edited by Karen S. Cook. New York: Russell Sage Foundation.

Macneil, Ian R. 1980. *The New Social Contract: An Inquiry into Modern Contractual Relations*. New Haven, Conn.: Yale University Press.

Macrae, C. Neil, Miles Hewstone, and Riana J. Griffiths. 1993. "Processing Load and Memory for Stereotype-Based Information." *European Journal of Social Psychology* 23(1): 77–87.

Mahon, John K. 1983. *History of the Militia and the National Guard*. New York: Macmillan.

Malakoff, David, and Martin Enserink. 2003. "Researchers Await Government Response to Self-regulation Plea." *Science* 302(October 17): 368–69.

Malhotra, Deepak, and J. Keith Murnighan. 2002. "The Effects of Contracts on Interpersonal Trust." *Administrative Science Quarterly* 47(3): 534–59.

Mansbridge, Jane J. 1999. "Altruistic Trust." In *Democracy and Trust*, edited by Mark Warren. Cambridge, U.K.: Cambridge University Press.

Mares, Isabela. 2003. *The Politics of Social Risk: Business and Welfare State Development*. New York: Cambridge University Press.

Marshall, Eliot. 1990. "When Commerce and Academe Collide." *Science* (new series) 248(4952): 152–56.

Marx, Karl. 1852/1963. *The Eighteenth Brumaire of Louis Bonaparte*. New York: International Publishers.

Massey, Douglas S. 1986. "The Settlement Process Among Mexican Migrants to the United States." *American Sociological Review* 51(5): 670–84.

Maurice, Marc, François Sellier, and Jean-Jacques Silvestre. 1986. *The Social Foundations of Industrial Power: A Comparison of France and Germany*. Translated by Arthur Goldhammer. Cambridge, Mass.: MIT Press.

McAllister, Daniel J. 1995. "Special Research Forum: Intra- and Interorganizational Cooperation Affect- and Cognition-Based Trust as Foundations for Inter-personal Cooperation in Organizations." *Academy of Management Journal* 38(1): 24–59.

McCabe, Kevin A., Stephen J. Rassenti, and Vernon L. Smith. 1998. "Reciprocity, Trust, and Payoff Privacy in Extensive Form Bargaining." *Games and Economic Behavior* 24(1): 10–24.

McGill, Ann. 1996. "Responsibility Judgments and the Causal Background." In *Codes of Conduct: Behavioral Research into Business Ethics*, edited by David M. Messick and Ann E. Tenbrunsel. New York: Russell Sage Foundation.

McKinlay, John B., and Lisa D. Marceau. 2002. "The End of the Golden Age of Doctoring." *International Journal of Health Services: Planning, Administration, Evaluation* 32(2): 379–416.

McMillan, John, and Christopher Woodruff. 2000. "Private Order Under Dysfunctional Public Order." *Michigan Law Review* 98(8): 2421–58.

McWilliam, Carol L., Judith Belle Brown, and Moira Stewart. 2000. "Breast Cancer Patients' Experiences of Patient-Doctor Communication: A Working Relationship." *Patient Education and Counseling* 39(2): 191–204.

Mechanic, David. 1998a. "Managed Care, Rationing, and Trust in Medical Care." *Journal of Urban Health* 75(1): 118–22.

———. 1998b. "The Functions and Limitations of Trust in the Provision of Medical Care." *Journal of Health Politics, Policy, and Law* 23(4): 661–86.

Mechanic, David, and Marsha Rosenthal. 1999. "Responses of HMO Medical Directors to Trust Building in Managed Care." *Milbank Quarterly* 77(3): 273, 283–303.

Mechanic, David, and Mark Schlesinger. 1996. "The Impact of Managed Care on Patients' Trust in Medical Settings." *Journal of the American Medical Association* 275: 1693.

Meeker, Barbara. 1994. "Performance Evaluation." In *Group Processes: Sociological Analyses,* edited by Margaret Foschi and Edward J. Lawler. Chicago: Nelson-Hall.

Meier, Nicholas, and Daryl Close Meier, eds. 1994. *Morality in Criminal Justice: An Introduction to Ethics.* Belmont, Calif.: Wadsworth.

Mérimée, Prosper. 1840/1989. "Colomba." In *Carmen and Other Stories,* by Prosper Mérimée. Oxford: Oxford University Press.

Merritt, Deborah Jones, and Kathryn Ann Barry. 1999. "Is the Tort System in Crisis? New Empirical Evidence." *Ohio State Law Journal* 60(2): 315–98.

Merton, Robert K. 1957/1968. *Social Theory and Social Structure.* 3rd ed. Glencoe, Ill.: Free Press.

Michaels, David, Eula Bingham, Les Boden, Richard Clapp, Lynn R. Goldman, Polly Hoppin, Sheldon Krimsky, Celeste Monforton, David Ozonoff, and Anthony Robbins. 2002. "Editorial: Advice Without Dissent." *Science* (October 25): 703.

Michaels, David, and Wendy Wagner. 2003. "Disclosure in Regulatory Science." *Science* 302(December 19): 2073.

Michels, Robert. 1919/1962. *Political Parties.* New York: Free Press.

Milgrom, Paul R., Douglass C. North, and Barry R. Weingast. 1990. "The Role of Institutions in the Revival of Trade: The Medieval Law Merchant, Private Judges, and the Champagne Fairs." *Economics and Politics* 2(1): 1–23.

Milgrom, Stanley. 1967. "The Small World Problem." *Psychology Today* 1(1): 60–67.

Mill, John Stuart. 1859/1977. *On Liberty.* In *Collected Works of John Stuart Mill,* vol. 18, edited by J. M. Robson. Toronto: University of Toronto Press.

Miller, Gary. 1992. *Managerial Dilemmas.* New York: Cambridge University Press.

———. 2000. "Why Is Trust Necessary in Organizations? The Moral Hazard of Profit Maximization." In *Trust in Society,* edited by Karen S. Cook. New York: Russell Sage Foundation.

———. 2004. "Monitoring, Rules, and the Control Paradox: Can the Good Soldier Svejk Be Trusted?" In *Trust and Distrust Within Organizations: Dilemmas and Approaches,* edited by Roderick M. Kramer and Karen S. Cook. New York: Russell Sage Foundation.

Miller, William Ian. 1990. *Bloodtaking and Peacemaking: Feud, Law, and Society in Saga Iceland.* Chicago: University of Chicago Press.

Minkel, J. R. 2002. "Reality Check: Alleged Fraud Gets Physicists Thinking About Misconduct." *Scientific American* (November): 20–22.

Mishler, William, and Richard Rose. 1997. "Trust, Distrust, and Skepticism: Popular Evaluations of Civil and Political Institutions in Post-Communist Societies." *Journal of Politics* 59(2): 419–51.

Misztal, Barbara A. 1996. *Trust in Modern Societies: The Search for the Bases of Social Order.* Cambridge, U.K.: Polity Press.

Mitroff, Ian I. 1974. "Norms and Counternorms in a Select Group of the Apollo Moon Scientists: A Case Study of the Ambivalence of Scientists." *American Sociological Review* 39(4): 579–95.

Mizruchi, Mark S., and Linda Brewster Stearns. 2001. "Getting Deals Done: The Use of Social Networks in Bank Decisionmaking." *American Sociological Review* 66(5): 647–71.

Mollering, Guido. 2002. "Perceived Trustworthiness and Interfirm Governance: Empirical Evidence from the U.K. Printing Industry." *Cambridge Journal of Economics* 26(2): 139–60.

Molm, Linda D. 1997. "Risk and Power Use: Constraints on the Use of Coercion in Exchange." *American Sociological Review* 62(1): 113–33.

Molm, Linda D., and Karen S. Cook. 1995. "Social Exchange and Exchange Networks." In *Sociological Perspectives on Social Psychology*, edited by Karen S. Cook, Gary Alan Fine, and James S. House. Boston: Allyn and Bacon.

Molm, Linda, Nobuyuki Takahashi, and Gretchen Peterson. 2000. "Risk and Trust in Social Exchange: An Experimental Test of a Classical Proposition." *American Journal of Sociology* 105(5): 1396–1427.

Montgomery, James D. 1999. "Adverse Selection and Employment Cycles." *Journal of Labor Economics* 17(2): 281–97.

Montinola, Gabriella. 2004. "Corruption, Distrust, and the Deterioration of the Rule of Law." In *Distrust*, edited by Russell Hardin. New York: Russell Sage Foundation.

Moore, Sally Falk. 1978. *Law as Process: An Anthropological Approach.* London: Routledge & Kegan Paul.

Morduch, Jonathan. 1999. "The Role of Subsidies in Microfinance: Evidence from the Grameen Bank." *Journal of Development Economics* 60(1): 228–48.

Morgan, Edmund S. 1999. "Just Say No." Review of Garry Wills, *A Necessary Evil: A History of American Distrust of Government. New York Review of Books* (November 18): 39–41.

Mueller, John. 1999. *Capitalism, Democracy, and Ralph's Pretty Good Grocery.* Princeton, N.J.: Princeton University Press.

Muldrew, Craig. 1993. "Interpreting the Market: The Ethics of Credit and Community Relations in Early Modern England." *Social History* 18(2): 163–83.

Murnighan, J. Keith, Deepak Malhotra, and J. Mark Weber. 2004. "Paradoxes of Trust: Empirical and Theoretical Departures from a Traditional Mode." In *Trust and Distrust Within Organizations: Emerging Perspectives, Enduring Questions*, edited by Roderick M. Kramer and Karen S. Cook. New York: Russell Sage Foundation.

National Center for Health Statistics. 2002. *Health, United States, 2002.* Hyattsville, Md.: National Center for Health Statistics.

Nature. 2003. "Survey Reveals Mixed Feelings over Scientific Misconduct." *Nature* 424(July 10): 117.

Nee, Victor, and Rebeccah Matthews. 1996. "Market Transition and Societal Transformation in Reforming State Socialism." *Annual Review of Sociology* 22: 401–35.

Nee, Victor, and Brett de Bar'y Nee. 1973. *Longtime Californ': A Documentary Study of an American Chinatown.* New York: Pantheon.

Nee, Victor, and Jimy Sanders. 2000. "Trust in Ethnic Ties: Social Capital and Immigrants." In *Trust in Society,* edited by Karen S. Cook. New York: Russell Sage Foundation.

Nelson, Bruce. 1988. *Workers on the Waterfront: Seamen, Longshoremen, and Unionism in the 1930s.* Urbana: University of Illinois Press.

Ness, Immanual. 1998. "Organizing Immigrant Communities: UNITE's Workers Center Strategy." In *Organizing to Win,* edited by Kate Bronfenbrenner, Sheldon Friedman, Richard W. Hurd, Rudolph Oswald, and Ronald L. Seeber. Ithaca, N.Y.: ILR Press, an imprint of Cornell University Press.

Nesse, Randolph M., ed. 2003. *The Evolution of Commitment.* New York: Russell Sage Foundation.

Neustadt, Richard E. 1980/1990. *Presidential Power and the Modern Presidents: The Politics of Leadership from Roosevelt to Reagan.* Rev. ed. New York: Free Press.

Newton, Kenneth. 1999. "Social and Political Trust." In *Critical Citizens: Global Support for Democratic Government,* edited by Pippa Norris. New York: Oxford University Press.

Newton, Kenneth, and Pippa Norris. 2000. "Confidence in Public Institutions: Faith, Culture, or Performance." In *Disaffected Democracies,* edited by Susan Pharr and Robert Putnam. Princeton, N.J.: Princeton University Press.

Nisbett, Richard, and Dov Cohen. 1996. *Culture of Honor.* Boulder, Colo.: Westview.

Norris, Pippa, ed. 1999. *Critical Citizens: Global Support for Democratic Government.* New York: Oxford University Press.

———. 2002. *Democratic Phoenix: Reinventing Political Activism.* New York: Cambridge University Press.

North, Douglass. 1981. *Structure and Change in Economic History.* New York: Norton.

———. 1990. *Institutions, Institutional Change, and Economic Performance.* Cambridge, U.K.: Cambridge University Press.

North, Douglass C., and Barry R. Weingast. 1989. "Constitutions and Commitment: The Evolution of Institutions Governing Public Choice in Seventeenth-Century England." *Journal of Economic History* 49(4): 803–32.

Offe, Claus. 1999. "How Can We Trust Our Fellow Citizens?" In *Democracy and Trust,* edited by Mark E. Warren. New York: Cambridge University Press.

Olson, Mancur, Jr. 1965. *The Logic of Collective Action.* Cambridge, Mass.: Harvard University Press.

———. 1982. *The Rise and Decline of Nations.* New Haven, Conn.: Yale University Press.

———. 1993. "Dictatorship, Democracy, and Development." *American Political Science Review* 87(3): 567–76.

Orbell, John M., and Robyn M. Dawes. 1993. "Social Welfare, Cooperators' Advantage, and the Option of Not Playing the Game." *American Sociological Review* 58(6): 787–800.

Ostrom, Elinor. 1990. *Governing the Commons: The Evolution of Institutions for Collective Action.* New York: Cambridge University Press.

————. 1998. "A Behavioral Approach to the Rational Choice Theory of Collective Action." *American Political Science Review* 92(1): 1–22.

Ostrom, Elinor, and T. K. Ahn, eds. 2003. *Foundations of Social Capital*. Cheltenham, Eng.: Edward Elgar.

Pagden, Anthony. 1988. "The Destruction of Trust and Its Economic Consequences in Eighteenth-Century Naples." In *Trust: Making and Breaking Cooperative Relations*, edited by Diego Gambetta. New York: Blackwell.

Palay, Thomas M. 1985. "Avoiding Regulatory Constraints: Contracting Safeguards and the Role of Informal Agreements." *Journal of Law, Economics, and Organizations* 1(1): 155–75.

Palca, Joseph. 1992. "Lead Researcher Confronts Accusers in Public Hearing." *Science* (April 24): 437–38.

Papon, Pierre. 2003. "Editorial: A Challenge for the EU." *Science* (August 1): 565.

Parsons, Talcott. 1937/1968. *The Structure of Social Action*. New York: Free Press.

Pearson, Steven D., and Tracey Hyams. 2002. "Talking About Money: How Primary Care Physicians Respond to a Patient's Question About Financial Incentives." *Journal of General Internal Medicine* 17(1): 75–79.

Peel, Mark. 1995. *Good Times, Hard Times*. Melbourne, Aust.: Melbourne University Press.

————. 1998. "Trusting Disadvantaged Citizens." In *Trust and Governance*, edited by Valerie Braithwaite and Margaret Levi. New York: Russell Sage Foundation.

Peirce, Charles Sanders. 1935. *Scientific Metaphysics*, vol. 6 of *Collected Papers of Charles Sanders Peirce*, edited by Charles Hartshorne and Paul Weiss. Cambridge, Mass.: Harvard University Press.

Pereira, Alexius A. 2000. "State Collaboration with Transnational Corporations: The Case of Singapore's Industrial Programs (1965–1999)." *Competition and Change* 4(4): 1–29.

Perrow, Charles. 1972. *Complex Organizations: A Critical Essay*. Glenview, Ill.: Scott, Foresman.

Peterson, Charles H., Stanley D. Rice, Jeffrey W. Short, Daniel Esler, James L. Bodkin, Brenda Ballachey, and David B. Irons. 2003. "Long-term Ecosystem Response to the *Exxon Valdez* Oil Spill." *Science* 302(December 19): 2082–86.

Pettit, Philip. 1995. "The Cunning of Trust." *Philosophy and Public Affairs* 24: 202–25.

Pharr, Susan J. 2000. "Officials' Misconduct and Public Distrust: Japan and the Trilateral Democracies." In *Disaffected Democracies*, edited by Susan J. Pharr and Robert D. Putnam. Princeton, N.J.: Princeton University Press.

Pharr, Susan J., and Robert D. Putnam, eds. 2000. *Disaffected Democracies: What's Troubling the Trilateral Democracies*. Princeton, N.J.: Princeton University Press.

Philpott, Stuart B. 1968. "Remittance Obligations, Social Networks, and Choice Among Montserratian Migrants in Britain." *Man* 3(3): 465–76.

Pinney, Neil, and John T. Scholz. 1995. "Duty, Fear, and Tax Compliance: The Heuristic Basis of Citizenship Behavior." *American Journal of Political Science* 39: 490–512.

Popkin, Samuel. 1991. *The Reasoning Voter*. Chicago: University of Chicago Press.

Portes, Alejandro, and Saskia Sassen-Koob. 1987. "Making It Underground: Comparative Material on the Informal Sector in Western Market Economies." *American Journal of Sociology* 93(July): 30–61.

Portes, Alejandro, and Julia Sensenbrenner. 1993. "Embeddedness and Immigration: Notes on the Social Determinants of Economic Action." *American Journal of Sociology* 98(6): 1320–50.

Posner, Richard. 1980. "A Theory of Primitive Society, with Special Reference to Law." *Journal of Law and Economics* 23(1): 1–53.

Prendergast, Canice. 1999. "The Provision of Incentives in Firms." *Journal of Economic Literature* 37(1): 7–63.

Przeworski, Adam, Susan C. Stokes, and Bernard Manin, eds. 1999. *Democracy, Accountability, and Representation.* New York: Cambridge University Press.

Putnam, Robert. 1993a. *Making Democracy Work: Civic Traditions in Modern Italy.* Princeton, N.J.: Princeton University Press.

———. 1993b. "The Prosperous Community: Social Capital and Public Life." *American Prospect* 13: 35–42.

———. 1995a. "Tuning In, Tuning Out: The Strange Disappearance of Social Capital in America." *PS: Political Science and Politics* 28(4): 664–83.

———. 1995b. "Bowling Alone: America's Declining Social Capital." *Journal of Democracy* 6(1, January): 65–78.

———. 2000. *Bowling Alone: The Collapse and Revival of American Community.* New York: Simon & Schuster.

Quirk, Paul. 1990. "Deregulation and the Politics of Ideas in Congress." In *Beyond Self-interest,* edited by Jane J. Mansbridge. Chicago: University of Chicago Press.

Radaev, Vadim. 2002. "Entrepreneurial Strategies and the Structure of Transaction Costs in Russian Business." *Problems of Economic Transition* 44(12): 57–84.

———. 2004a. "Coping with Distrust in the Emerging Russian Markets." In *Distrust,* edited by Russell Hardin. New York: Russell Sage Foundation.

———. 2004b. "How Trust Is Established in Economic Relationships When Institutions and Individuals Are Not Trustworthy: The Case of Russia." In *Building a Trustworthy State in Post-Socialist Transition,* edited by Janos Kornai and Susan Rose-Ackerman. New York: Palgrave Macmillan.

Rahn, Wendy, John Brehm, and Neil Carlson. 1999. "National Elections as Institutions for Generating Social Capital." In *Civic Engagement in American Democracy,* edited by Theda Skocpol and Morris P. Fiorina. Washington, D.C., and New York: Brookings Institution and Russell Sage Foundation.

Rahn, Wendy, and Thomas J. Rudolph. 2000. *Report on the NES 2000 Pilot Election Items.* Ann Arbor, Mich.: National Election Studies.

Raiser, Martin, Alan Rousso, and Franklin Steves. 2004. "Measuring Trust in Transition: Preliminary Findings from Twenty-six Transition Economies." In *Building a Trustworthy State in Post-Socialist Transition,* edited by Janos Kornai and Susan Rose-Ackerman. New York: Palgrave Macmillan.

Rappoport, Alfred. 1999. "New Thinking on How to Link Executive Pay with Performance." *Harvard Business Review* (March–April): 91–101.

Raub, Werner, and Jeroen Weesie. 2000. "Cooperation Via Hostages." *Analyse und Kritik* 22: 19–43.

Rebitzer, James B. 1995. "Is There a Trade-off Between Supervision and Wages? An Empirical Test of Efficiency Wage Theory." *Journal of Economic Behavior and Organization* 28(1): 107–29.

Reiss, Albert J. 1971. *The Police and the Public.* New Haven, Conn.: Yale University Press.

Richardson, Laurel. 1988. "Secrecy and Status: The Social Construction of Forbidden Relationships." *American Sociological Review* 53(2): 209–19.

Ridgeway, Cecilia, and Henry Walker. 1995. "Status Structures." In *Sociological Perspectives on Social Psychology,* edited by Karen S. Cook, Gary Alan Fine, and James House. Boston: Allyn and Bacon.

Roberts, M. D. 1967. *The Persistence of Interpersonal Trust.* Storrs: University of Connecticut.

Rodwin, M. A. 1992. "The Organized American Medical Profession's Response to Financial Conflicts of Interest: 1890–1992." *Milbank Quarterly* 70(4): 703–41.

Roniger, Luis. 1990. *Hierarchy and Trust in Modern Mexico and Brazil.* New York: Praeger.

Root, Hilton L. 1989. "Tying the King's Hands: Credible Commitments and Royal Fiscal Policy During the Old Regime." *Rationality and Society* 1: 240–58.

Rose, Richard. 1994. "Postcommunism and the Problem of Trust." *Journal of Democracy* 5(3): 18–30.

Rose, Richard, William Mishler, and Christian Haerpfer. 1998. *Democracy and Its Alternatives: Understanding Post-Communist Societies.* Baltimore: Johns Hopkins University Press.

Rose-Ackerman, Susan. 2001. "Trust and Honesty in Post-Socialist Societies." *Kyklos* 54(2–3): 415–43.

Rotenburg, Ken J. 1995. "The Socialization of Trust: Parents' and Children's Interpersonal Trust." *International Journal of Behavioral Development* 18(4): 713–26.

Rothstein, Bo. 2001. "The Universal Welfare State as a Social Dilemma." *Rationality and Society* 13(2): 213–33.

———. 2004. "Social Trust and Honesty in Government: A Causal Mechanisms Approach." In *Building a Trustworthy State in Post-Socialist Transition,* edited by Janos Kornai and Susan Rose-Ackerman. New York: Palgrave Macmillan.

Rothstein, Bo, and Dietlind Stolle. 2003. "Social Capital, Impartiality, and the Welfare State: An Institutional Approach." In *Generating Social Capital: The Role of Voluntary Associations, Institutions, and Government Policy,* edited by Dietlind Stolle and Marc Hooghe. New York: Palgrave Macmillan.

Rotter, Julian B. 1967. "A New Scale for the Measurement of Interpersonal Trust." *Journal of Personality* 35(4): 651–65.

———. 1971. "Generalized Expectancies for Interpersonal Trust." *American Psychologist* 26(5): 443–50.

———. 1980. "Interpersonal Trust, Trustworthiness, and Gullibility." *American Psychologist* 35(1): 1–7.

Safran, Dana Gelb, Mark Kosinski, Alvin R. Tarlov, William H. Rogers, Deborah A. Taira, Naomi Lieberman, and John E. Ware. 1998. "The Primary Care Assessment Survey: Tests of Data Quality and Measurement Performance." *Medical Care* 36: 728.

Saha, Somnath, Miriam Komaromy, Thomas Koepsell, and Andrew S. Bindman. 1998. "Patient-Physician Racial Concordance and the Perceived Quality and Use of Health Care." *Archives of Internal Medicine* 159: 997–1004.

Sanders, Jimy, and Victor Nee. 1987. "Limits of Ethnic Solidarity in the Enclave Economy." *American Sociological Review* 52(6): 745–73.

Sanders, Will. 1994. "Reconciling Public Accountability and Aboriginal Self-determination/Self-management: Is ASTIC Succeeding?" *Australian Journal of Public Administration* 53(4): 475–88.

Schelling, Thomas C. 1978. *Micromotives and Macrobehavior.* New York: Norton.

———. 2001. "Commitment: Deliberate Versus Involuntary." In *Evolution and the Capacity for Commitment,* edited by Randolph M. Nesse. New York: Russell Sage Foundation.

Schmitt, Frederick F., ed. 1994. *Socializing Epistemology: The Social Dimensions of Knowledge.* Lanham: Rowman and Littlefield.

Scholz, John T. 1984. "Cooperation, Deterrence, and the Ecology of Regulatory Enforcement." *Law and Society Review* 18(2): 179–224.

———. 1998. "Trust, Taxes, and Compliance." In *Trust and Governance,* edited by Valerie Braithwaite and Margaret Levi. New York: Russell Sage Foundation.

Scholz, John T., and Mark Lubell. 1998. "Adaptive Political Attitudes: Duty, Trust, and Fear as Monitors of Tax Policy." *American Journal of Political Science* 42(3): 903–20.

Schwartz, Al. 1996. "Will Competition Change the Physician Workforce? Early Signals from the Market." *Academic Medicine: Journal of the Association of American Medical Colleges* 71(1): 15–22.

Schwartz, Warren F., Keith Baxter, and David Ryan. 1984. "The Duel: Can These Gentlemen Be Acting Efficiently?" *Journal of Legal Studies* 13(June): 321–55.

Scott, W. Richard. 1965. "Reactions to Supervision in a Heteronomous Professional Organization." *Administrative Science Quarterly* 10(June): 65–81.

Searle, Eleanor. 1988. *Predatory Kinship and the Creation of Norman Power, 840–1066.* Berkeley: University of California Press.

Seidman, Gay. 1994. *Manufacturing Militance: Workers' Movements in Brazil and South Africa, 1970–1985.* Berkeley: University of California Press.

Seligman, Adam. 1997. *The Problem of Trust.* Princeton, N.J.: Princeton University Press.

Service, Robert F. 2002. "Breakdown of the Year: Physics Fraud." *Science* (December 20): 2303.

Sewell, Graham. 1998. "The Discipline of Teams: The Control of Team-Based Industrial Work Through Electronic and Peer Surveillance." *Administrative Science Quarterly* 43(2): 397–428.

Sewell, Graham, and Barry Wilkinson. 1992. "Someone to Watch over Me: Surveillance, Discipline, and the Just-in-Time Labor Process." *Sociology* 26(2): 271–98.

Shamir, Boas, and Yael Lapidot. 2003. "Trust in Organizational Superiors: Systemic and Collective Considerations." *Organization Studies* 24(3): 463–91.

Shanteau, James, and Paul Harrison. 1987. "The Perceived Strength of an Implied Contract: Can It Withstand Financial Temptation?" *Organizational Behavior and Human Decision Processes* 49(1): 1–21.

Shortell, Stephen M., Teresa M. Waters, Kenneth W. B. Clarke, and Peter P. Budetti. 1998. "Physicians as Double Agents: Maintaining Trust in an Era of Multiple Accountabilities." *Journal of the American Medical Association* 280(12): 1102–08.

Simmel, Georg. 1902/1964. "The Metropolis and Mental Life." In *The Sociology of Georg Simmel,* edited by Kurt H. Wolff. New York: Free Press.

————. 1908/1955. *Conflict and the Web of Group Affiliations.* New York: Free Press.

Simon, Herbert A. 1947. *Administrative Behavior.* New York: Macmillan.

Singer, Eleanor. 1981. "Reference Groups and Social Evaluations." In *Social Psychology: Sociological Perspectives,* edited by Morris Rosenberg and Ralph H. Turner. New York: Basic Books.

Singleton, Sara. 1998. *Constructing Cooperation: The Evolution of Institutions of Comanagement.* Ann Arbor: University of Michigan Press.

Sitkin, Sim B., and Darryl Stickel. 1996. "The Road to Hell: The Dynamics of Distrust in an Era of Quality." In *Trust in Organizations: Frontiers of Theory and Research,* edited by Roderick M. Kramer and Tom R. Tyler. Thousand Oaks, Calif.: Sage Publications.

Skocpol, Theda. 1997. "The Tocqueville Problem: Civic Engagement in American Democracy." *Social Science History* 21(4): 455–79.

————. 2003. *Diminished Democracy: From Membership to Management in American Civic Life.* Norman: University of Oklahoma Press.

Skocpol, Theda, Marshall Ganz, Ziad Munson, Bayliss Camp, Michele Swers, and Jennifer Oser. 1999. "How Americans Became Civic." In *Civic Engagement in American Democracy,* edited by Theda Skocpol and Morris P. Fiorina. Washington, D.C., and New York: Brookings Institution and Russell Sage Foundation.

Slemrod, Joel. 2003. "Trust in Public Finance." In *Public Finances and Public Policy in the New Millennium,* edited by Sijbren Cnossen and Hans-Werner Sinn. Cambridge, Mass.: MIT Press.

Smith, Adam. 1776/1976. *An Inquiry into the Nature and Causes of the Wealth of Nations.* Oxford: Oxford University Press; reprint, Indianapolis, Ind.: Liberty Classics, 1981.

Snijders, Chris, and Vincent Buskens. 2001. "How to Convince Someone That You Can Be Trusted? The Role of 'Hostages.' " *Journal of Mathematical Sociology* 25(4): 355–83.

Solzhenitsyn, Alexander. 1977. *Lenin in Zurich: Chapters.* Translated by T. H. Willetts. New York: Bantam Books.

Stahl, Charles W., and Fred Arnold. 1986. "Economic Causes, Roles, and Consequences of Temporary Worker Migrations Overseas Workers' Remittances in Asian Development." *International Migration Review* 20(4): 899–925.

Standifird, Stephen S. 2001. "Reputation and E-commerce: eBay Auctions and the Asymmetrical Impact of Positive and Negative Ratings." *Journal of Management* 27(3): 279–95.

Steingraber, Sandra. 1998. *Living Downstream: An Ecologist Looks at Cancer.* Cambridge, Mass.: Perseus.

Stewart, Frank Henderson. 1994. *Honor.* Chicago: University of Chicago Press.

Stiglitz, Joseph E. 1987. "The Causes and Consequences of the Dependence of Quality on Price." *Journal of Economic Literature* 25(1): 1–48.

Stinchcombe, Arthur L. 1999. "Ending Revolutions and Building New Governments." *Annual Review of Political Science* 2: 49–73.

Stokes, Susan C. 2001a. *Mandates and Democracy: Neoliberalism by Surprise in Latin America.* New York: Cambridge University Press.

————, ed. 2001b. *Public Support for Market Reforms in New Democracies.* New York: Cambridge University Press.

Strickland, Lloyd H. 1958. "Surveillance and Trust." *Journal of Personality* 26(June): 200–15.

Sturm, Roland. 2002. "Effect of Managed Care and Financing on Practice Constraints and Career Satisfaction in Primary Care." *Journal of American Board of Family Physicians* 15(5): 367–77.

Surowiecki, James. 2003. "In Wall Street We Trust." *New Yorker* (May 26): 40.

Swenson, Peter. 2002. *Capitalists Against Markets*. New York: Oxford.

Sztompka, Piotr. 1996. "Trust and Emerging Democracy." *International Sociology* 11(1): 37–62.

———. 1998. "Trust, Distrust, and Two Paradoxes of Democracy." *European Journal of Social Theory* 1(1): 19–32.

———. 1999. *Trust*. New York: Cambridge University Press.

Tamanaha, Brian Z. 1995. "The Lessons of Law-and-Development Studies." *American Journal of International Law* 89(2, April): 470–86.

Tarrow, Sidney. 1996. "Making Social Science Work Across Space and Time: A Critical Reflection on Robert Putnam's *Making Democracy Work*." *American Political Science Review* 90(2): 389–97.

———. 2000. "Mad Cows and Activists: Contentious Politics in the Trilateral Democracies." In *Disaffected Democracies: What's Troubling the Trilateral Democracies*, edited by Susan Pharr and Robert Putnam. Princeton, N.J.: Princeton University Press.

Taylor, Michael. 1982. *Community, Anarchy, and Liberty*. Cambridge, U.K.: Cambridge University Press.

———, ed. 1988. *The Rationality of Revolution*. New York: Cambridge University Press.

Thelen, Kathleen. 2004. *How Institutions Evolve: The Political Economy of Skills in Comparative-Historical Perspective*. New York: Cambridge University Press.

Thom, David H., Kurt M. Ribisl, Anita L. Stewart, and Douglas A. Luke. 1999. "Further Validation and Reliability Testing of the Trust in Physician Scale." *Medical Care* 37(5, May): 510–17.

Thucydides. 431 B.C.E./1972. *History of the Peloponnesian War*, translated by Richard Crawley. Baltimore: Penguin Books.

Tilly, Charles. 1998. *Durable Inequality*. Berkeley: University of California Press.

———. 2004. "Social Boundary Mechanisms." *Philosophy of the Social Sciences* 34: 211–36.

———. 2005. *Trust and Rule*. New York: Cambridge University Press.

Tocqueville, Alexis de. 1835/1990. *Democracy in America*. Vol. 1. New York: Vintage.

———. 1840/1990. *Democracy in America*. Vol. 2. New York: Vintage.

Troy, Patrick. 2004. "Distrust and the Development of Urban Regulations." In *Distrust*, edited by Russell Hardin. New York: Russell Sage Foundation.

Tsai, Kellee S. 1998. "A Circle of Friends, a Web of Troubles: Rotating Credit Associations in China." *Harvard China Review* 1(1): 81–83.

Tsoukas, Haridimos. 1997. "The Tyranny of Light: The Temptations and the Paradoxes of the Information Society." *Futures* 29: 827–43.

Tyler, Tom R. 1990a. "Justice, Self-interest, and the Legitimacy of Legal and Political Authority." In *Beyond Self-interest*, edited by Jane Mansbridge. Chicago: University of Chicago Press.

————. 1990b. *Why People Obey the Law*. New Haven, Conn.: Yale University Press.

————. 1998. "Trust and Democratic Government." In *Trust and Governance*, edited by Valerie Braithwaite and Margaret Levi. New York: Russell Sage Foundation.

————. 2001. "Why Do People Rely on Others? Social Identity and the Social Aspects of Trust." In *Trust in Society*, edited by Karen S. Cook. New York: Russell Sage Foundation.

Tyler, Tom R., and Peter Degoey. 1996. "Trust in Organizational Authorities: The Influence of Motive Attributions on Willingness to Accept Decisions." In *Trust in Organizations: Frontiers of Theory and Research*, edited by Roderick Kramer and Tom R. Tyler. Thousand Oaks, Calif.: Sage Publications.

Tyler, Tom R., and Yuen J. Huo. 2002. *Trust in the Law: Encouraging Public Cooperation with the Police and Courts*. New York: Russell Sage Foundation.

Ullmann-Margalit, Edna. 2004. "Trust, Distrust, and in Between." In *Distrust*, edited by Russell Hardin. New York: Russell Sage Foundation.

Uslaner, Eric M. 2002. *The Moral Foundations of Trust*. Cambridge: Cambridge University Press.

Uzzi, Brian. 1996. "The Sources and Consequences of Embeddedness for the Economic Performance of Organizations: The Network Effect." *American Sociological Review* 61(4): 674–98.

————. 1999. "Embeddedness in the Making of Financial Capital: How Social Relations and Networks Benefit Firms Seeking Financing." *American Sociological Review* 64(August): 481–505.

Varese, Federico. 2000. "There Is No Place Like Home: How Mafia Finds It Difficult to Expand from Its Geographical Place." *Times Literary Supplement* (February 23): 3–4.

————. 2001. *The Russian Mafia: Private Protection in a New Market Economy*. Oxford: Oxford University Press.

————. 2004. "Mafia Transplantation." In *Building a Trustworthy State in Post-Socialist Transition*, edited by Janos Kornai and Susan Rose-Ackerman. New York: Palgrave Macmillan.

Varshney, Ashutosh. 2002. *Ethnic Conflict and Civic Life*. New Haven, Conn.: Yale University Press.

Veatch, Robert. 1972. "Medical Ethics: Professional or Universal?" *Harvard Theological Review* 65(4, October): 531–59.

Velez-Ibanez, Carlos G. 1983. *Bonds of Mutual Trust: The Cultural Systems of Rotating Credit Associations Among Urban Mexicans and Chicanos*. New Brunswick, N.J.: Rutgers University Press.

Volkov, Vadim. 2002. *The Monopoly of Force*. Ithaca, N.Y.: Cornell University Press.

Wagenaar, Willem A. 1996. "The Ethics of Not Spending Money on Safety." In *Codes of Conduct: Behavioral Research into Business Ethics*, edited by David M. Messick and Ann E. Tenbrunsel. New York: Russell Sage Foundation.

Waldinger, Roger. 1986. "Immigrant Enterprise: A Critique and Reformulation." *Theory and Society* 15(1–2, special double issue, "Structures of Capital"): 249–85.

Warren, Christian. 2000. *Brush with Death: A Social History of Lead Poisoning*. Baltimore: Johns Hopkins University Press.

Warren, Mark E. 1999. "Democratic Theory and Trust." In *Democracy and Trust,* edited by Mark Warren. Cambridge, U.K.: Cambridge University Press.

Wason, P. C. 1960. "On the Failure to Eliminate Hypotheses in a Conceptual Task." *Quarterly Journal of Experimental Psychology* 12: 129–40.

Watts, Duncan J. 2003. *Six Degrees: The Science of a Connected Age.* New York: Norton.

Watts, Jonathan. 2002. "Japan's Newest Star: A Chemist." *Christian Science Monitor,* November 4.

Weatherford, M. Stephen. 1987. "How Does Government Performance Influence Political Support?" *Political Behavior* 9: 5–28.

Weber, Elke U., Christopher K. Hsee, and Joanna Sokolowska. 1998. "What Folklore Tells Us About Risk and Risk-Taking: Cross-cultural Comparisons of American, German, and Chinese Proverbs." *Organization Behavior and Human Decision Processes* 75(2): 170–86.

Weber, Eugen. 1976. *Peasants into Frenchmen: The Modernization of Rural France, 1870–1914.* Palo Alto, Calif.: Stanford University Press.

Weber, Max. 1968. *Economy and Society,* edited by Guenther Roth and Claus Wittich. Berkeley: University of California Press.

Weick, Karl. 1969. *The Social Psychology of Organization.* Reading, Mass.: Addison-Wesley.

Weingast, Barry R. 1997. "The Political Foundations of Democracy and the Rule of Law." *American Political Science Review* 91(2): 245–63.

Weiss, Andrew. 1990. *Efficiency Wages: Models of Unemployment, Layoffs, and Wage Dispersion.* Princeton, N.J.: Princeton University Press.

Weiss, P. 2004. "Two New Elements Made." *Science News,* February 7, 84.

Weissman, Marsha, and Candace Mayer LaRue. 1998. "Earning Trust from Youths with None to Spare." *Child Welfare* 77(5): 579–94.

Wellman, Barry, ed. 1998. *Networks in the Global Village.* Boulder, Colo.: Westview.

Westacott, George H., and Lawrence K. Williams. 1976. "Interpersonal Trust and Modern Attitudes in Peru." *International Journal of Contemporary Society* 13: 117–37.

Whiteley, Paul F. 2000. "Economic Growth and Social Capital." *Political Studies* 48(3): 443–66.

Whiteley, Richard D., Alan Thomas, and Jane Marceau. 1981. *Masters of Business? Business Schools and Business Graduates in Britain and France.* London: Tavistock.

Whiting, Susan. 1998. "The Mobilization of Private Investment as a Problem of Trust in Local Governance Structures." In *Trust and Governance,* edited by Valerie Braithwaite and Margaret Levi. New York: Russell Sage Foundation.

———. 2000. *Power and Wealth in Rural China.* New York: Cambridge University Press.

Widner, Jennifer A. 2001. *Building the Rule of Law.* New York: Norton.

Wielers, Rudi. 1997. "The Wages of Trust: The Case of Child Minders." *Rationality and Society* 9(3): 351–72.

Wiener, Jon. 2002. "Fire at Will: How the Critics Shot Up Michael Bellesisles's Book *Arming America.*" *The Nation* (November 4): 28–32.

Wilkinson, Steven. 2004. *Votes and Violence: Electoral Competition and Ethnic Riots in India.* New York: Cambridge University Press.

Williamson, Oliver E. 1975. *Markets and Hierarchies.* New York: Free Press.

————. 1980. "The Organization of Work." *Journal of Economic Behavior and Organization* 1: 5–38.

————. 1985. *The Economic Institutions of Capitalism.* New York: The Free Press.

————. 1993. "Calculativeness, Trust, and Economic Organization." *Journal of Law and Economics* 36(1, pt. 2): 453–86.

————. 1996. *The Mechanisms of Governance.* New York: Oxford University Press.

Wills, Garry. 1999. *A Necessary Evil: A History of American Distrust of Government.* New York: Simon & Schuster.

Wilson, William Julius. 1987. *The Truly Disadvantaged.* Chicago: University of Chicago Press.

Windt, Peter, Peter C. Appleby, Margaret P. Battin, Leslie P. Francis, and Bruce M. Landesman, eds. 1989. *Ethical Issues in the Professions.* Englewood Cliffs, N.J.: Prentice-Hall.

Wintrobe, Ronald. 1995. "Some Economics of Ethnic Capital Formation and Conflict." In *Nationalism and Rationality,* edited by Albert Breton, Gianluigi Galeotti, Pierre Salmon, and Ronald Wintrobe. Cambridge: Cambridge University Press.

Wissow, Lawrence S., Susan M. Larson, Debra Roter, Mei-Cheng Wang, Wei-Ting Hwang, Xianghua Luo, Rachel Johnson, Andrea Gielen, Modena H. Wilson, and Eileen McDonald. 2003. "Longitudinal Care Improves Disclosure of Psychosocial Information." For the SAFE Home Project. *Archives of Pediatric and Adolescent Medicine* 157(5): 419–24.

World Bank. 1993. *The East Asian Miracle: Economic Growth and Public Policy.* New York: Oxford University Press.

Wright, Thomas L. 1972. *Situational and Personality Parameters of Interpersonal Trust in a Modified Prisoner's Dilemma Game.* Storrs: University of Connecticut.

Wright, Thomas L., and Richard G. Tedeschi. 1975. "Factor Analysis of the Interpersonal Trust Scale." *Journal of Consulting and Clinical Psychology* 43(4): 470–77.

Yamagishi, Toshio. 2001. "Trust as a Form of Social Intelligence." In *Trust in Society,* edited by Karen S. Cook. New York: Russell Sage Foundation.

Yamagishi, Toshio, and Karen S. Cook. 1993. "Generalized Exchange and Social Dilemmas." *Social Psychology Quarterly* 56(4): 235–48.

Yamagishi, Toshio, Masako Kikuchi, and Motoko Kosugi. 1999. "Trust, Gullibility, and Social Intelligence." *Asian Journal of Social Psychology* 2(1): 145–61.

Yamagishi, Toshio, Masafumi Matsuda, Noriaki Yoshikai, Hiroyuki Takahashi, and Yukihiro Usui. 2003. "Solving Lemons Problem with Reputation: An Experimental Study of Online Trading." Working paper CEFOM/21. Sapporo, Japan: Hokkaido University.

Yamagishi, Toshio, and Midori Yamagishi. 1994. "Trust and Commitment in the United States and Japan." *Motivation and Emotion* 18(2): 129–66.

Yoon, In-Jin. 1991. "The Changing Significance of Ethnic and Class Resources in Immigrant Businesses: The Case of Korean Immigrant Businesses in Chicago." *International Migration Review* 25(2): 303–32.

Young-Ybarra, Candace, and Margarethe Wiersema. 1999. "Strategic Flexibility in Information Technology Alliances: The Influence of Transaction Cost Economics and Social Exchange Theory." *Organization Science* 10(4): 439–59.

Yunus, Muhammad. 1998. "Alleviating Poverty Through Technology." *Science* (October 16): 409–10.

———. 1999. *Banker to the Poor: Micro-Lending and the Battle Against World Poverty.* New York: Public Affairs.

Zak, Paul, and Stephen Knack. 2001. "Trust and Growth." *Economic Journal* 3: 295–321.

Zand, Dale E. 1972. "Trust and Managerial Problem-Solving." *Administrative Studies Quarterly* 17(2): 229–39.

Zinberg, Dorothy. 1996. "Editorial: A Cautionary Tale." *Science* (July 26): 411.

Zucker, Lynn. 1986. "Production of Trust: Institutional Sources of Economic Structure, 1840–1920." In *Research in Organizational Behavior*, edited by Barry M. Staw and Larry L. Cummings. Greenwich, Conn.: JAI Press.

Index

Boldface numbers refer to figures and tables.

243